Magical Angel
Creamy Mami
and the
Spoiled Princess

①

story & art: **Emi Mitsuki**
original concept: **Studio Pierrot**

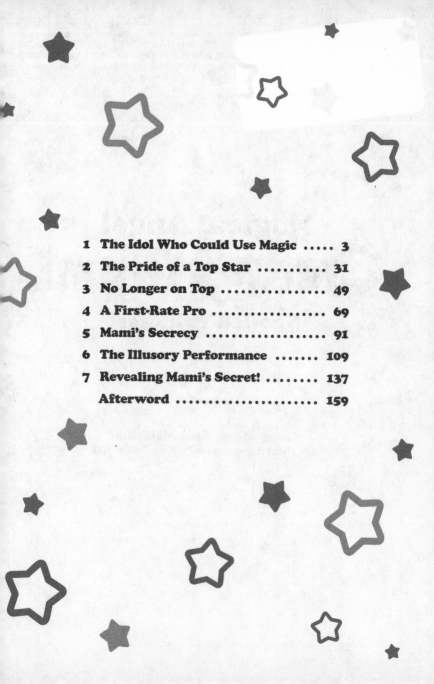

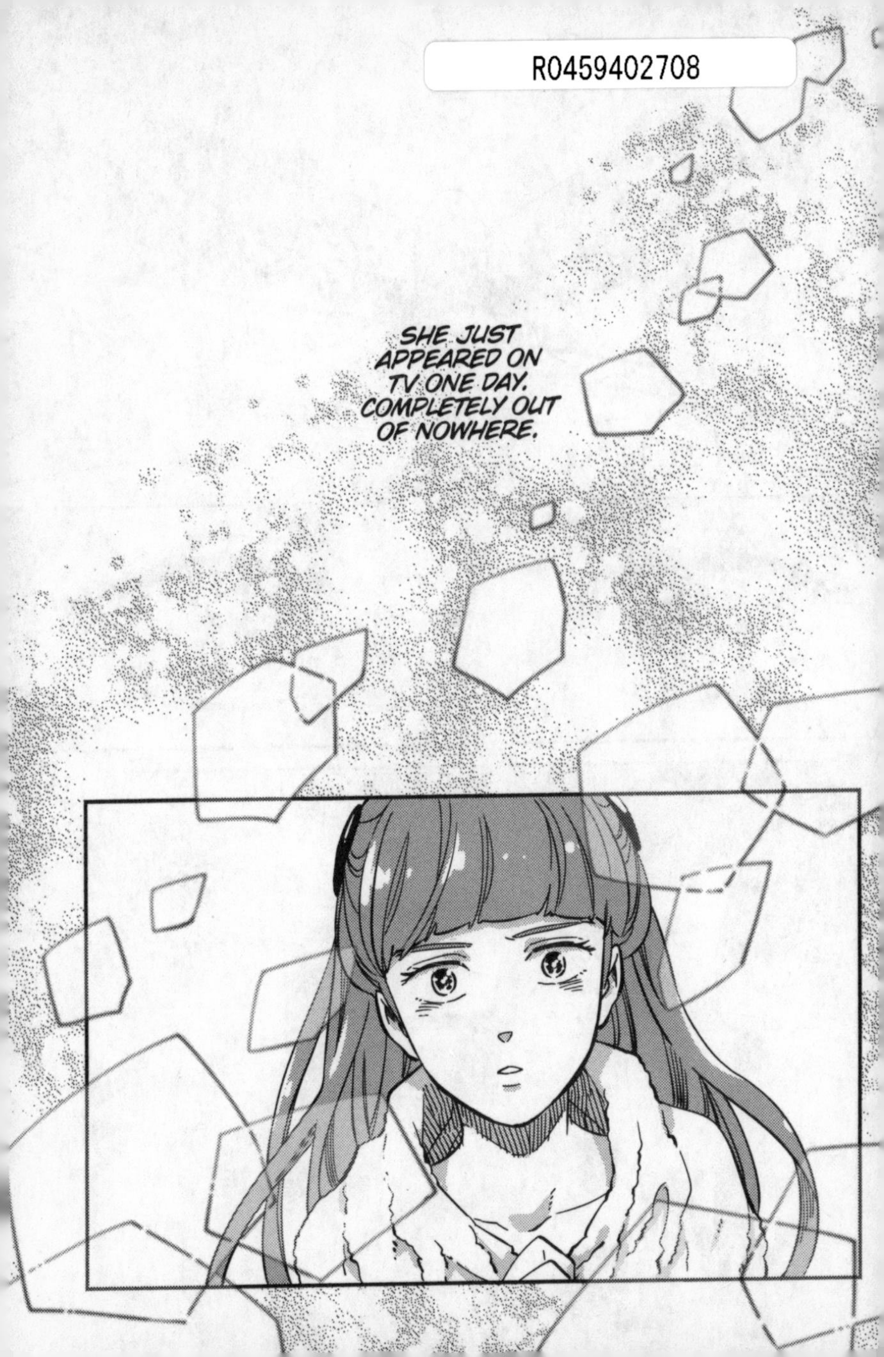
SHE JUST APPEARED ON TV ONE DAY. COMPLETELY OUT OF NOWHERE.

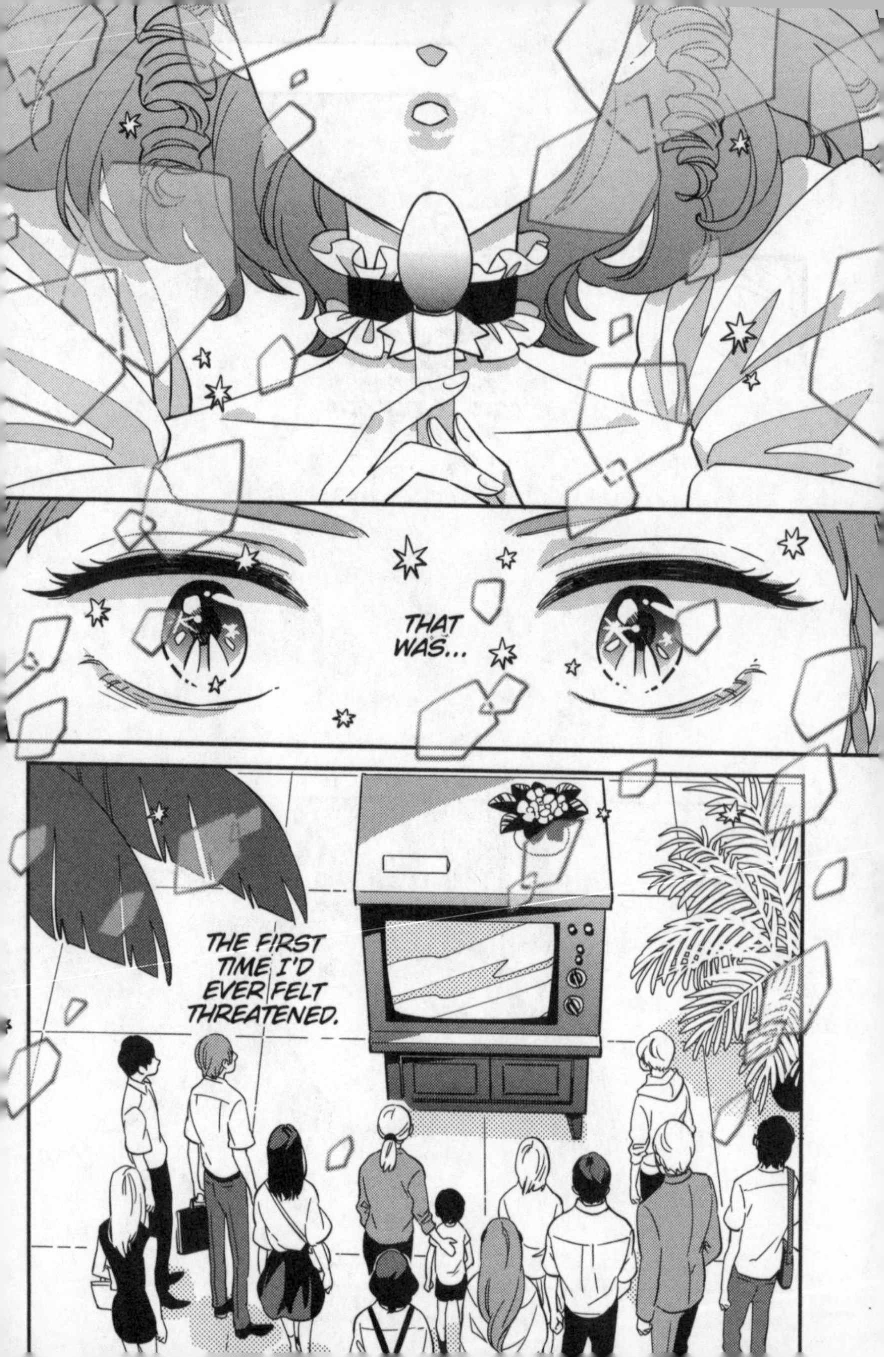
THAT WAS...
THE FIRST TIME I'D EVER FELT THREATENED.

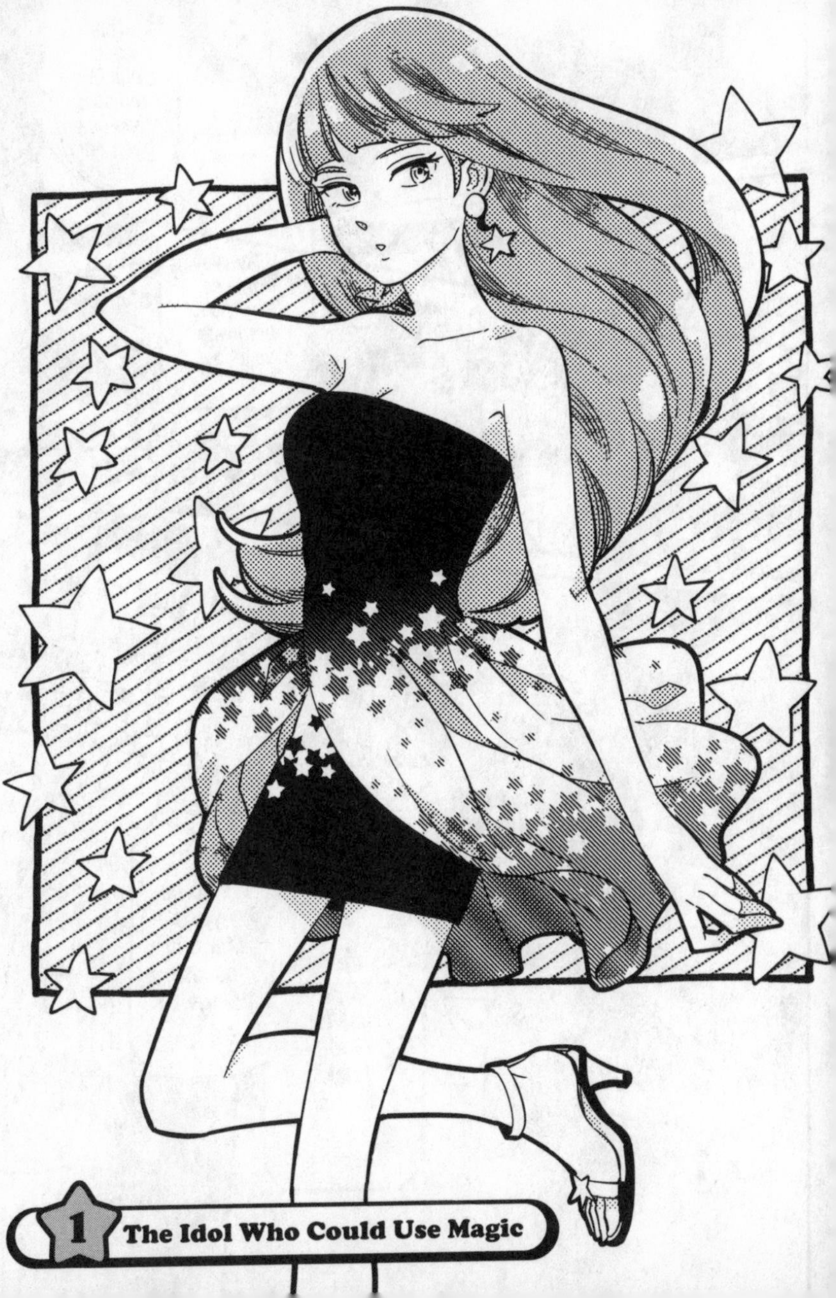

1 The Idol Who Could Use Magic

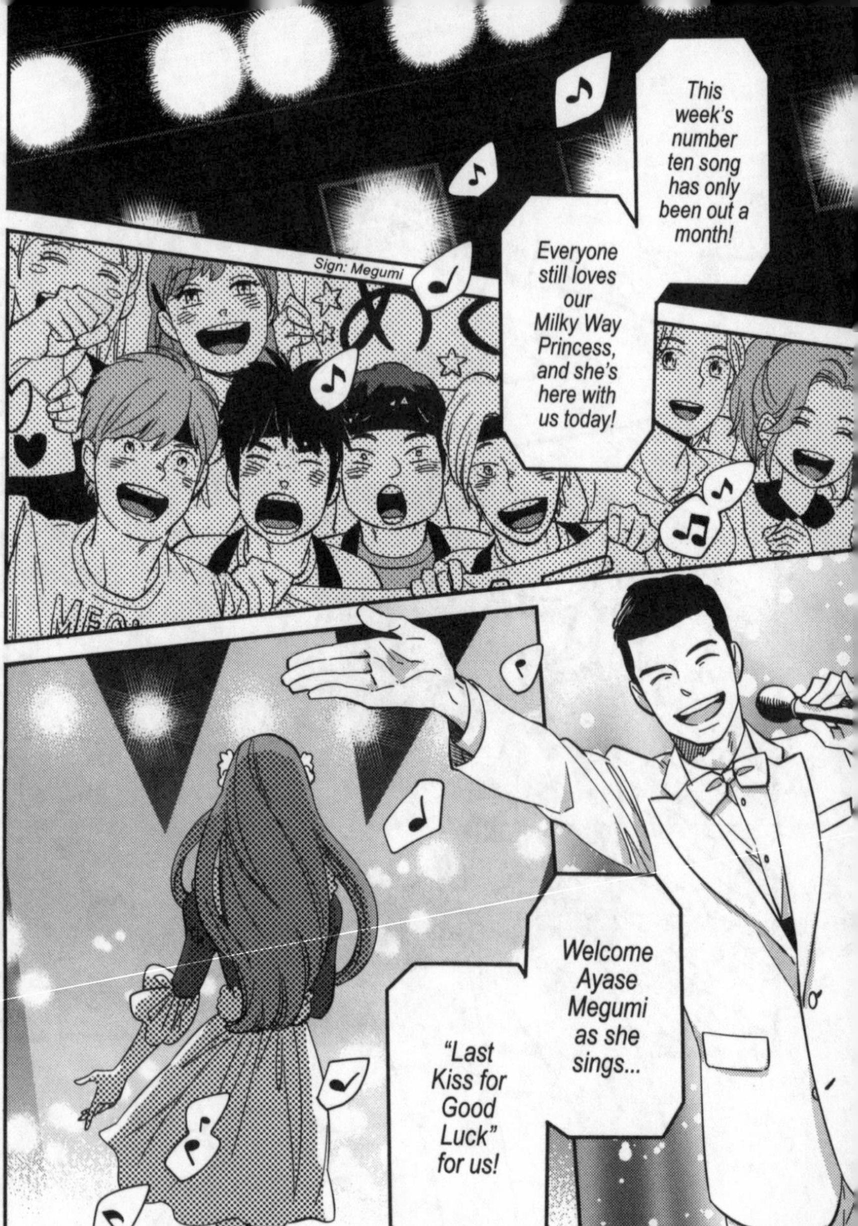
This week's number ten song has only been out a month!
Everyone still loves our Milky Way Princess, and she's here with us today!
Sign: Megumi
Welcome Ayase Megumi as she sings...
"Last Kiss for Good Luck" for us!

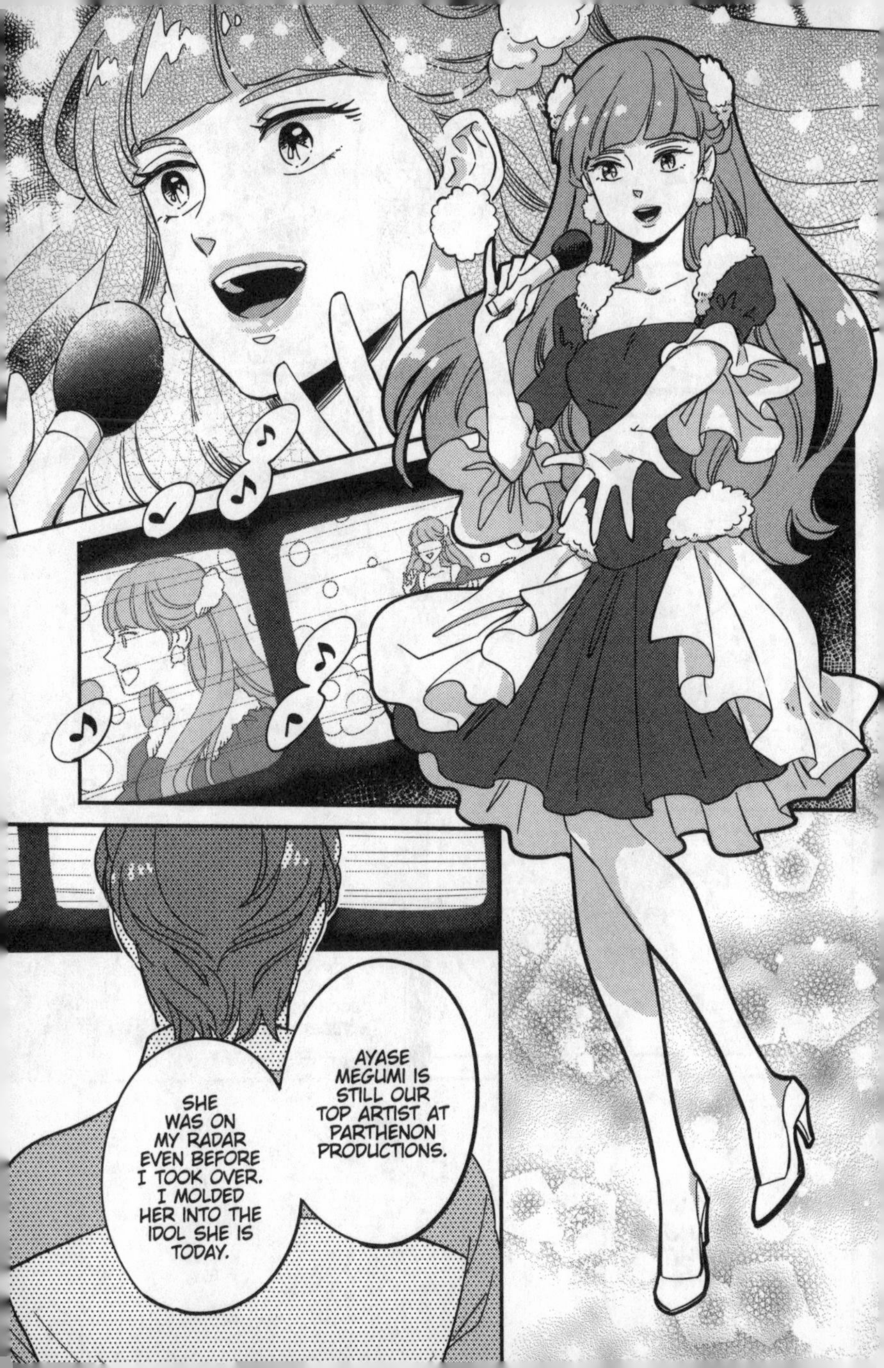
AYASE MEGUMI IS STILL OUR TOP ARTIST AT PARTHENON PRODUCTIONS.
SHE WAS ON MY RADAR EVEN BEFORE I TOOK OVER. I MOLDED HER INTO THE IDOL SHE IS TODAY.

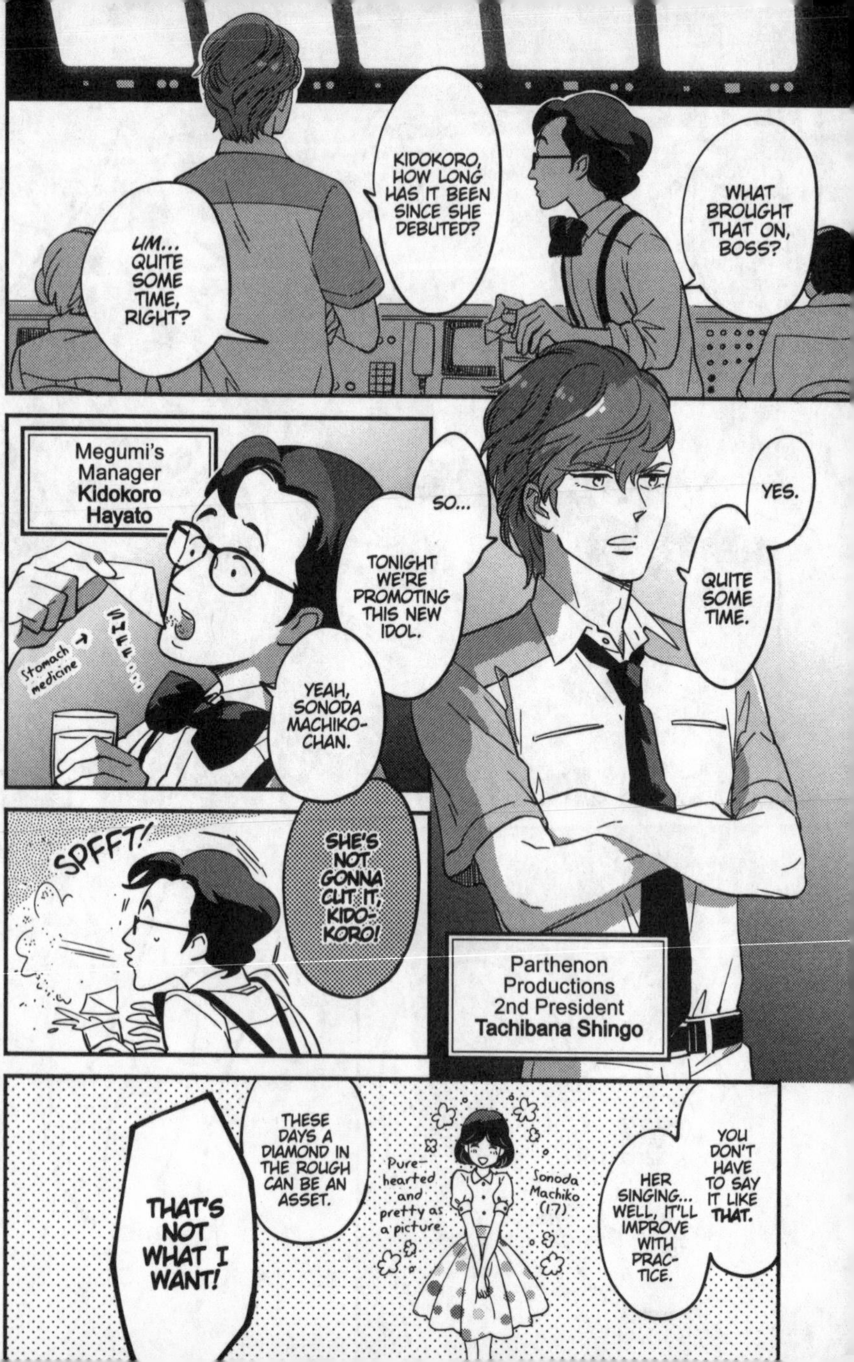

KIDOKORO, HOW LONG HAS IT BEEN SINCE SHE DEBUTED?
WHAT BROUGHT THAT ON, BOSS?
UM... QUITE SOME TIME, RIGHT?
YES.
QUITE SOME TIME.
SO...
TONIGHT WE'RE PROMOTING THIS NEW IDOL.
YEAH, SONODA MACHIKO-CHAN.
SHE'S NOT GONNA CUT IT, KIDOKORO!
Parthenon Productions 2nd President Tachibana Shingo
Megumi's Manager Kidokoro Hayato
SHFF...
Stomach medicine
SPFFT!
YOU DON'T HAVE TO SAY IT LIKE THAT.
HER SINGING... WELL, IT'LL IMPROVE WITH PRACTICE.
Sonoda Machiko (17)
Pure-hearted and pretty as a picture.
THESE DAYS A DIAMOND IN THE ROUGH CAN BE AN ASSET.
THAT'S NOT WHAT I WANT!

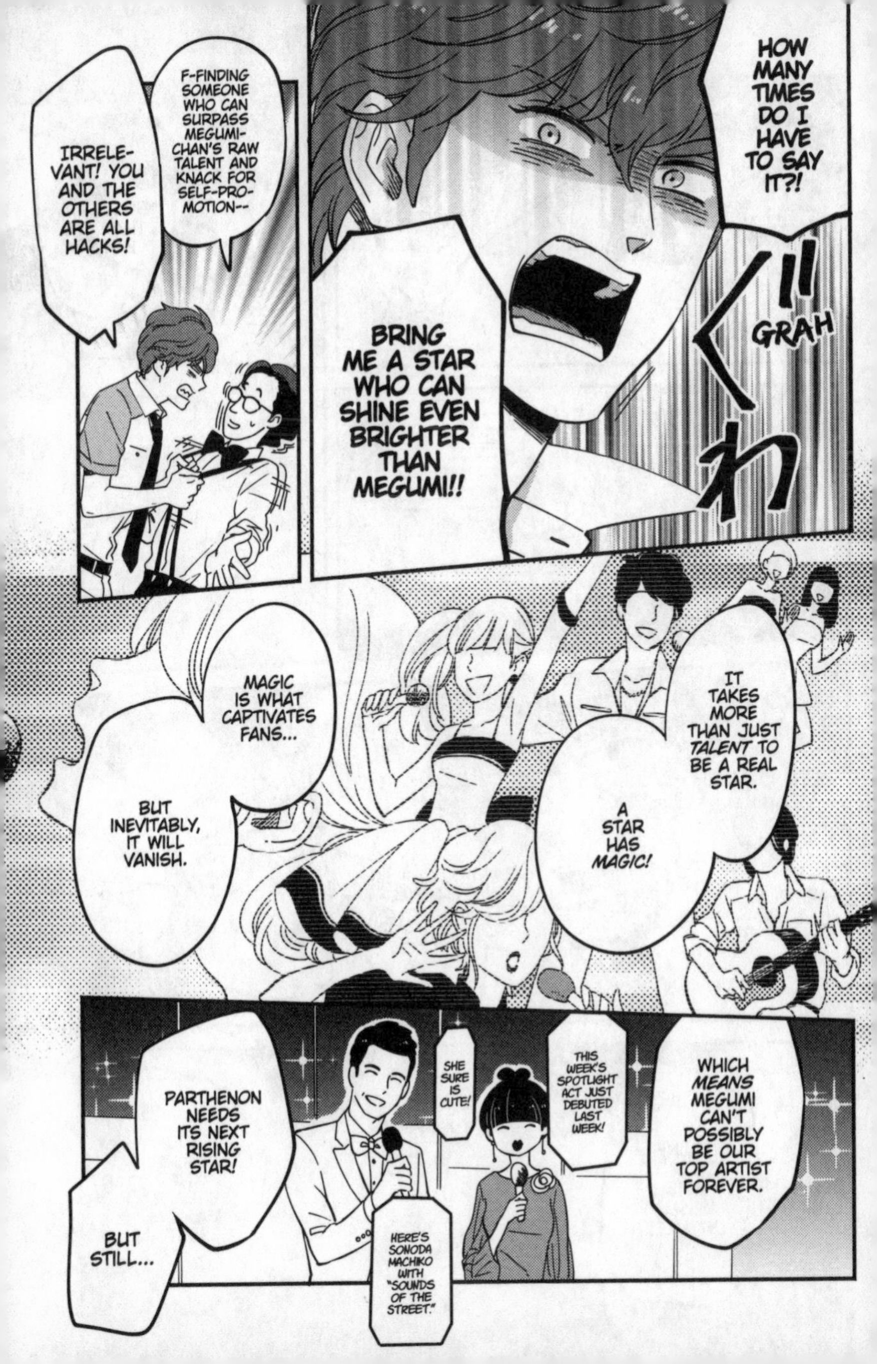
HOW MANY TIMES DO I HAVE TO SAY IT?!
GRAH
BRING ME A STAR WHO CAN SHINE EVEN BRIGHTER THAN MEGUMI!!
F-FINDING SOMEONE WHO CAN SURPASS MEGUMI-CHAN'S RAW TALENT AND KNACK FOR SELF-PRO-MOTION--
IRRELE-VANT! YOU AND THE OTHERS ARE ALL HACKS!
IT TAKES MORE THAN JUST *TALENT* TO BE A REAL STAR.
A STAR HAS *MAGIC!*
MAGIC IS WHAT CAPTIVATES FANS...
BUT INEVITABLY, IT WILL VANISH.
WHICH *MEANS* MEGUMI CAN'T POSSIBLY BE OUR TOP ARTIST FOREVER.
THIS WEEK'S SPOTLIGHT ACT JUST DEBUTED LAST WEEK!
SHE SURE IS CUTE!
HERE'S SONODA MACHIKO WITH "SOUNDS OF THE STREET."
PARTHENON NEEDS ITS NEXT RISING STAR!
BUT STILL...

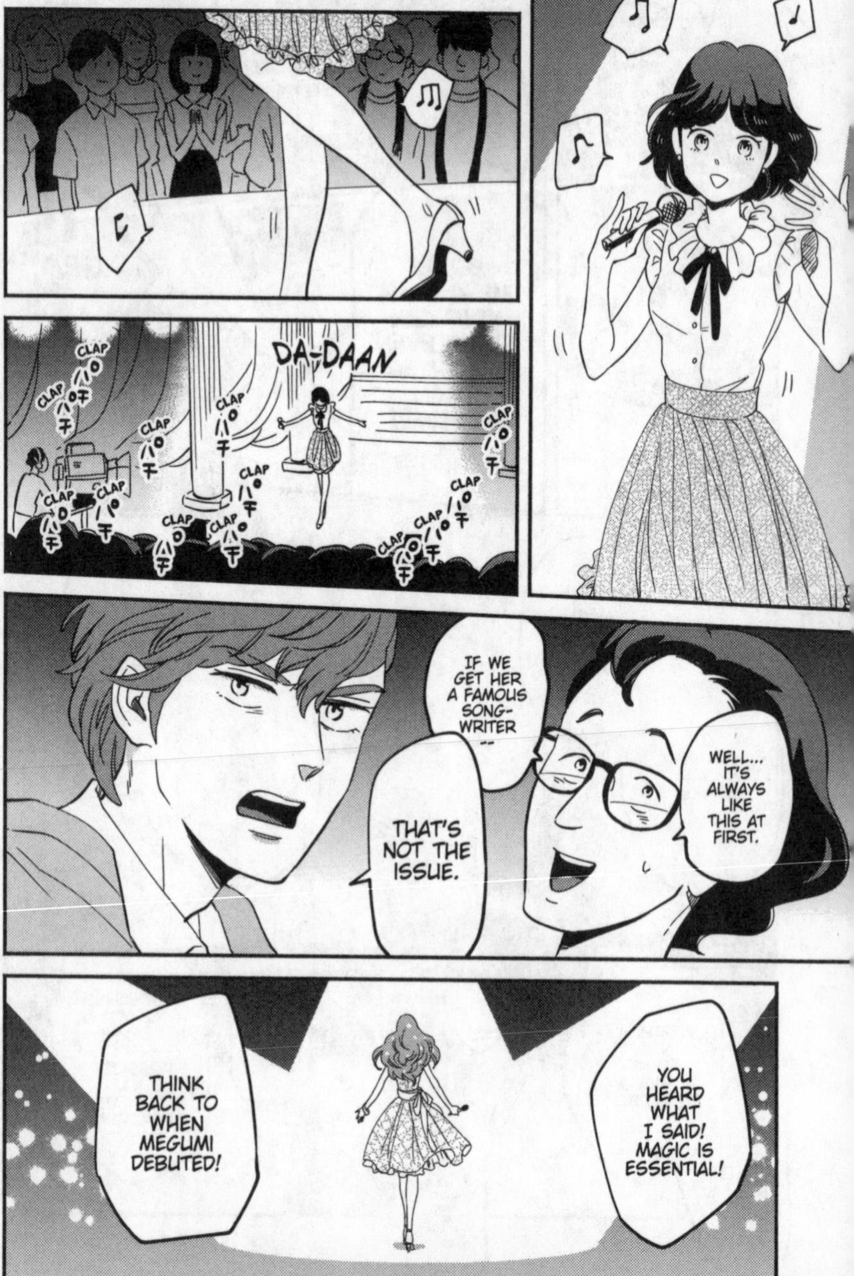
DA-DAAN
CLAP パチ
CLAP パチ
CLAP パチ
CLAP パチ
CLAP パチ
CLAP パチ
CLAP パチ
CLAP パチ
CLAP パチ
CLAP パチ
CLAP パチ
CLAP パチ
CLAP パチ
WELL... IT'S ALWAYS LIKE THIS AT FIRST.
IF WE GET HER A FAMOUS SONG-WRITER--
THAT'S NOT THE ISSUE.
YOU HEARD WHAT I SAID! MAGIC IS ESSENTIAL!
THINK BACK TO WHEN MEGUMI DEBUTED!

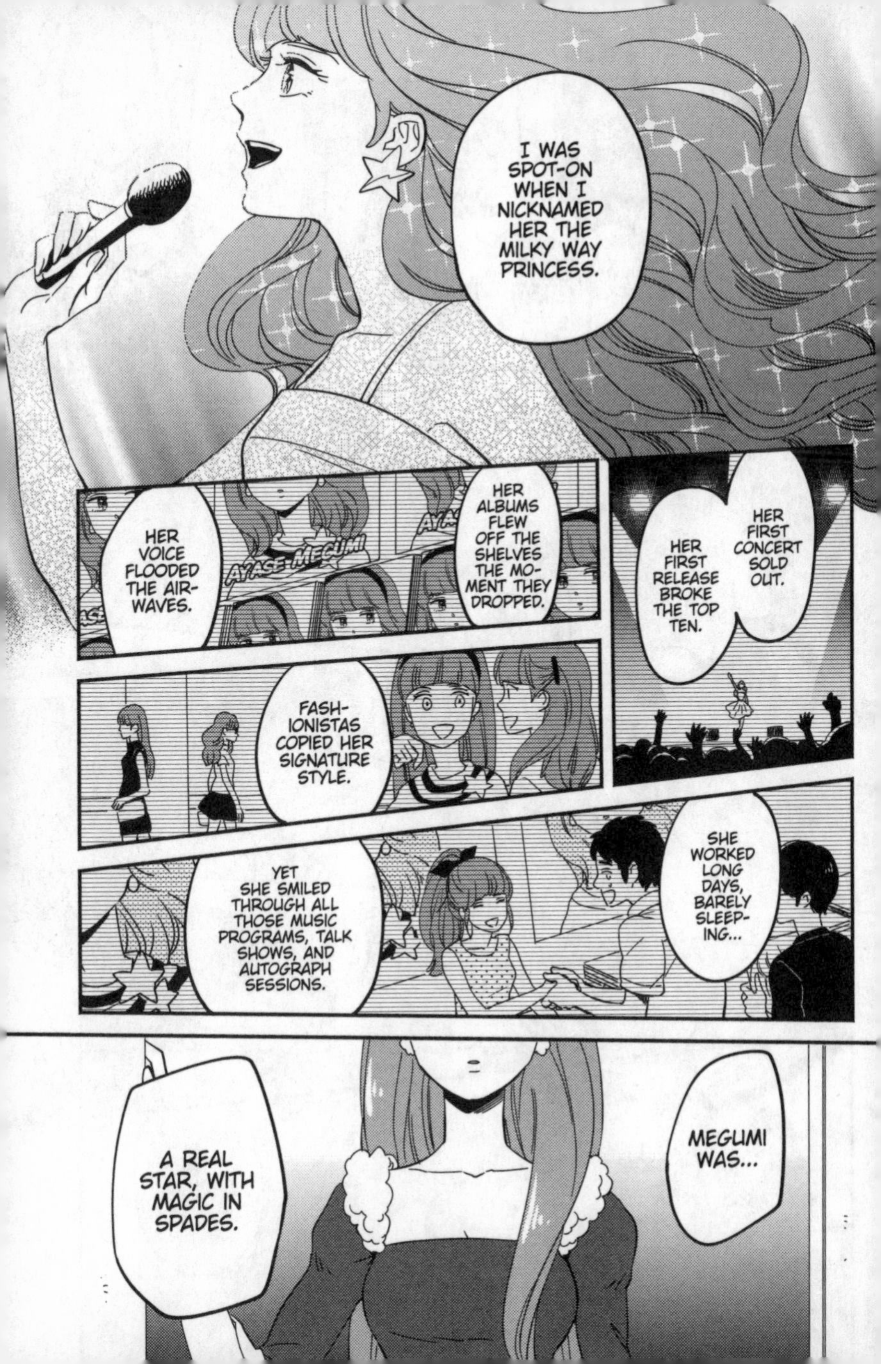
I WAS SPOT-ON WHEN I NICKNAMED HER THE MILKY WAY PRINCESS.
HER FIRST CONCERT SOLD OUT.
HER FIRST RELEASE BROKE THE TOP TEN.
AYASE MEGUMI
HER ALBUMS FLEW OFF THE SHELVES THE MOMENT THEY DROPPED.
HER VOICE FLOODED THE AIRWAVES.
FASHIONISTAS COPIED HER SIGNATURE STYLE.
SHE WORKED LONG DAYS, BARELY SLEEPING...
YET SHE SMILED THROUGH ALL THOSE MUSIC PROGRAMS, TALK SHOWS, AND AUTOGRAPH SESSIONS.
MEGUMI WAS...
A REAL STAR, WITH MAGIC IN SPADES.

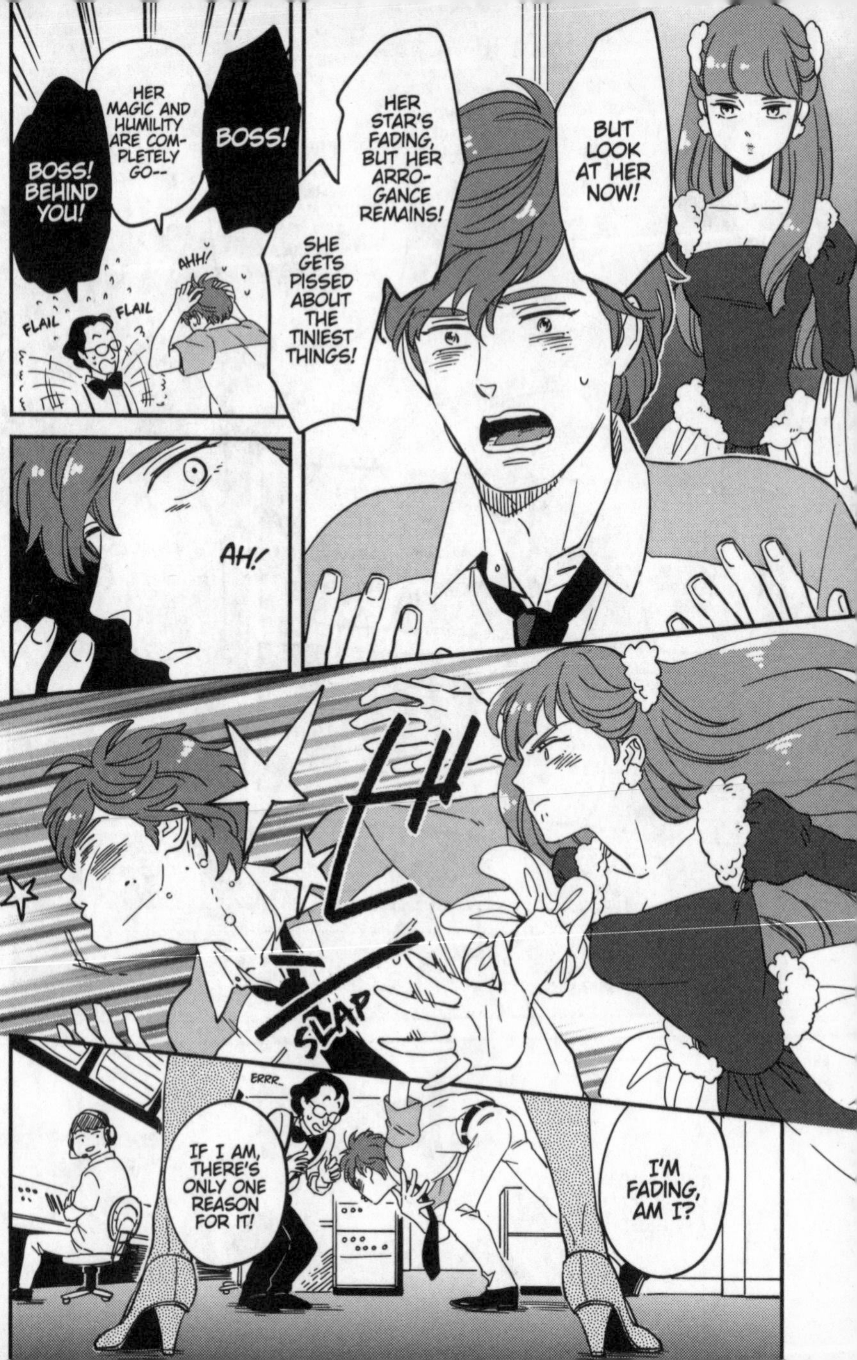

BUT LOOK AT HER NOW!
HER STAR'S FADING, BUT HER ARROGANCE REMAINS!
SHE GETS PISSED ABOUT THE TINIEST THINGS!
BOSS!
HER MAGIC AND HUMILITY ARE COMPLETELY GO--
BOSS! BEHIND YOU!
AHH!
FLAIL
FLAIL
AH!
SLAP
I'M FADING, AM I?
IF I AM, THERE'S ONLY ONE REASON FOR IT!
ERRR..

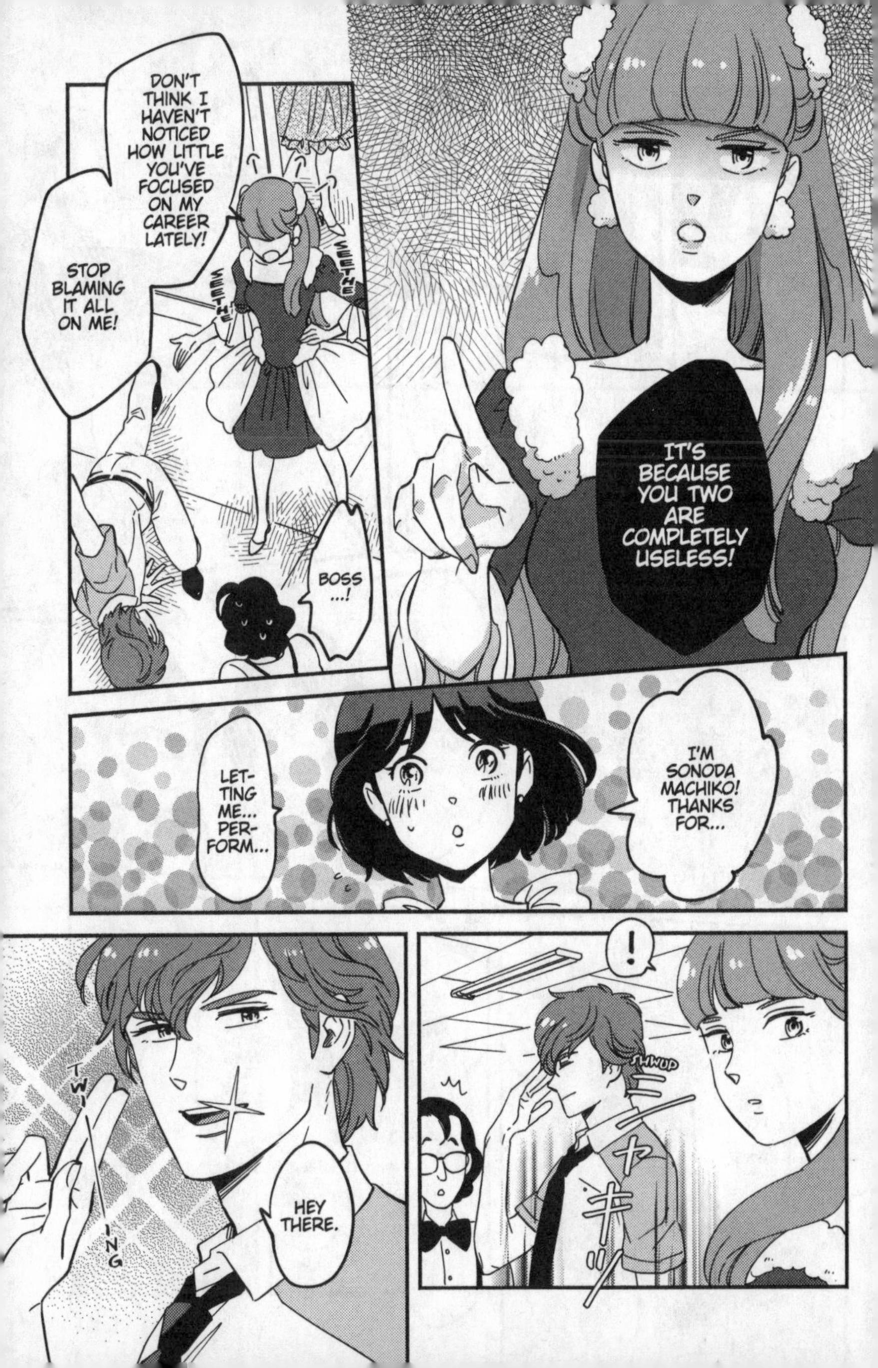
IT'S BECAUSE YOU TWO ARE COMPLETELY USELESS!
DON'T THINK I HAVEN'T NOTICED HOW LITTLE YOU'VE FOCUSED ON MY CAREER LATELY!
SEETHE
SEETHE
STOP BLAMING IT ALL ON ME!
BOSS ...!
I'M SONODA MACHIKO! THANKS FOR...
LET-TING ME... PER-FORM...
!
SHWUP
TWI-ING
HEY THERE.

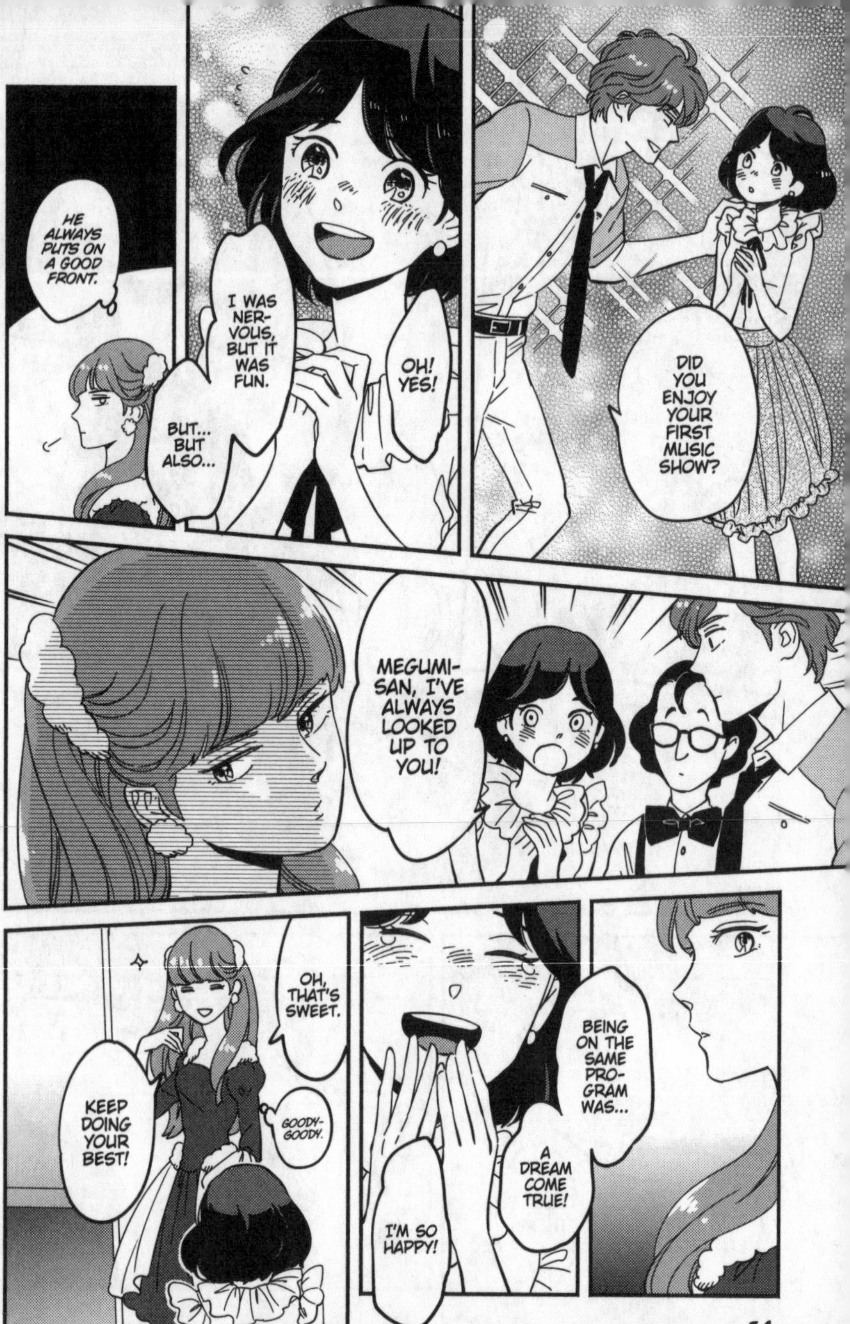
DID YOU ENJOY YOUR FIRST MUSIC SHOW?
OH! YES!
I WAS NERVOUS, BUT IT WAS FUN.
BUT... BUT ALSO...
HE ALWAYS PUTS ON A GOOD FRONT.
MEGUMI-SAN, I'VE ALWAYS LOOKED UP TO YOU!
BEING ON THE SAME PROGRAM WAS...
A DREAM COME TRUE!
I'M SO HAPPY!
OH, THAT'S SWEET.
KEEP DOING YOUR BEST!
GOODY-GOODY.

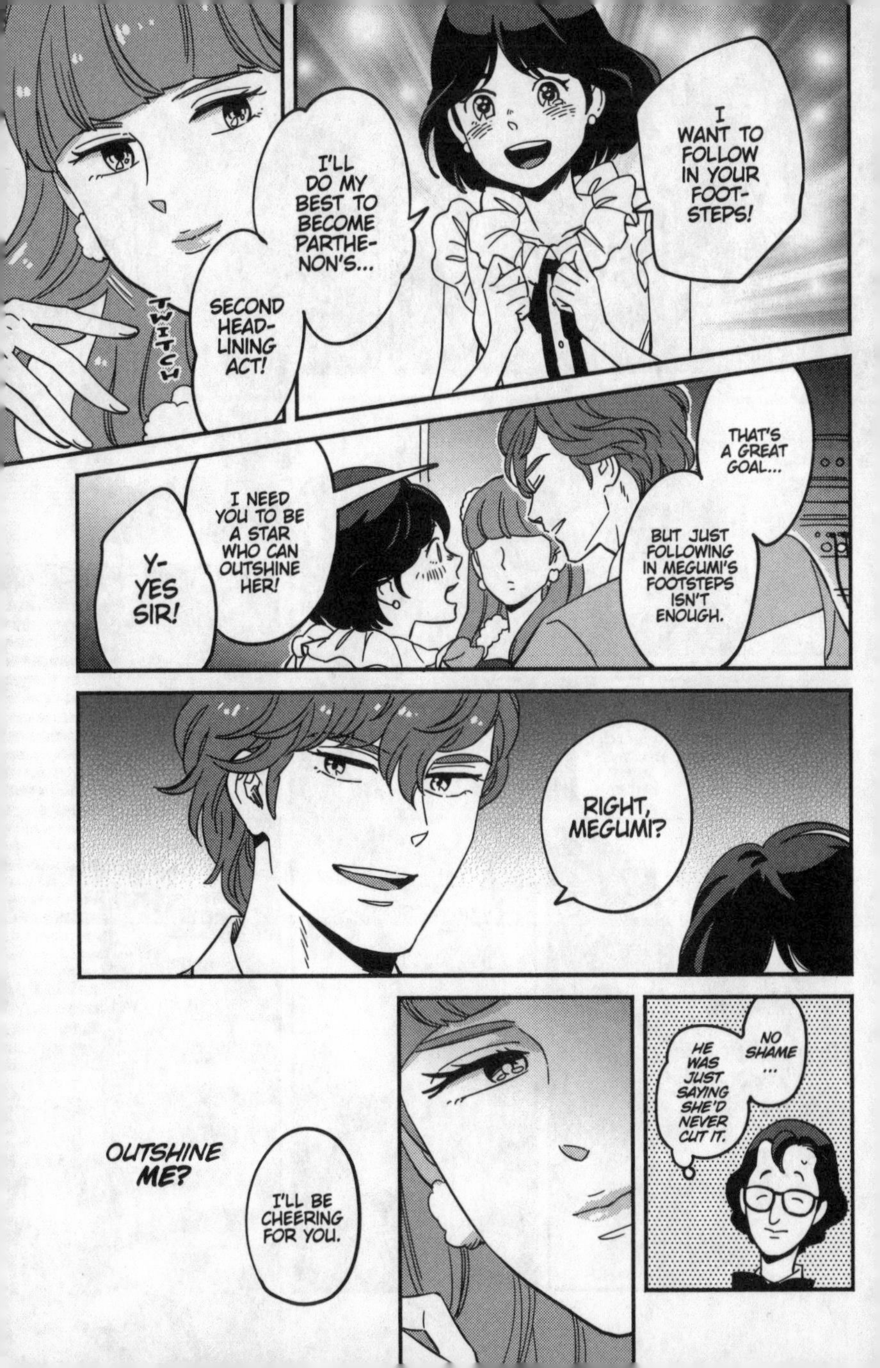
I WANT TO FOLLOW IN YOUR FOOT-STEPS!
I'LL DO MY BEST TO BECOME PARTHE-NON'S...
SECOND HEAD-LINING ACT!
TWITCH
THAT'S A GREAT GOAL...
BUT JUST FOLLOWING IN MEGUMI'S FOOTSTEPS ISN'T ENOUGH.
I NEED YOU TO BE A STAR WHO CAN OUTSHINE HER!
Y-YES SIR!
RIGHT, MEGUMI?
NO SHAME...
HE WAS JUST SAYING SHE'D NEVER CUT IT.
I'LL BE CHEERING FOR YOU.
OUTSHINE ME?

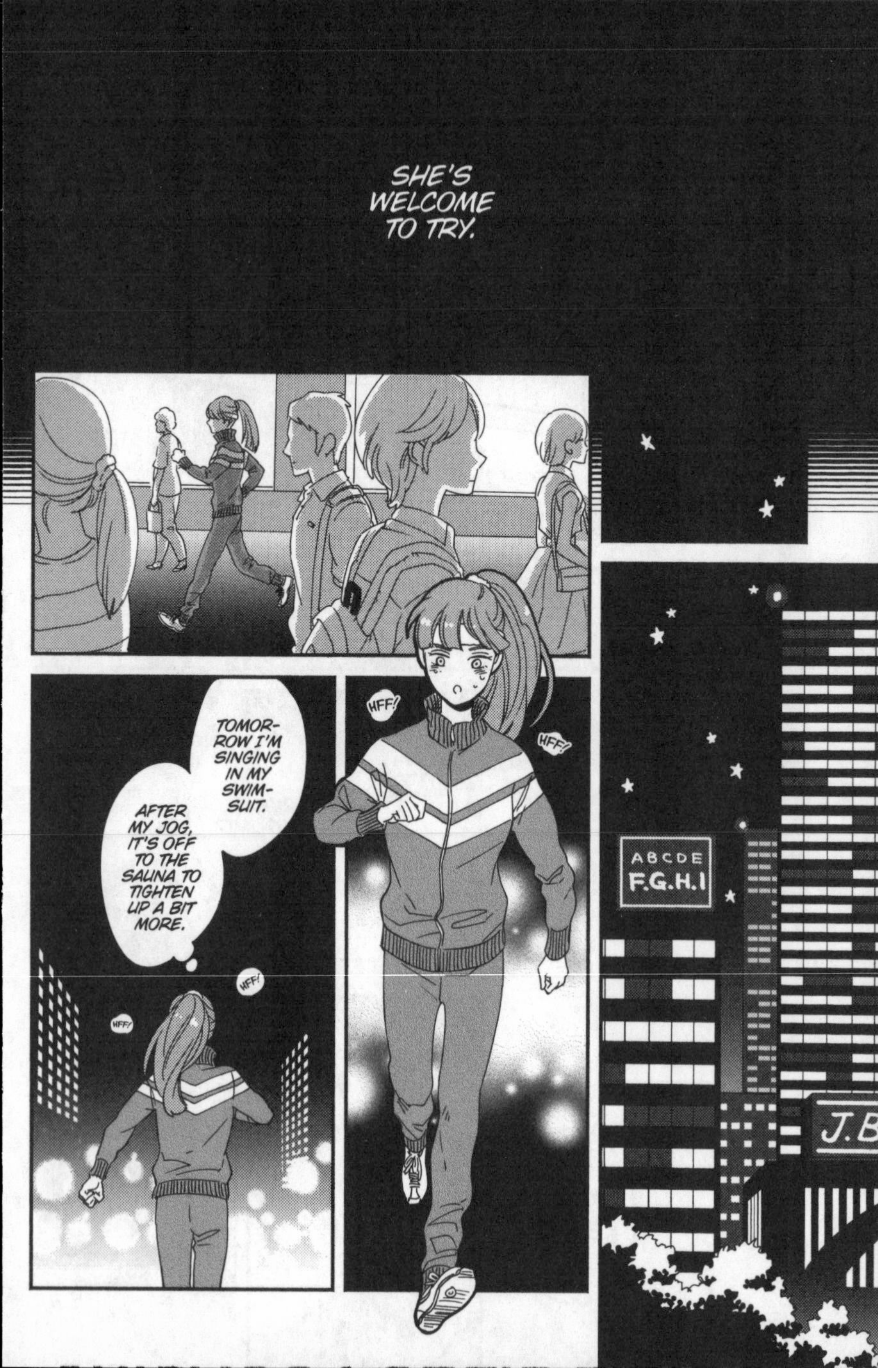
SHE'S WELCOME TO TRY.
ABCDE F.G.H.I
HFF!
HFF!
TOMORROW I'M SINGING IN MY SWIMSUIT.
AFTER MY JOG, IT'S OFF TO THE SAUNA TO TIGHTEN UP A BIT MORE.
HFF!
HFF!

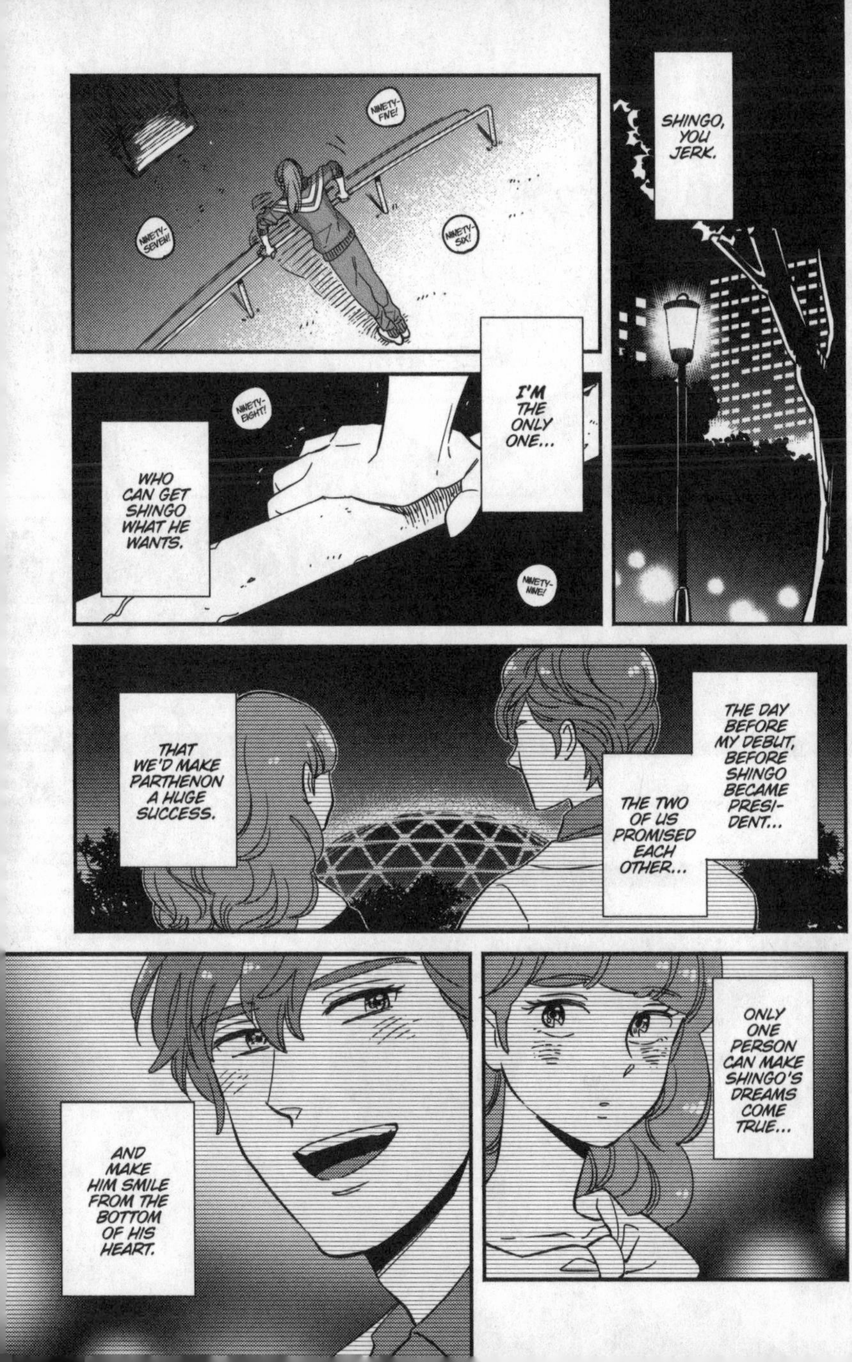
SHINGO, YOU JERK.
NINETY-FIVE!
NINETY-SIX!
NINETY-SEVEN!
I'M THE ONLY ONE...
NINETY-EIGHT!
WHO CAN GET SHINGO WHAT HE WANTS.
NINETY-NINE!
THE DAY BEFORE MY DEBUT, BEFORE SHINGO BECAME PRESI-DENT...
THE TWO OF US PROMISED EACH OTHER...
THAT WE'D MAKE PARTHENON A HUGE SUCCESS.
ONLY ONE PERSON CAN MAKE SHINGO'S DREAMS COME TRUE...
AND MAKE HIM SMILE FROM THE BOTTOM OF HIS HEART.

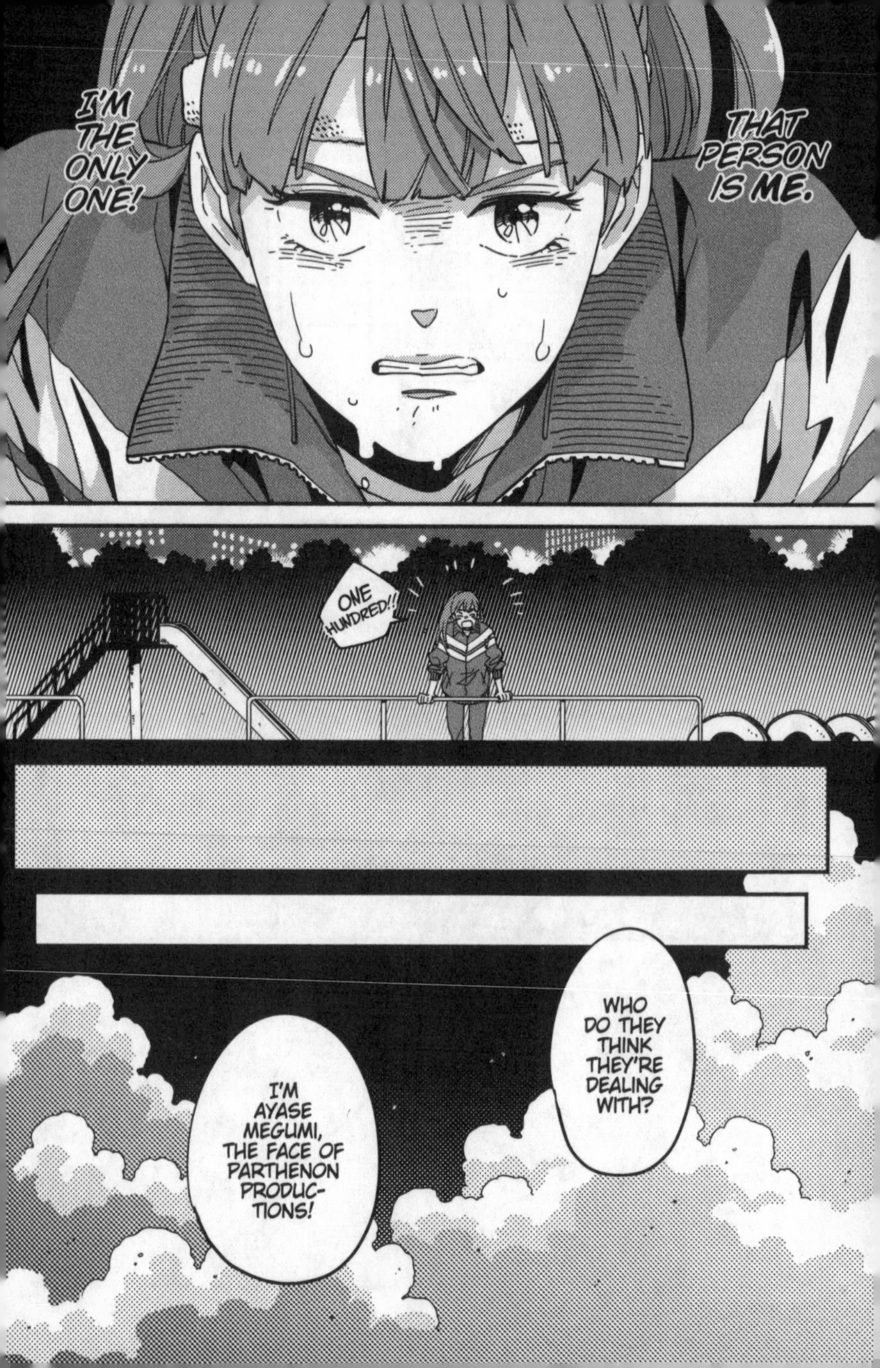
THAT PERSON IS ME.
I'M THE ONLY ONE!
ONE HUNDRED!!
WHO DO THEY THINK THEY'RE DEALING WITH?
I'M AYASE MEGUMI, THE FACE OF PARTHENON PRODUC-TIONS!

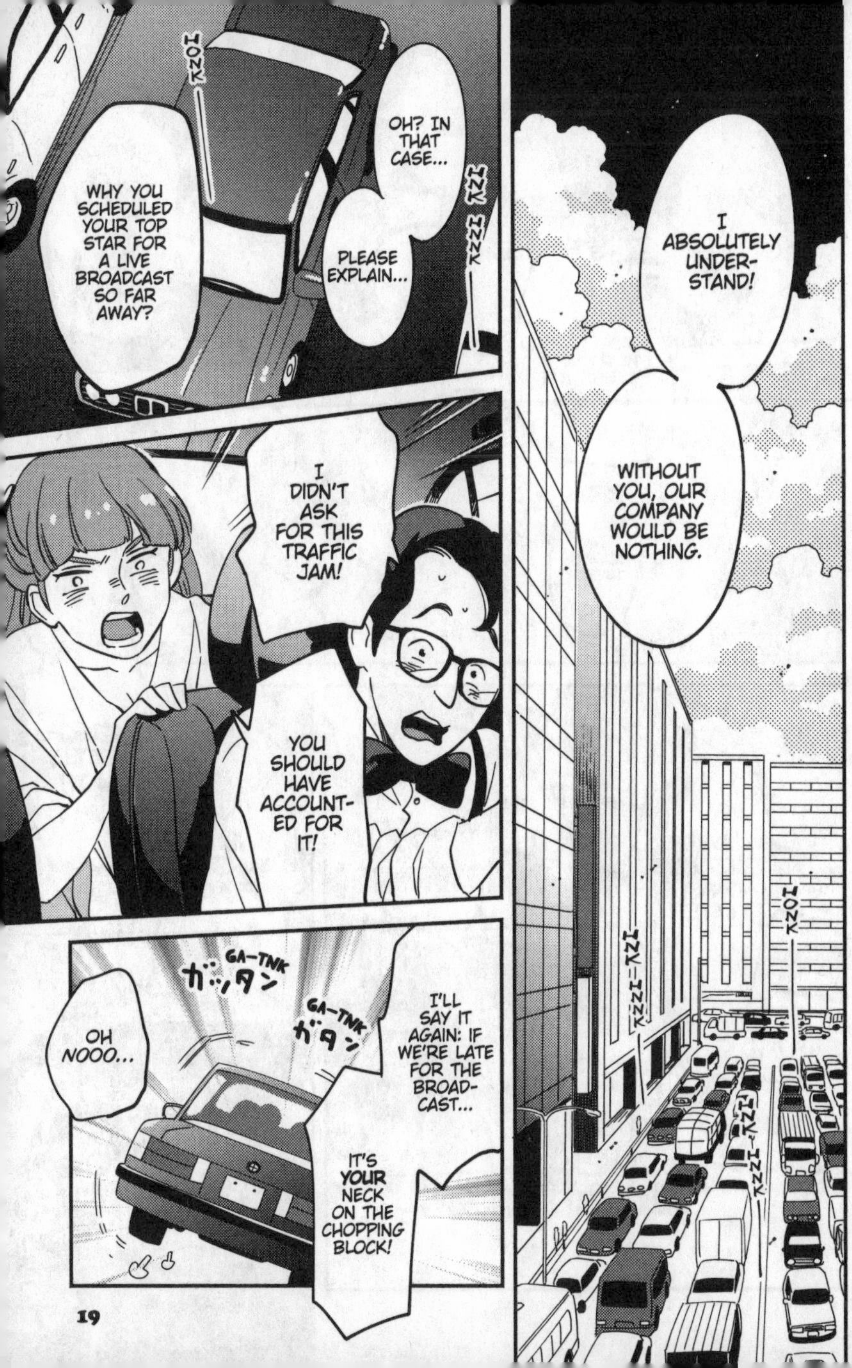
I ABSOLUTELY UNDER-STAND!
WITHOUT YOU, OUR COMPANY WOULD BE NOTHING.
HONK
INNK-HNNK
INNK-INNK
OH? IN THAT CASE...
PLEASE EXPLAIN...
WHY YOU SCHEDULED YOUR TOP STAR FOR A LIVE BROADCAST SO FAR AWAY?
HONK
INNK HNNK
I DIDN'T ASK FOR THIS TRAFFIC JAM!
YOU SHOULD HAVE ACCOUNT-ED FOR IT!
I'LL SAY IT AGAIN: IF WE'RE LATE FOR THE BROAD-CAST...
IT'S YOUR NECK ON THE CHOPPING BLOCK!
GA-TNK
ガタン
GA-TNK
ガッタン
OH NOOO...

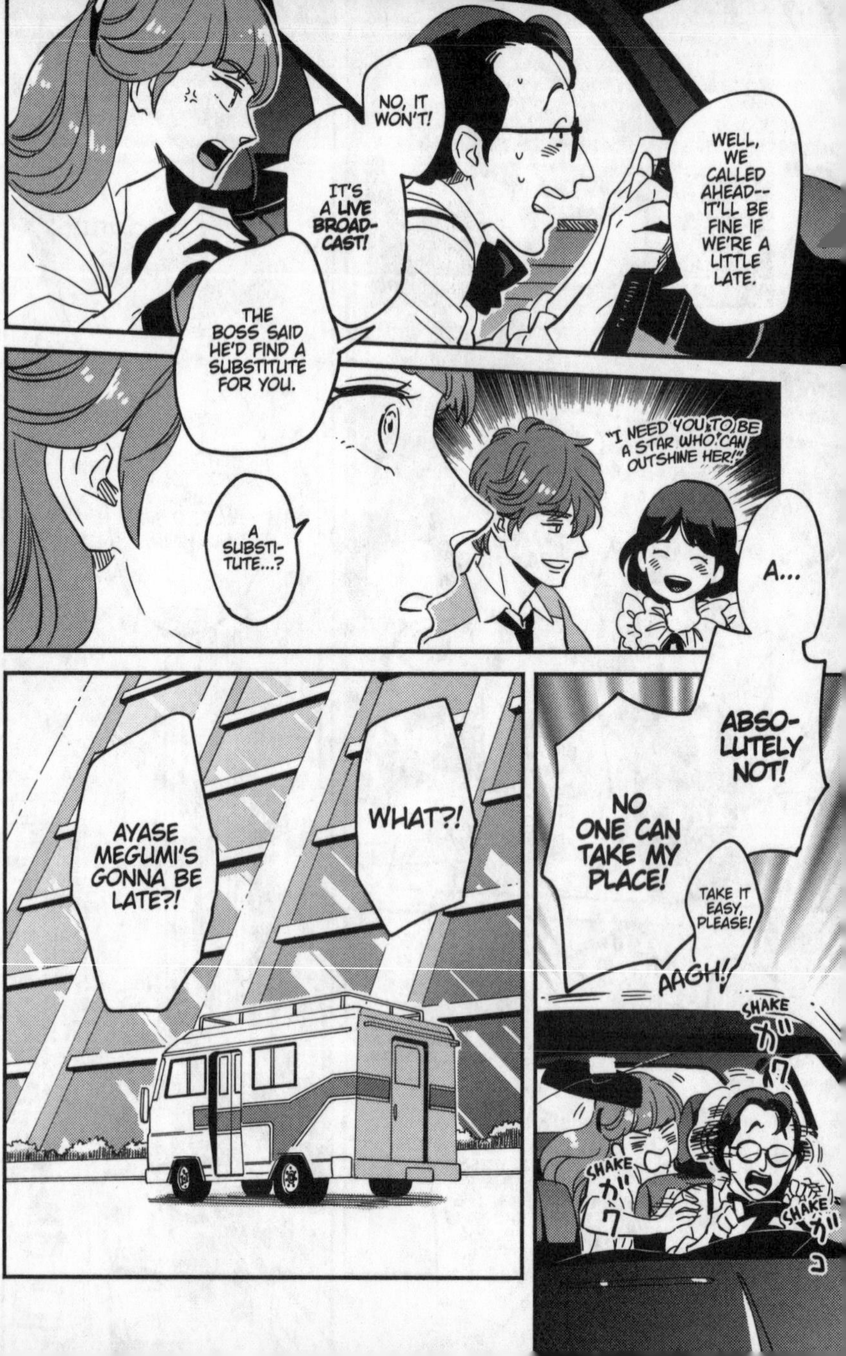

WELL, WE CALLED AHEAD-- IT'LL BE FINE IF WE'RE A LITTLE LATE.
NO, IT WON'T!
IT'S A LIVE BROADCAST!
THE BOSS SAID HE'D FIND A SUBSTITUTE FOR YOU.
"I NEED YOU TO BE A STAR WHO CAN OUTSHINE HER!"
A SUBSTITUTE...?
A...
ABSOLUTELY NOT!
NO ONE CAN TAKE MY PLACE!
TAKE IT EASY, PLEASE!
AAGH!
SHAKE
SHAKE
SHAKE
WHAT?!
AYASE MEGUMI'S GONNA BE LATE?!

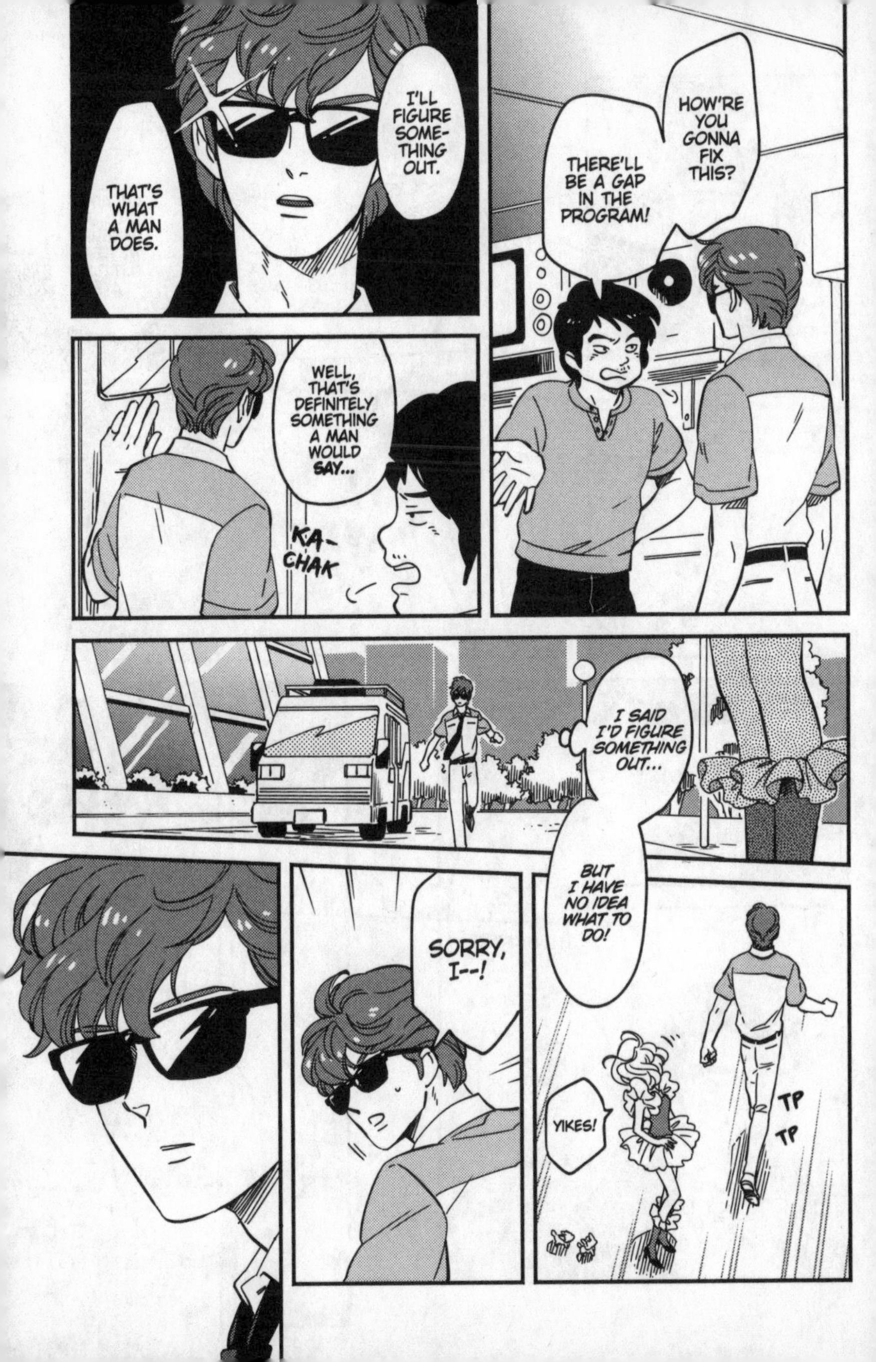
HOW'RE YOU GONNA FIX THIS?
THERE'LL BE A GAP IN THE PROGRAM!
I'LL FIGURE SOMETHING OUT.
THAT'S WHAT A MAN DOES.
WELL, THAT'S DEFINITELY SOMETHING A MAN WOULD SAY...
KA-CHAK
I SAID I'D FIGURE SOMETHING OUT...
BUT I HAVE NO IDEA WHAT TO DO!
YIKES!
TP
TP
SORRY, I--!

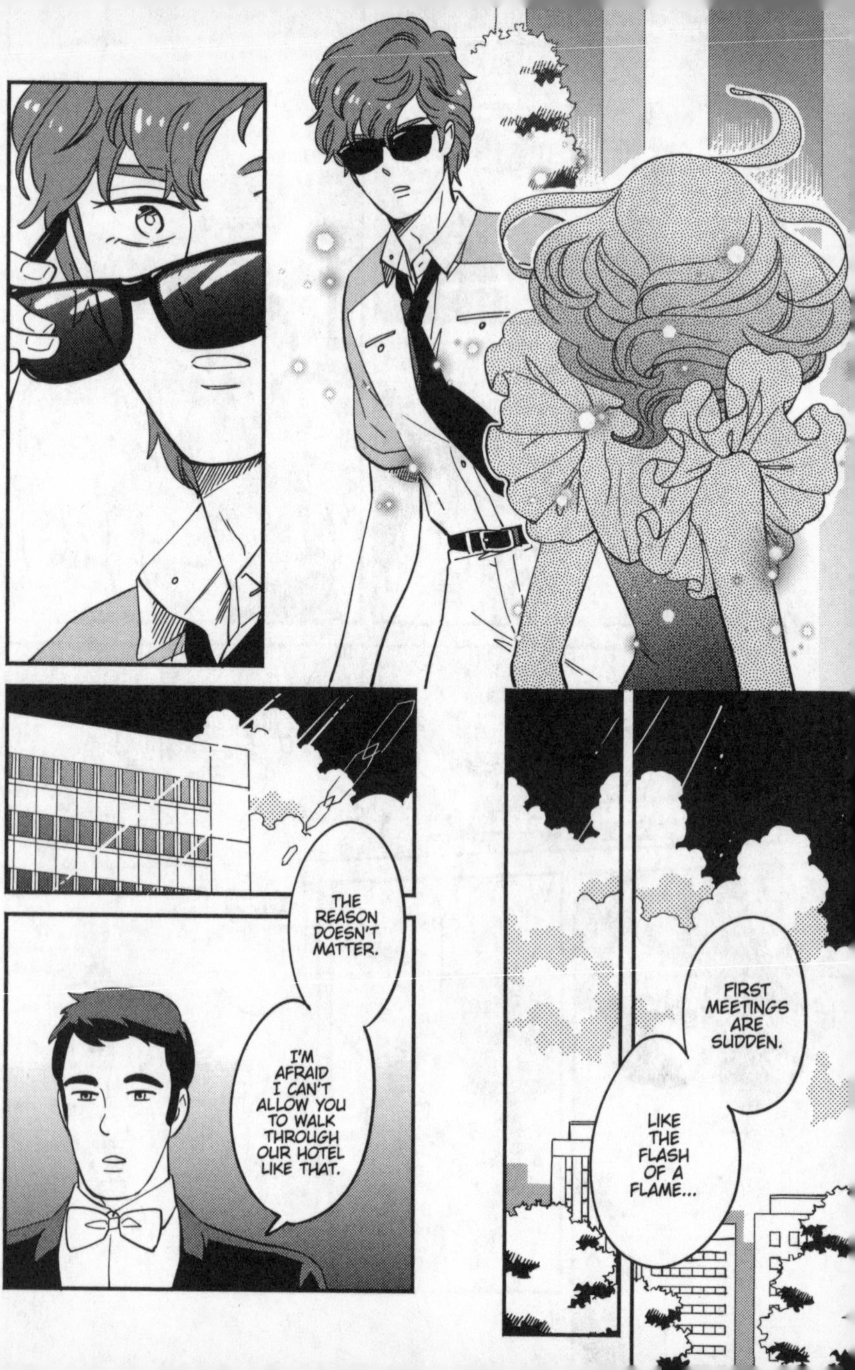
FIRST MEETINGS ARE SUDDEN.
LIKE THE FLASH OF A FLAME...
THE REASON DOESN'T MATTER.
I'M AFRAID I CAN'T ALLOW YOU TO WALK THROUGH OUR HOTEL LIKE THAT.

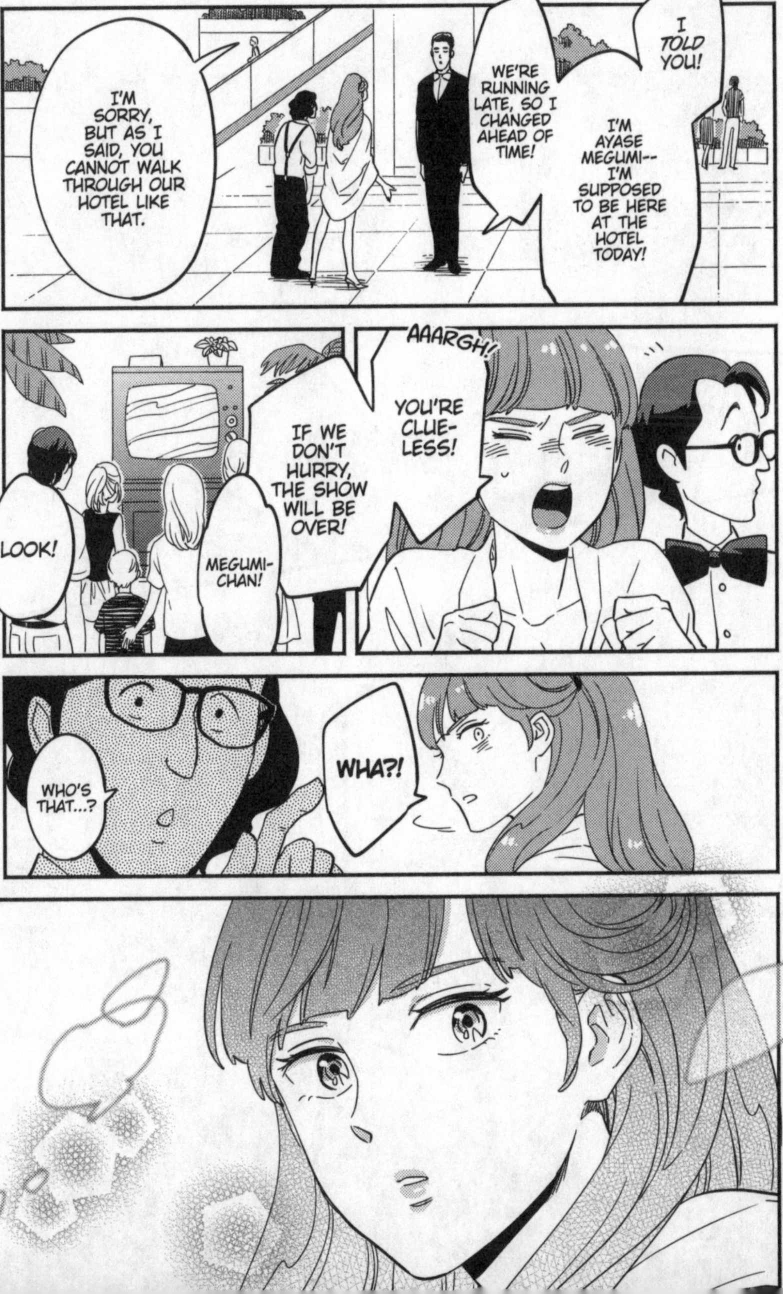
I TOLD YOU!
I'M AYASE MEGUMI-- I'M SUPPOSED TO BE HERE AT THE HOTEL TODAY!
WE'RE RUNNING LATE, SO I CHANGED AHEAD OF TIME!
I'M SORRY, BUT AS I SAID, YOU CANNOT WALK THROUGH OUR HOTEL LIKE THAT.
AAARGH!
YOU'RE CLUE-LESS!
IF WE DON'T HURRY, THE SHOW WILL BE OVER!
MEGUMI-CHAN!
LOOK!
WHA?!
WHO'S THAT...?

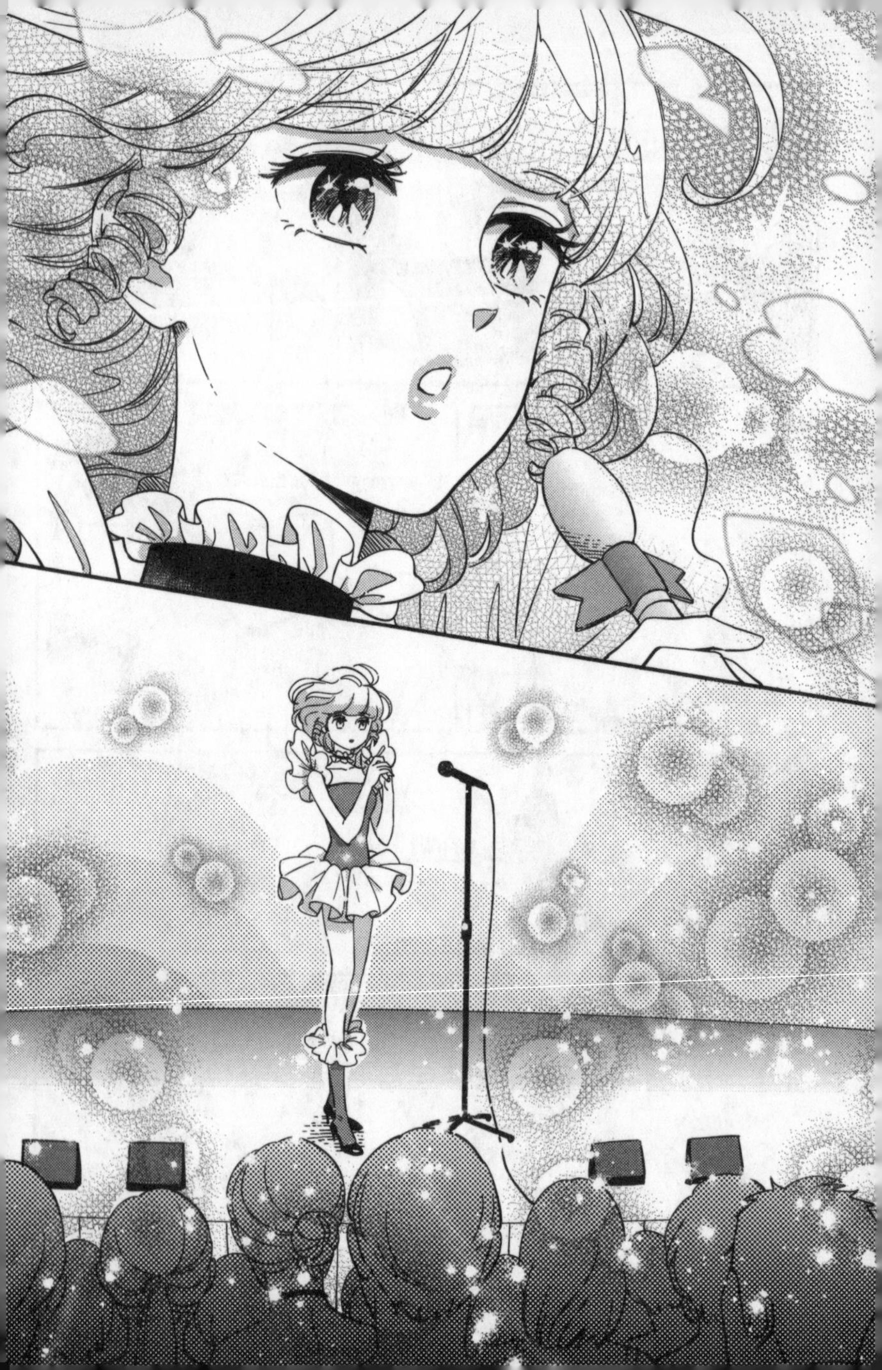

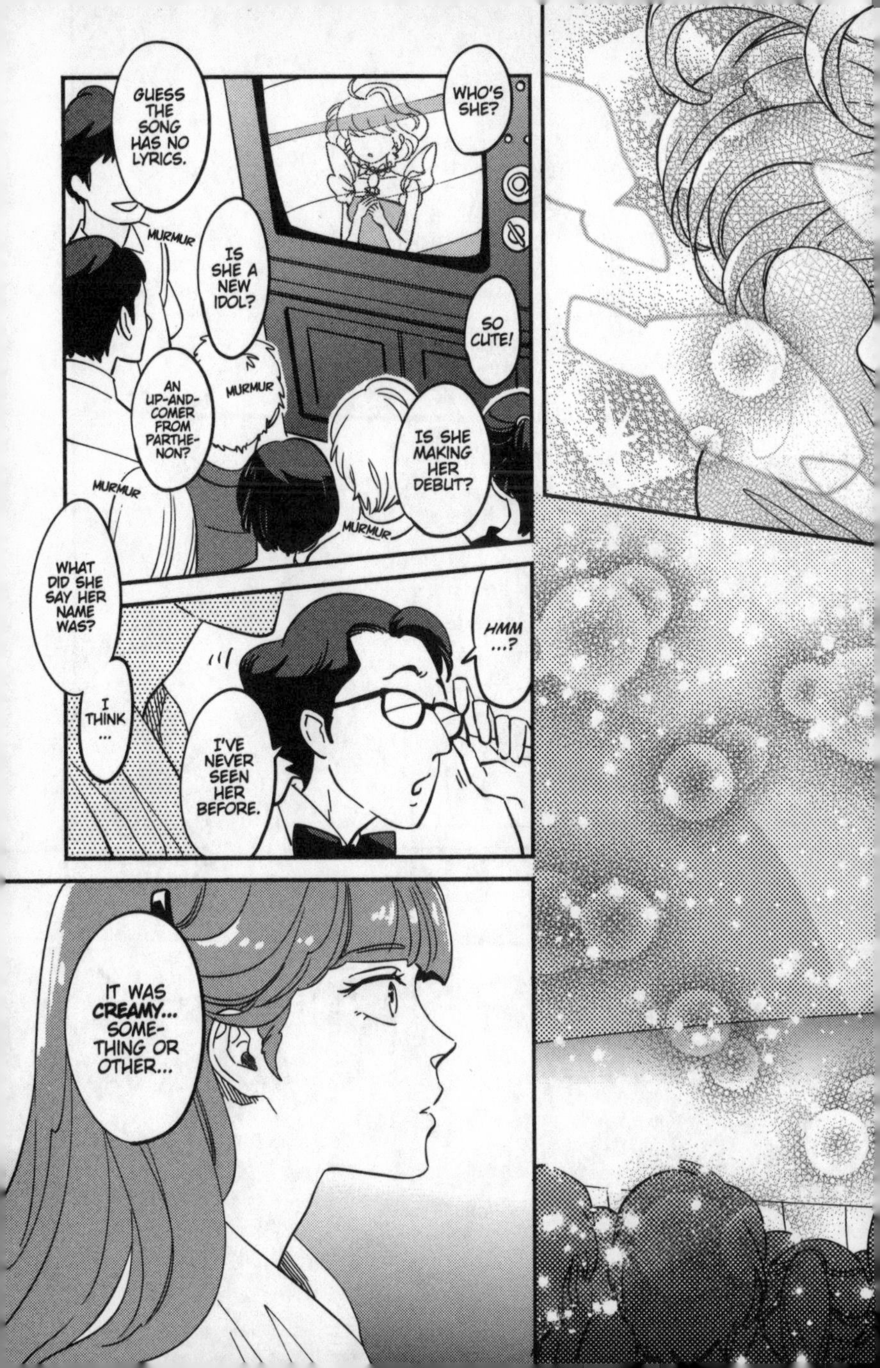
WHO'S SHE?
GUESS THE SONG HAS NO LYRICS.
MURMUR
IS SHE A NEW IDOL?
SO CUTE!
MURMUR
AN UP-AND-COMER FROM PARTHENON?
IS SHE MAKING HER DEBUT?
MURMUR
MURMUR
HMM ...?
WHAT DID SHE SAY HER NAME WAS?
I'VE NEVER SEEN HER BEFORE.
I THINK ...
IT WAS **CREAMY...** SOMETHING OR OTHER...

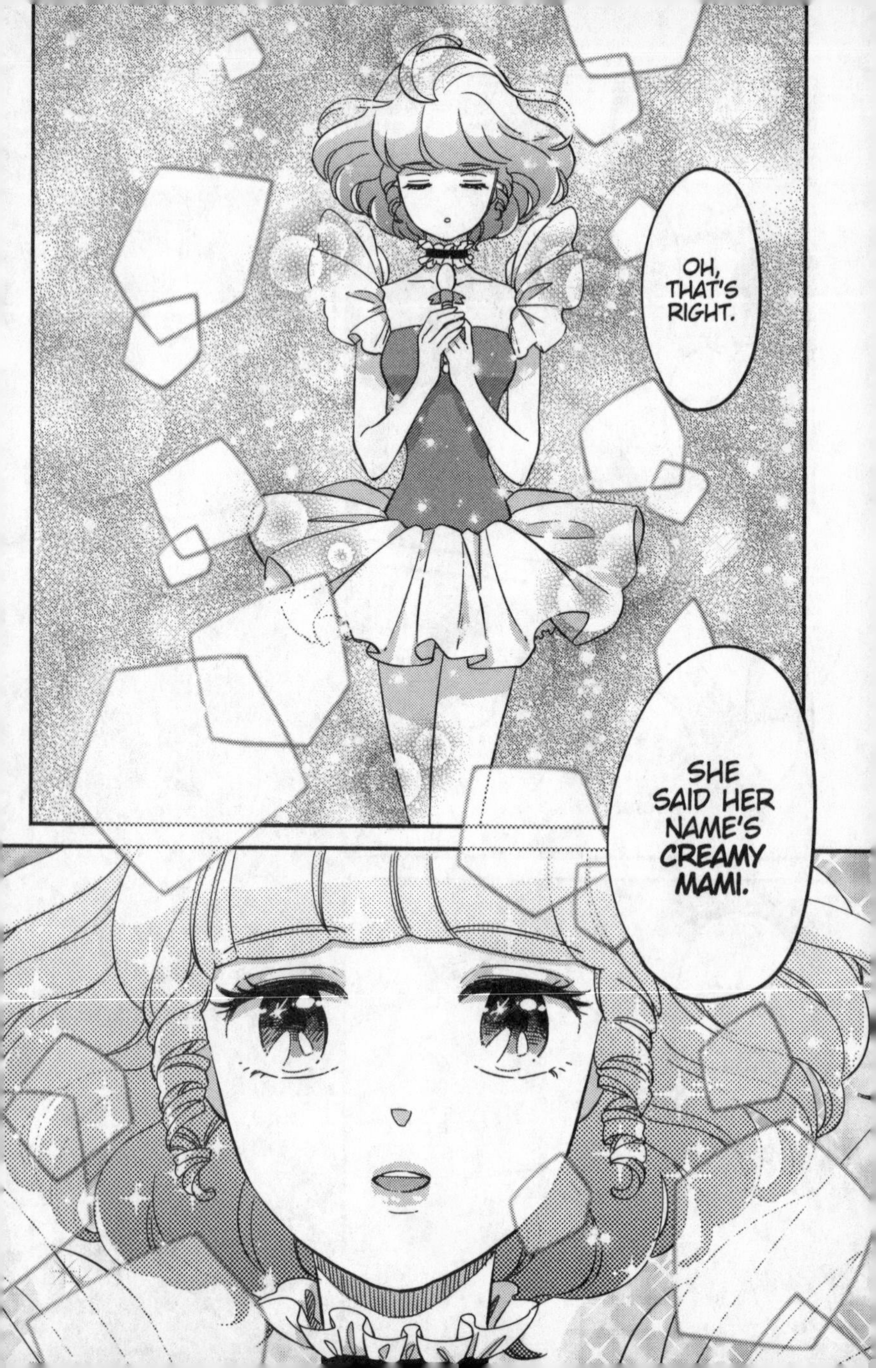
OH, THAT'S RIGHT.
SHE SAID HER NAME'S CREAMY MAMI.

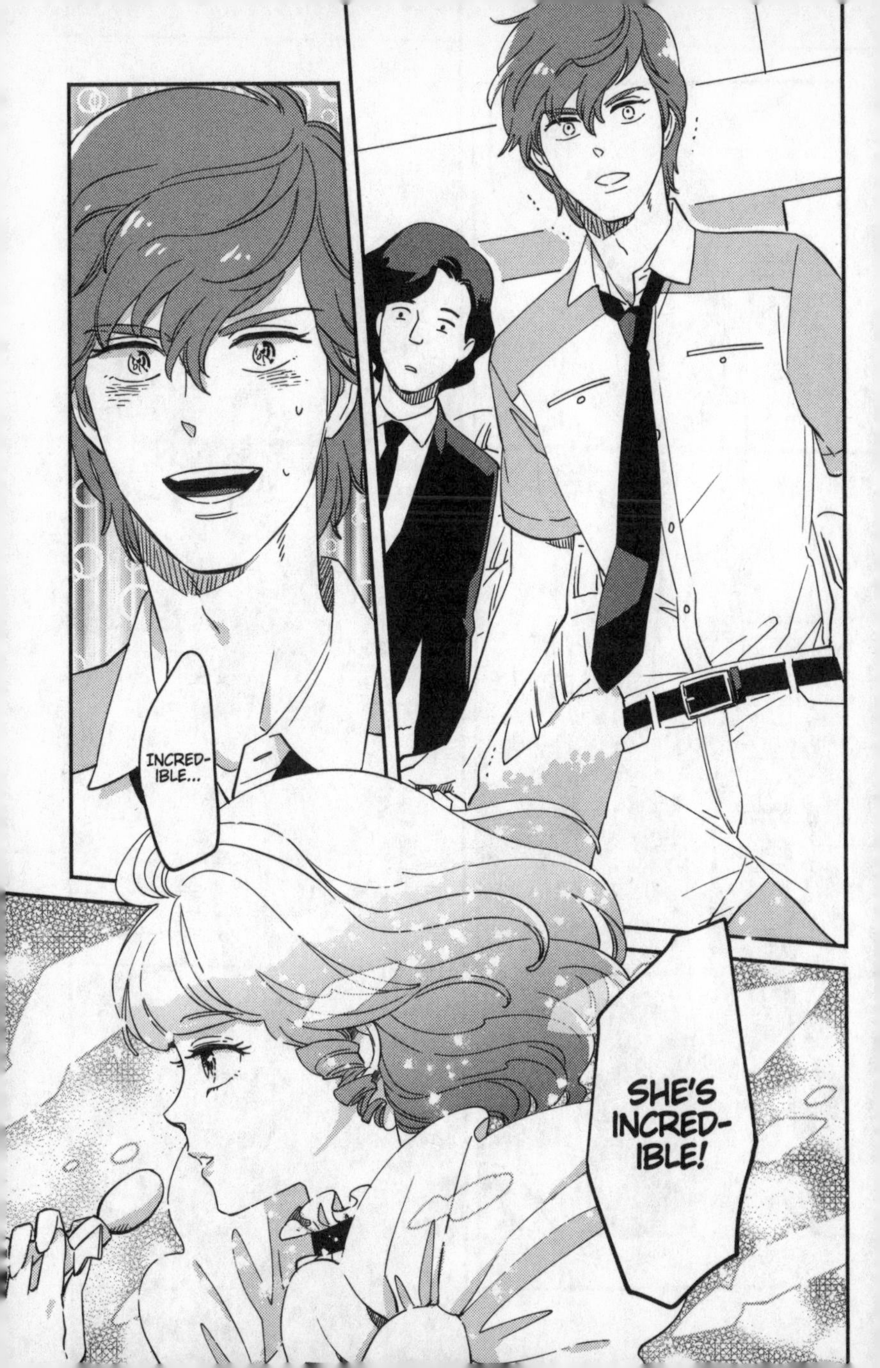
INCRED-IBLE...
SHE'S INCRED-IBLE!

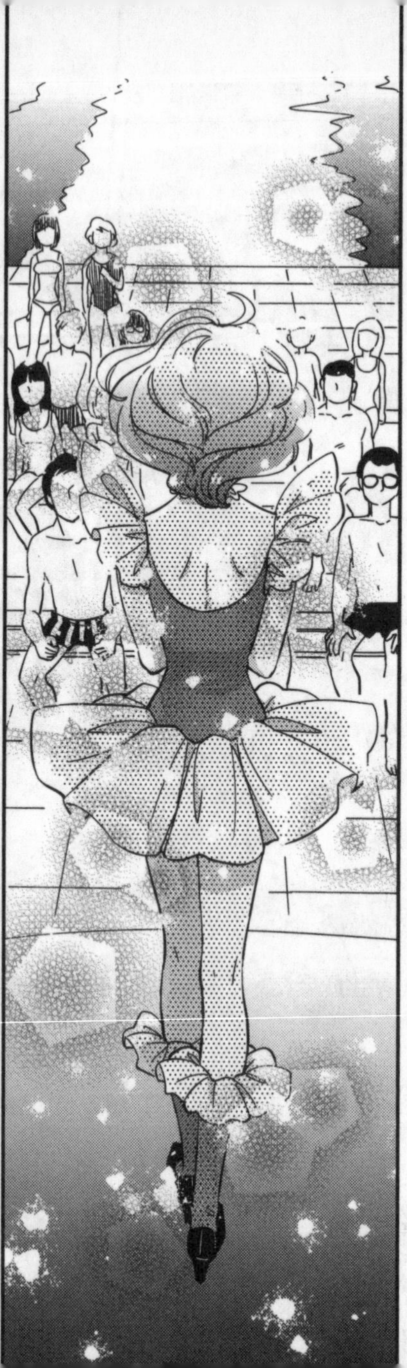

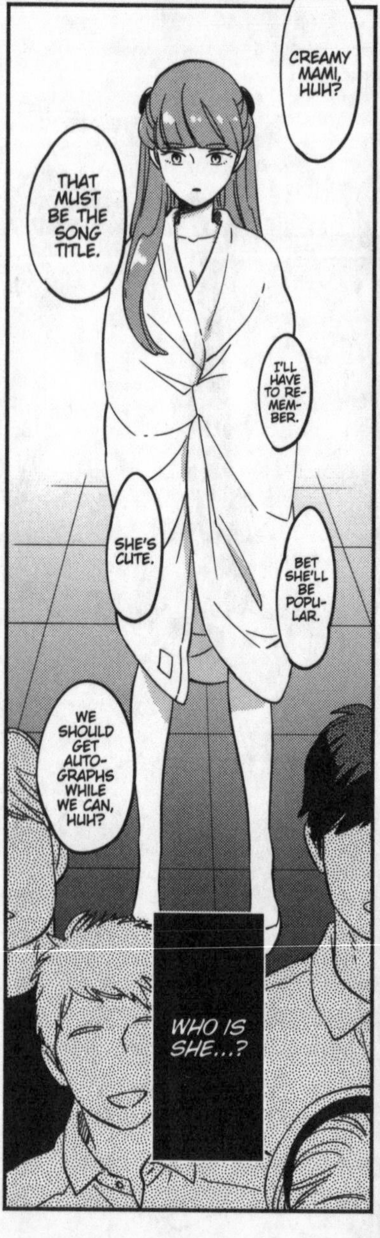
CREAMY MAMI, HUH?
THAT MUST BE THE SONG TITLE.
I'LL HAVE TO REMEMBER.
BET SHE'LL BE POPULAR.
SHE'S CUTE.
WE SHOULD GET AUTOGRAPHS WHILE WE CAN, HUH?
WHO IS SHE...?

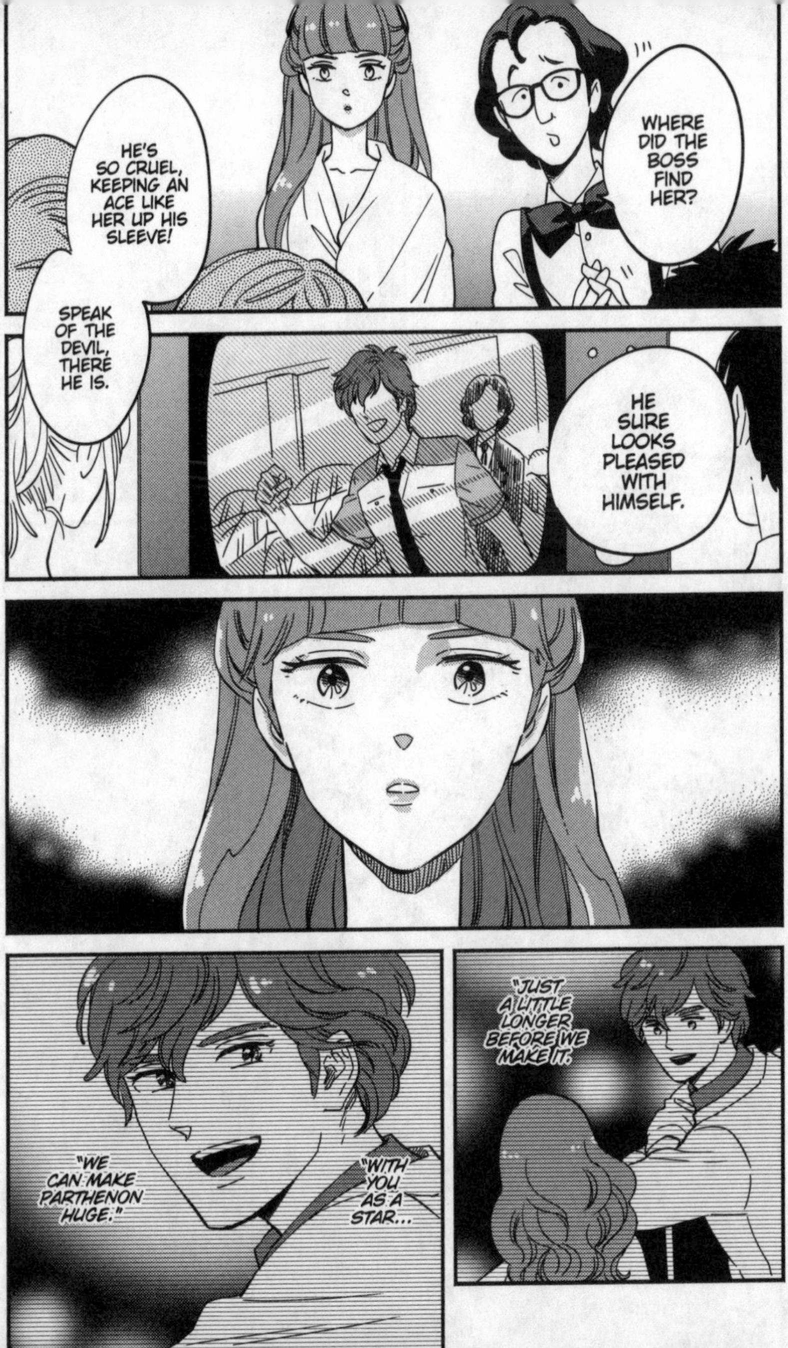
WHERE DID THE BOSS FIND HER?
HE'S SO CRUEL, KEEPING AN ACE LIKE HER UP HIS SLEEVE!
SPEAK OF THE DEVIL, THERE HE IS.
HE SURE LOOKS PLEASED WITH HIMSELF.
"JUST A LITTLE LONGER BEFORE WE MAKE IT.
"WITH YOU AS A STAR...
"WE CAN MAKE PARTHENON HUGE."

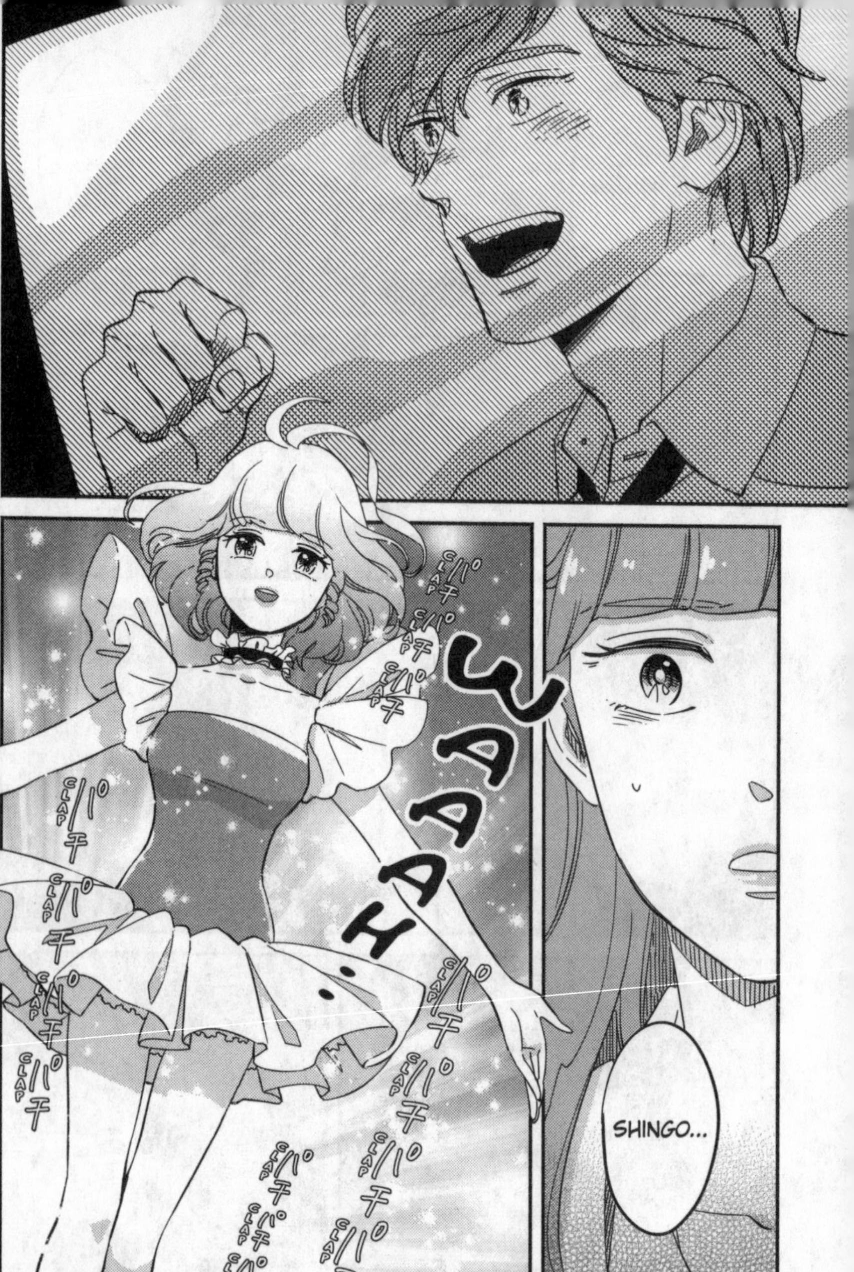
SHINGO...
WAAAH...
パチ CLAP
パチ CLAP
パチ CLAP
パチ CLAP
パチ CLAP
パチ CLAP
パチ CLAP
パチ CLAP
パチ CLAP
パチ CLAP
パチ CLAP
パチ CLAP
パチ CLAP
パチ CLAP

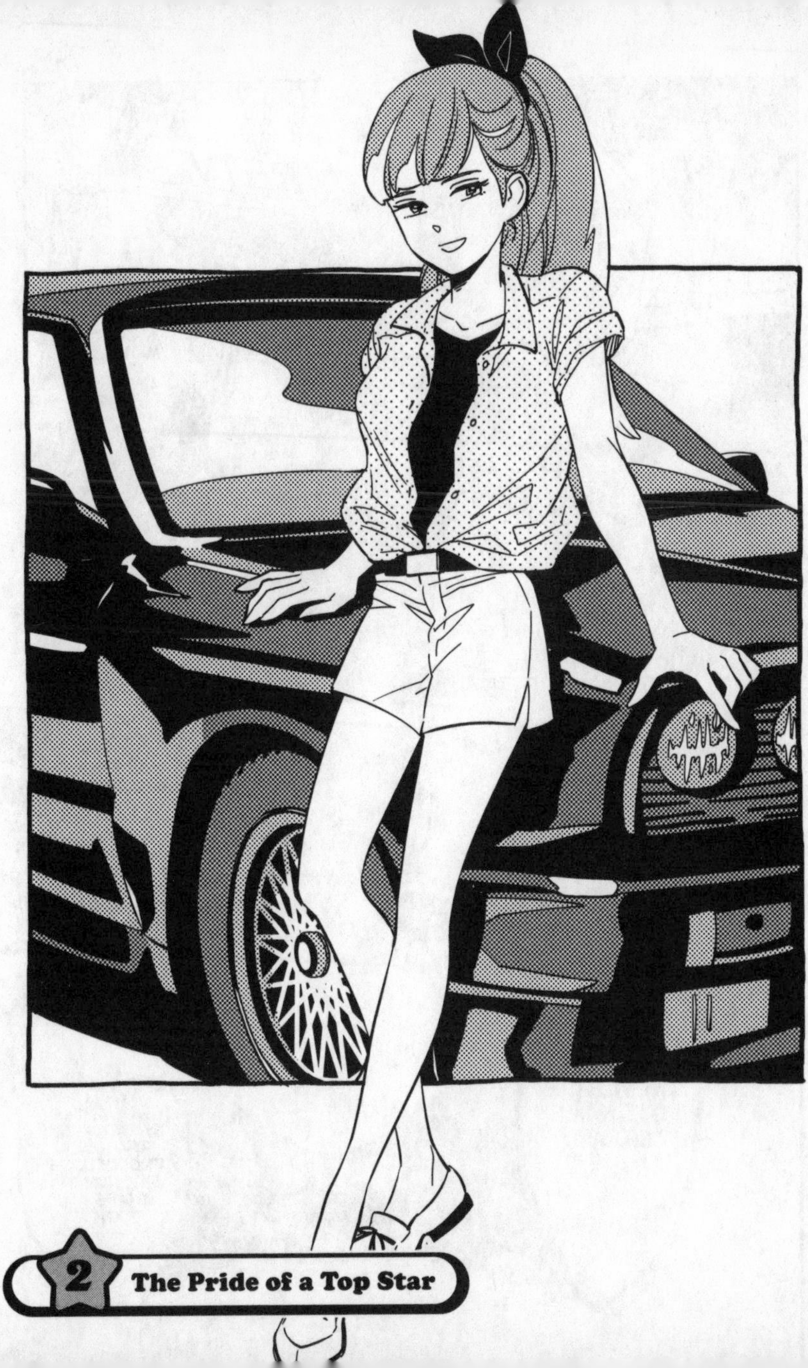
2
The Pride of a Top Star

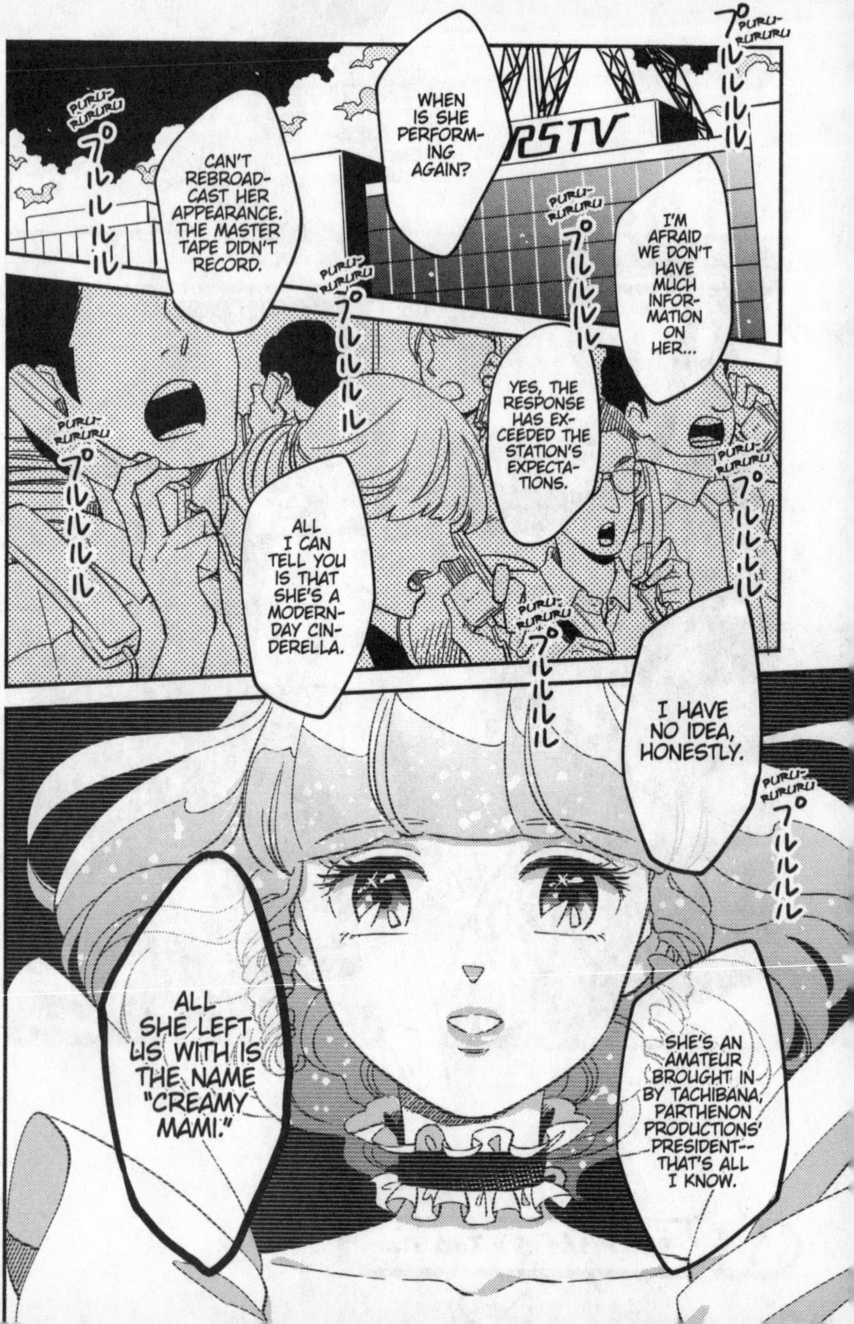
PURU-RURURU
プルルルル
WHEN IS SHE PERFORMING AGAIN?
PURU-RURURU
プルルルル
I'M AFRAID WE DON'T HAVE MUCH INFORMATION ON HER...
PURU-RURURU
プルルルル
CAN'T REBROADCAST HER APPEARANCE. THE MASTER TAPE DIDN'T RECORD.
PURU-RURURU
プルルルル
PURU-RURURU
プルルルル
YES, THE RESPONSE HAS EXCEEDED THE STATION'S EXPECTATIONS.
PURU-RURURU
プルルルル
ALL I CAN TELL YOU IS THAT SHE'S A MODERN-DAY CINDERELLA.
PURU-RURURU
プルルルル
I HAVE NO IDEA, HONESTLY.
PURU-RURURU
プルルルル
SHE'S AN AMATEUR BROUGHT IN BY TACHIBANA, PARTHENON PRODUCTIONS' PRESIDENT--THAT'S ALL I KNOW.
ALL SHE LEFT US WITH IS THE NAME "CREAMY MAMI."

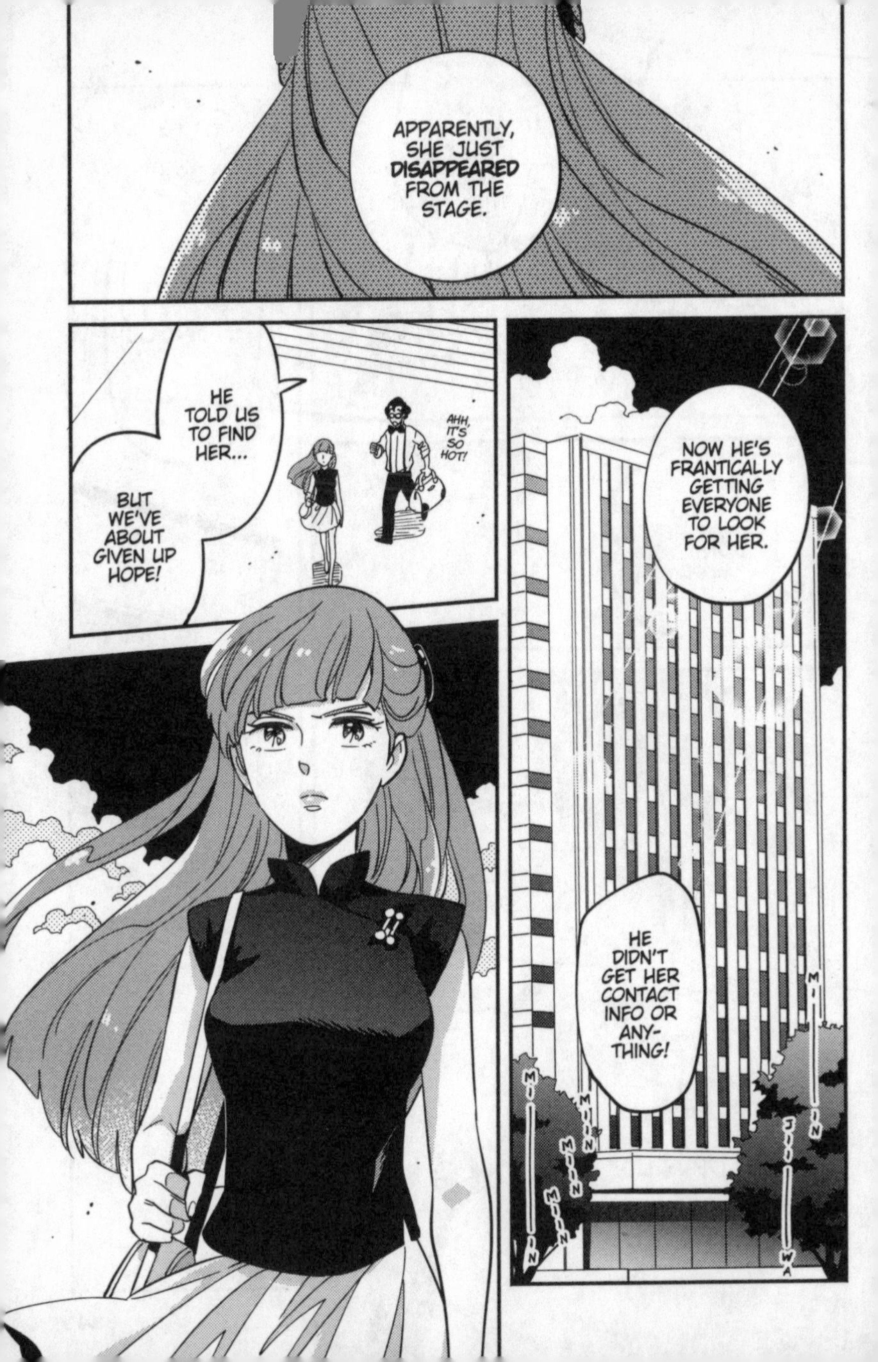
APPARENTLY, SHE JUST DISAPPEARED FROM THE STAGE.
NOW HE'S FRANTICALLY GETTING EVERYONE TO LOOK FOR HER.
HE DIDN'T GET HER CONTACT INFO OR ANY-THING!
MI-I-N
JI-I-WA
MI-I-N
MI-N
MI-N
MI-N
HE TOLD US TO FIND HER...
BUT WE'VE ABOUT GIVEN UP HOPE!
AHH, IT'S SO HOT!

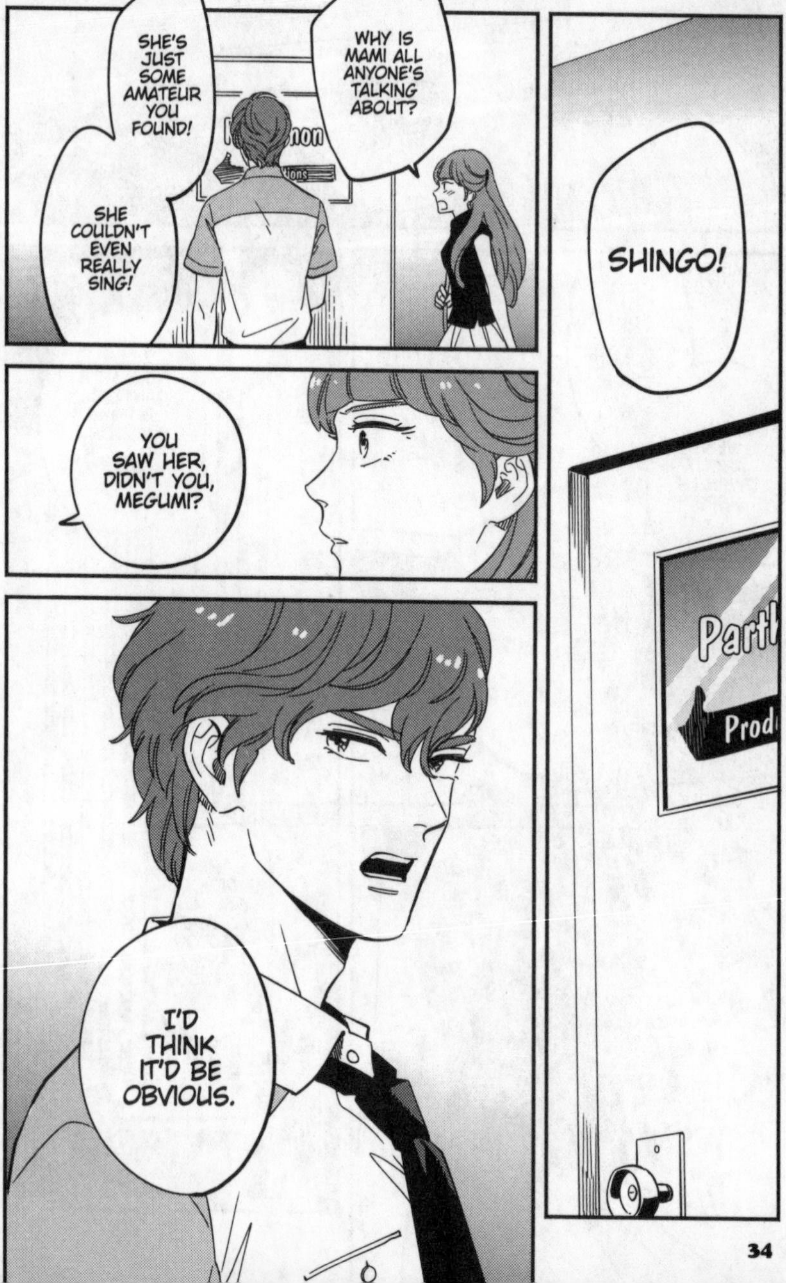
SHINGO!
WHY IS MAMI ALL ANYONE'S TALKING ABOUT?
SHE'S JUST SOME AMATEUR YOU FOUND!
SHE COULDN'T EVEN REALLY SING!
YOU SAW HER, DIDN'T YOU, MEGUMI?
I'D THINK IT'D BE OBVIOUS.

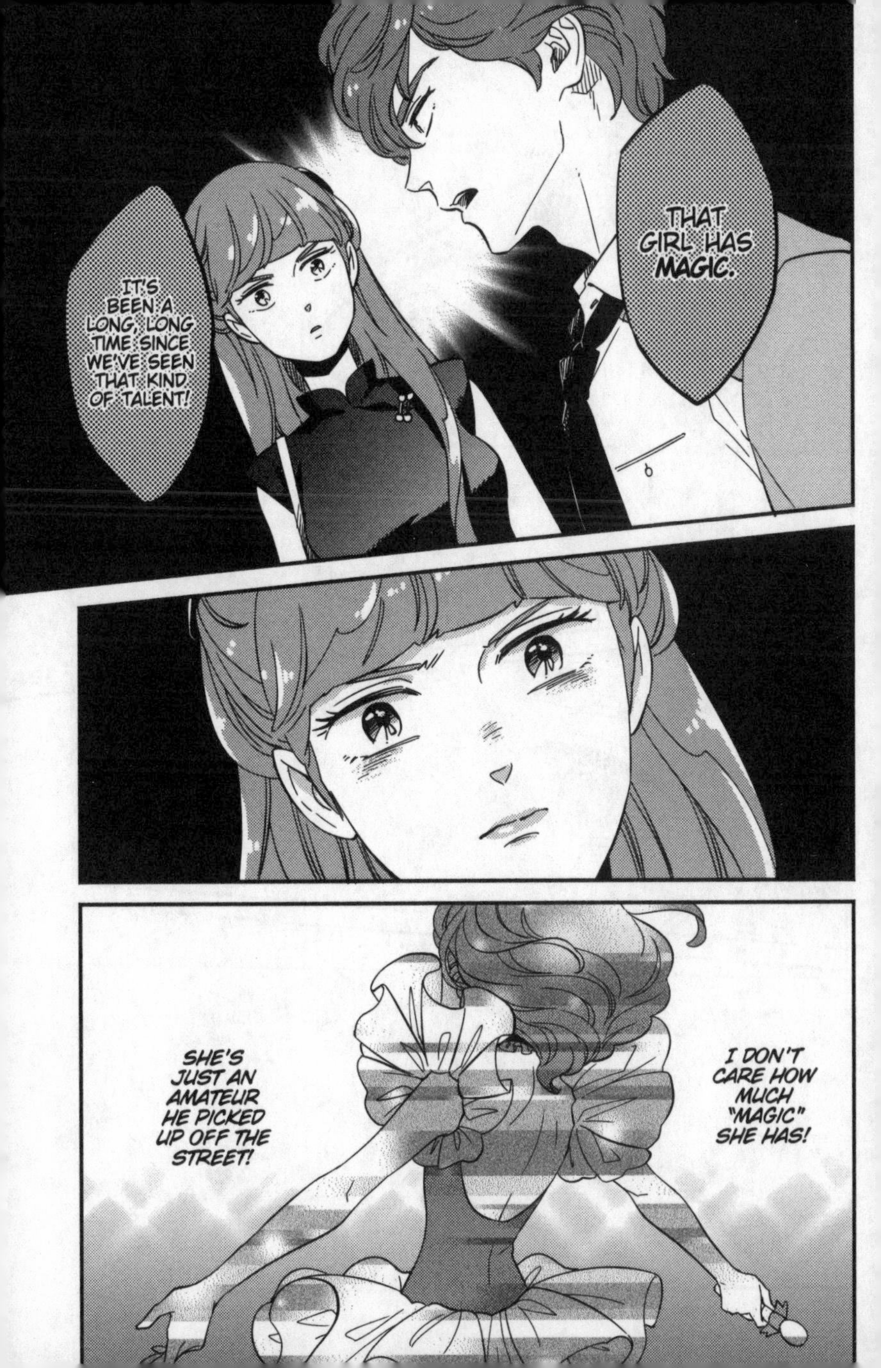
THAT GIRL HAS MAGIC.
IT'S BEEN A LONG, LONG TIME SINCE WE'VE SEEN THAT KIND OF TALENT!
I DON'T CARE HOW MUCH "MAGIC" SHE HAS!
SHE'S JUST AN AMATEUR HE PICKED UP OFF THE STREET!

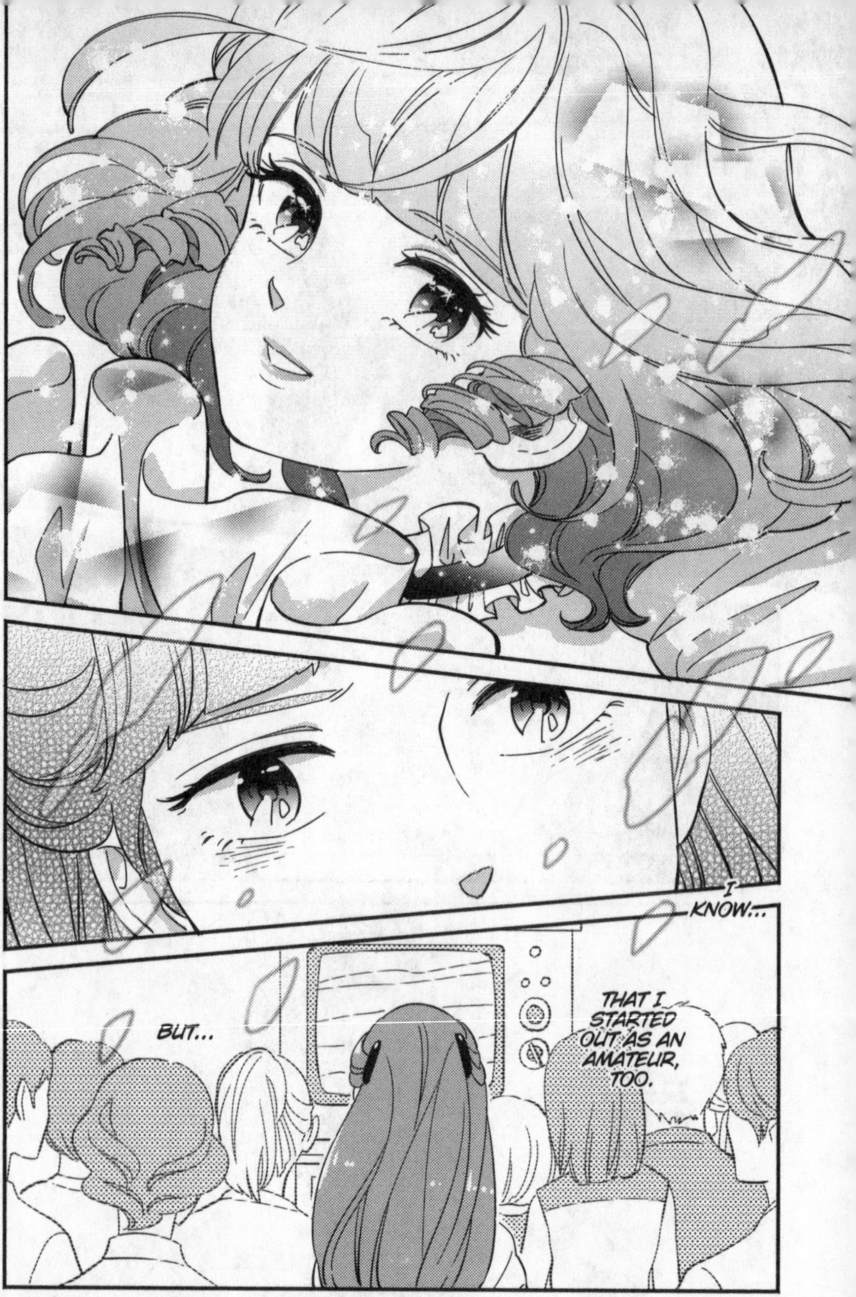
I KNOW...
THAT I STARTED OUT AS AN AMATEUR, TOO.
BUT...

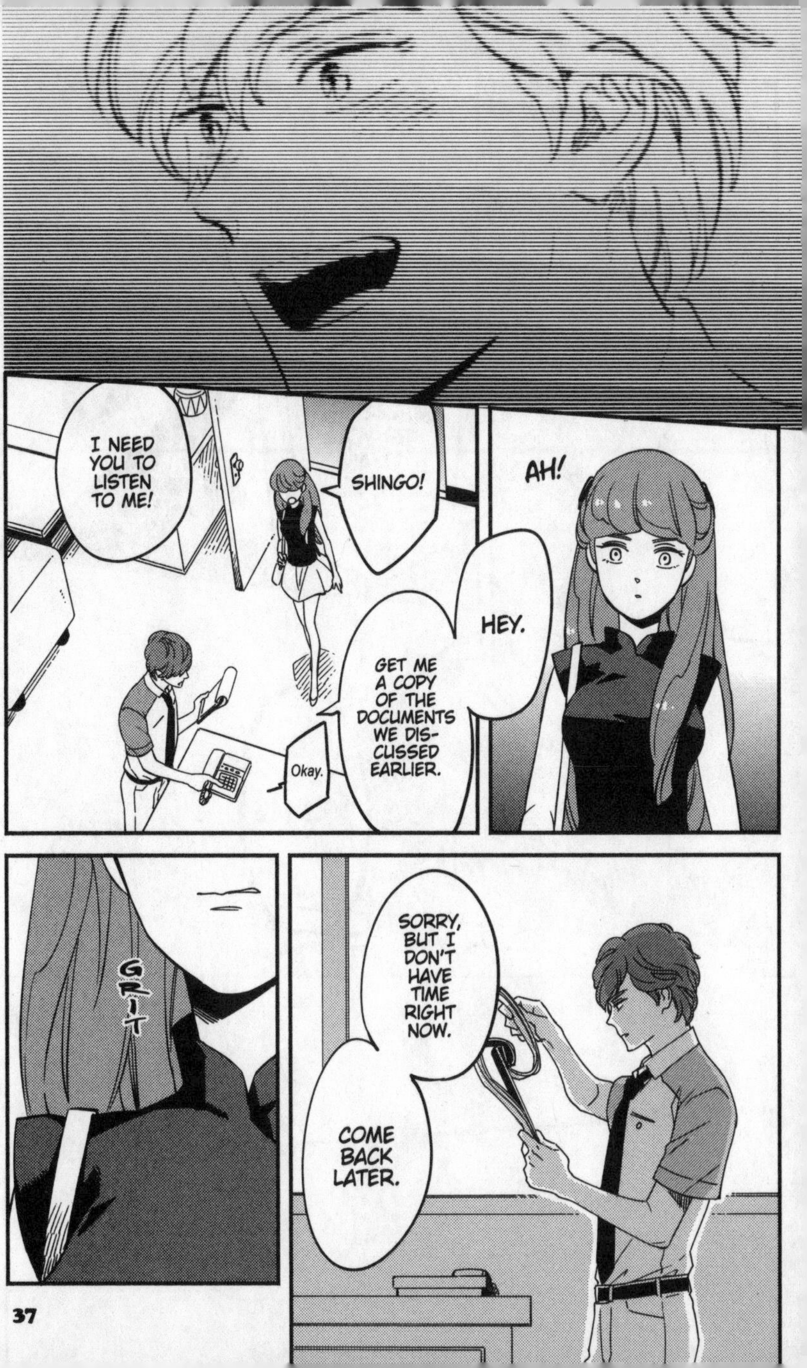
AH!
HEY.
GET ME A COPY OF THE DOCUMENTS WE DIS-CUSSED EARLIER.
Okay.
SHINGO!
I NEED YOU TO LISTEN TO ME!
SORRY, BUT I DON'T HAVE TIME RIGHT NOW.
COME BACK LATER.
GRIT

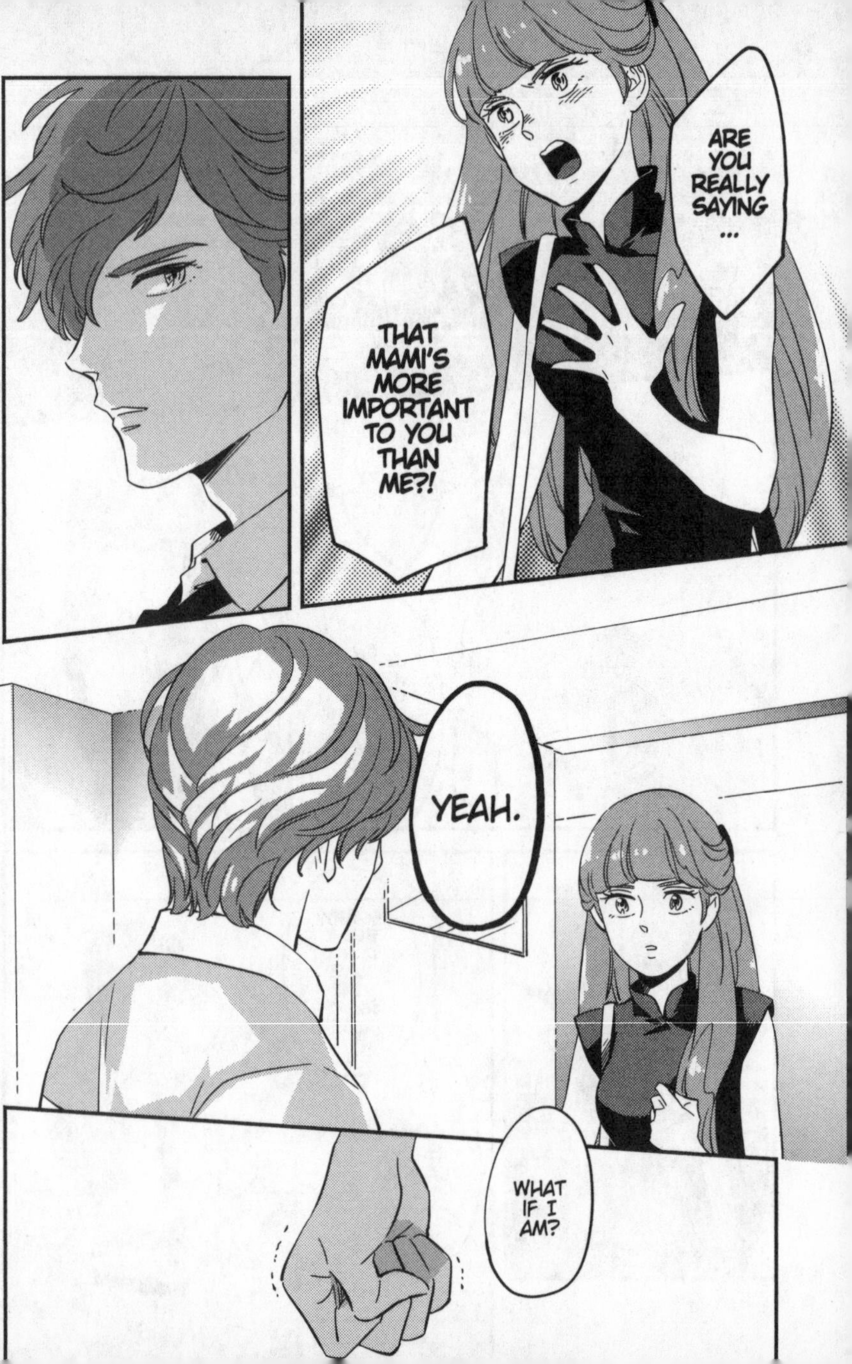
ARE YOU REALLY SAYING ...
THAT MAMI'S MORE IMPORTANT TO YOU THAN ME?!
YEAH.
WHAT IF I AM?

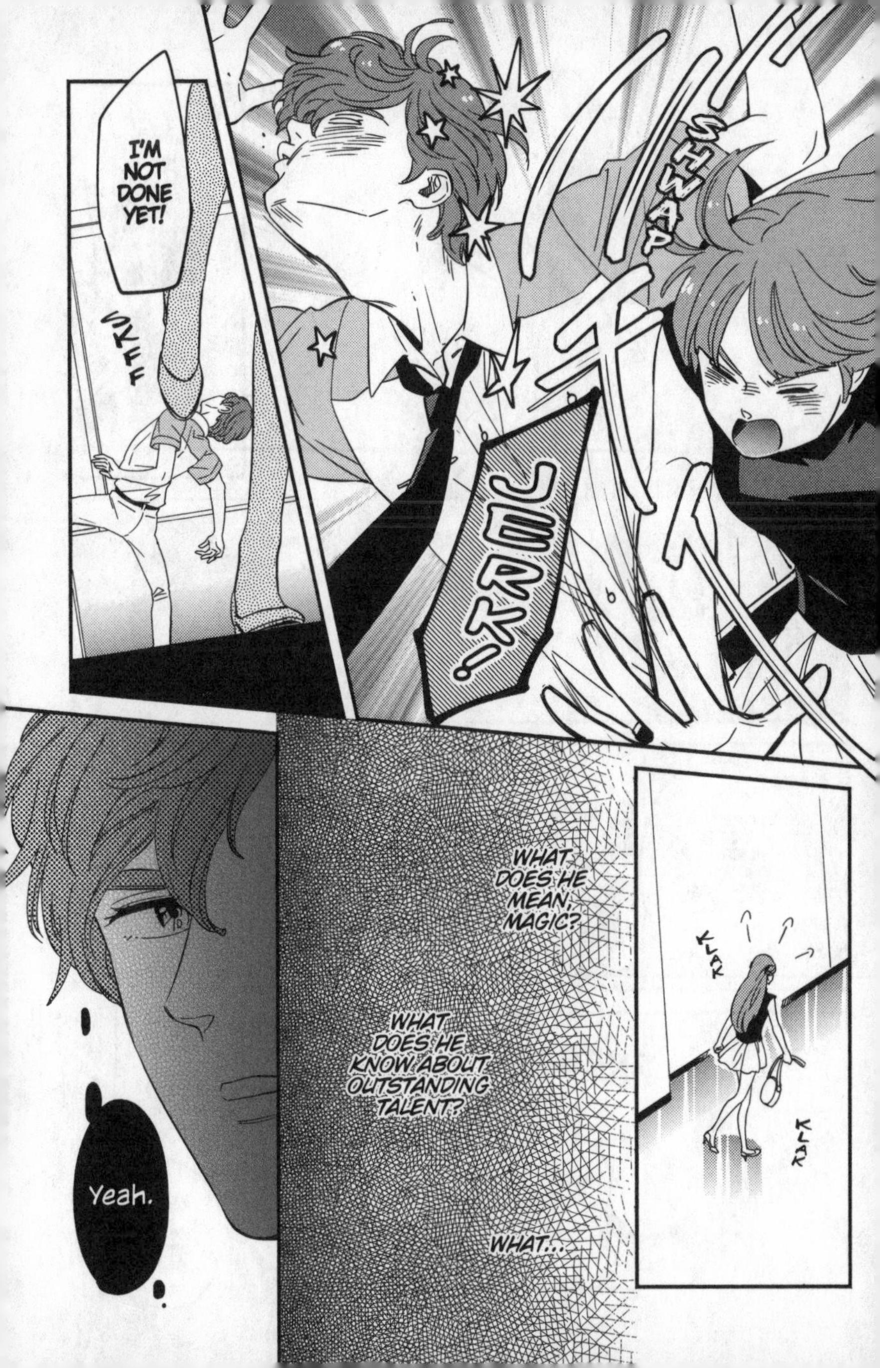
SHWAP
JERK!
I'M NOT DONE YET!
SKFF
KLAK
KLAK
WHAT DOES HE MEAN, MAGIC?
WHAT DOES HE KNOW ABOUT OUTSTANDING TALENT?
WHAT...
Yeah.

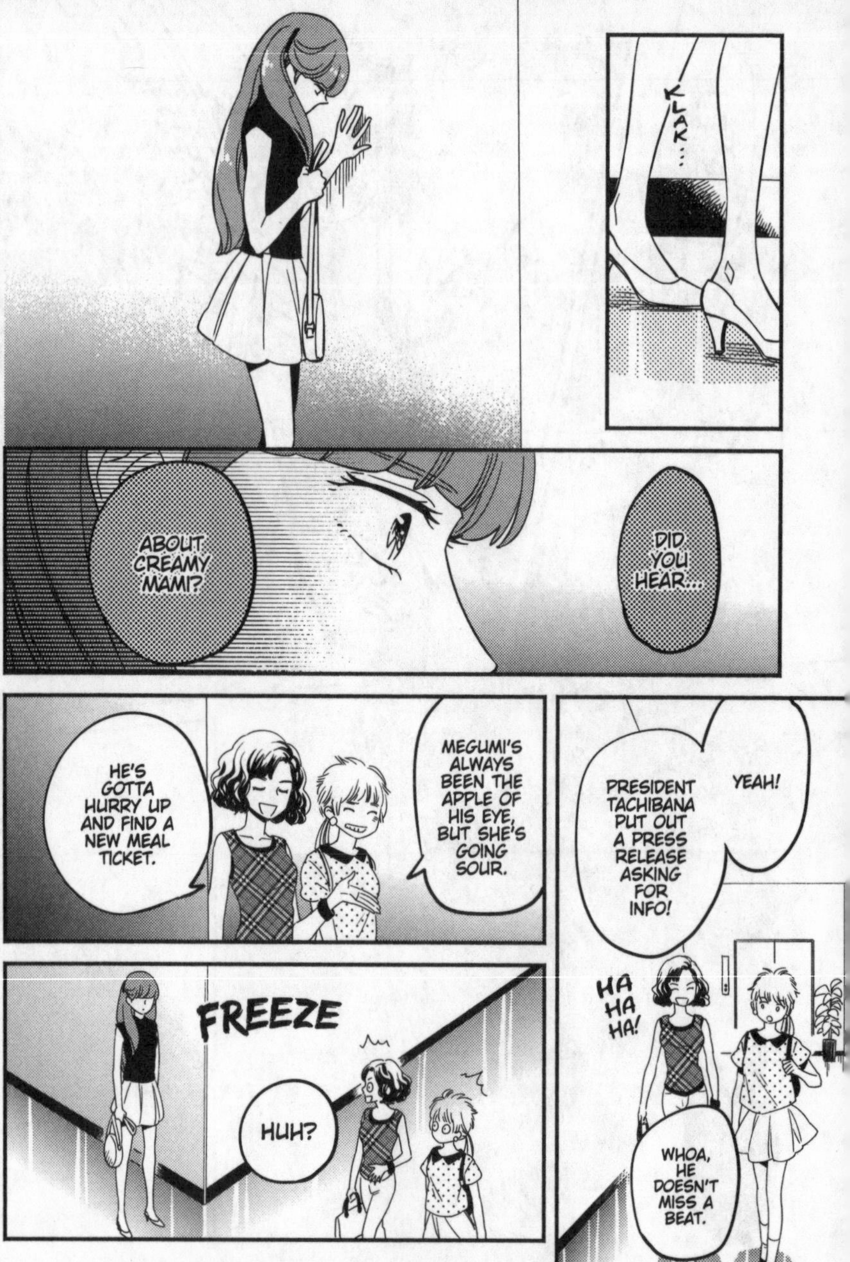
KLAK...
DID YOU HEAR...
ABOUT CREAMY MAMI?
YEAH!
PRESIDENT TACHIBANA PUT OUT A PRESS RELEASE ASKING FOR INFO!
HA HA HA!
WHOA, HE DOESN'T MISS A BEAT.
MEGUMI'S ALWAYS BEEN THE APPLE OF HIS EYE, BUT SHE'S GOING SOUR.
HE'S GOTTA HURRY UP AND FIND A NEW MEAL TICKET.
FREEZE
HUH?

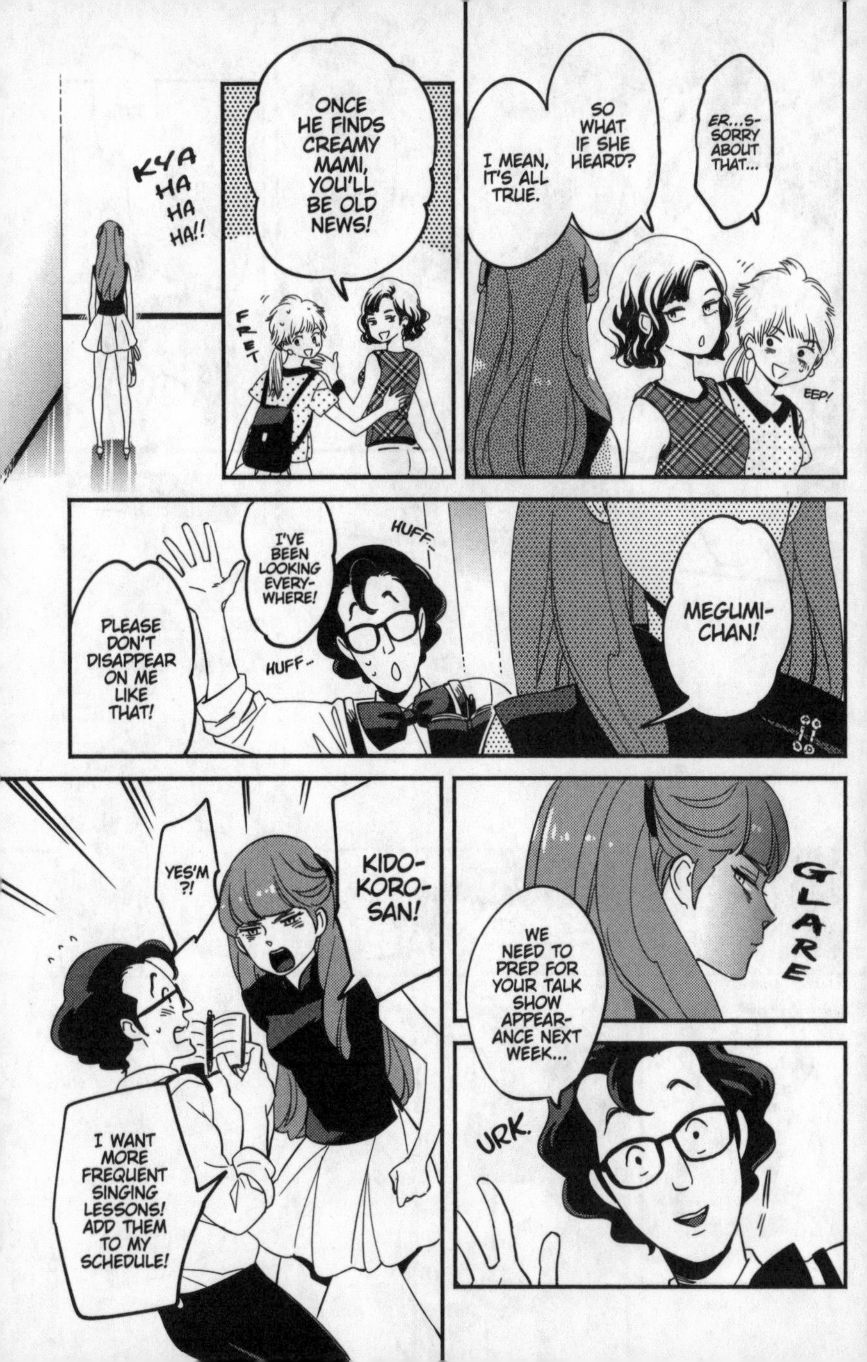
ER...S-SORRY ABOUT THAT...
SO WHAT IF SHE HEARD?
I MEAN, IT'S ALL TRUE.
EEP!
ONCE HE FINDS CREAMY MAMI, YOU'LL BE OLD NEWS!
FRET
KYA HA HA HA!!
MEGUMI-CHAN!
HUFF...
I'VE BEEN LOOKING EVERYWHERE!
HUFF...
PLEASE DON'T DISAPPEAR ON ME LIKE THAT!
GLARE
WE NEED TO PREP FOR YOUR TALK SHOW APPEARANCE NEXT WEEK...
URK.
KIDO-KORO-SAN!
YES'M?!
I WANT MORE FREQUENT SINGING LESSONS! ADD THEM TO MY SCHEDULE!

QUIT ARGU-ING!

JUST DO IT!

OKAY! OKAY!

B-BUT... YOU COULD STRAIN YOUR VOCAL CORDS!

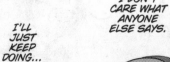

I DON'T CARE WHAT ANYONE ELSE SAYS.

I'LL JUST KEEP DOING...

WHAT I'VE ALWAYS DONE.

......

I'LL GIVE MY WORK EVERYTHING I'VE GOT.

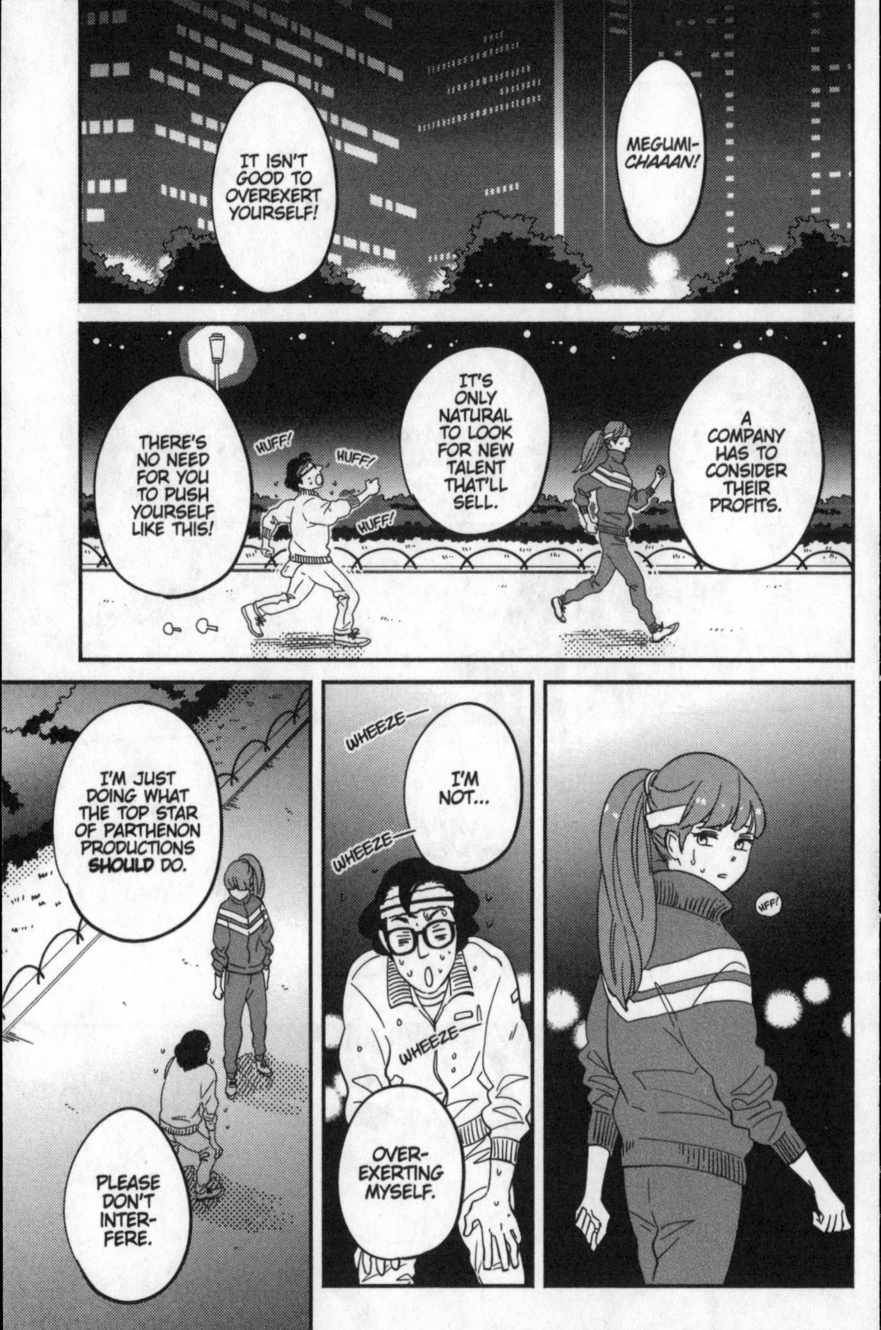
MEGUMI-CHAAAN!
IT ISN'T GOOD TO OVEREXERT YOURSELF!
A COMPANY HAS TO CONSIDER THEIR PROFITS.
IT'S ONLY NATURAL TO LOOK FOR NEW TALENT THAT'LL SELL.
HUFF!
HUFF!
HUFF!
THERE'S NO NEED FOR YOU TO PUSH YOURSELF LIKE THIS!
WHEEZE—
I'M NOT...
WHEEZE—
WHEEZE—
OVER-EXERTING MYSELF.
I'M JUST DOING WHAT THE TOP STAR OF PARTHENON PRODUCTIONS **SHOULD** DO.
PLEASE DON'T INTER-FERE.

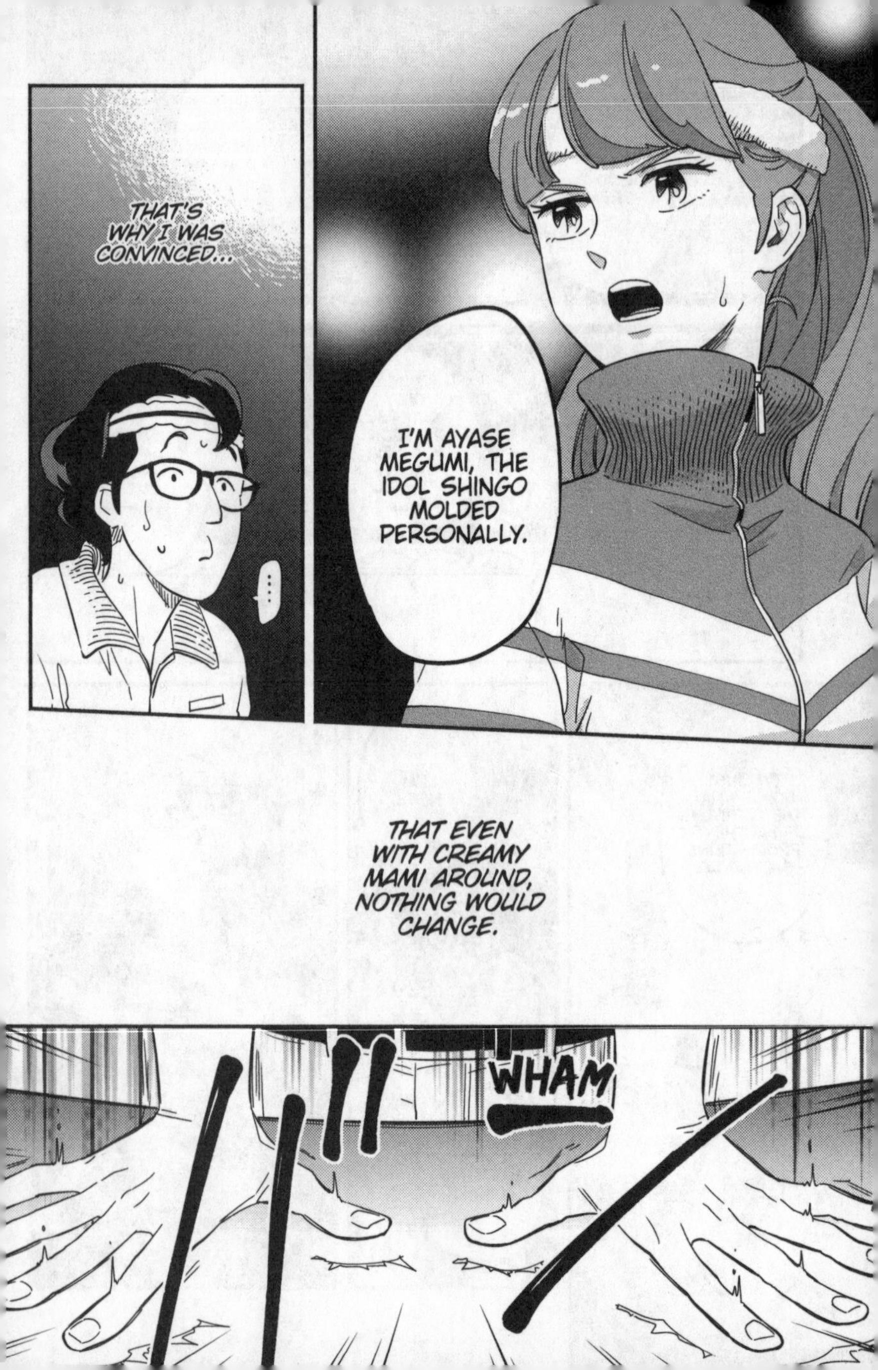
I'M AYASE MEGUMI, THE IDOL SHINGO MOLDED PERSONALLY.
THAT'S WHY I WAS CONVINCED...
...
THAT EVEN WITH CREAMY MAMI AROUND, NOTHING WOULD CHANGE.
WHAM

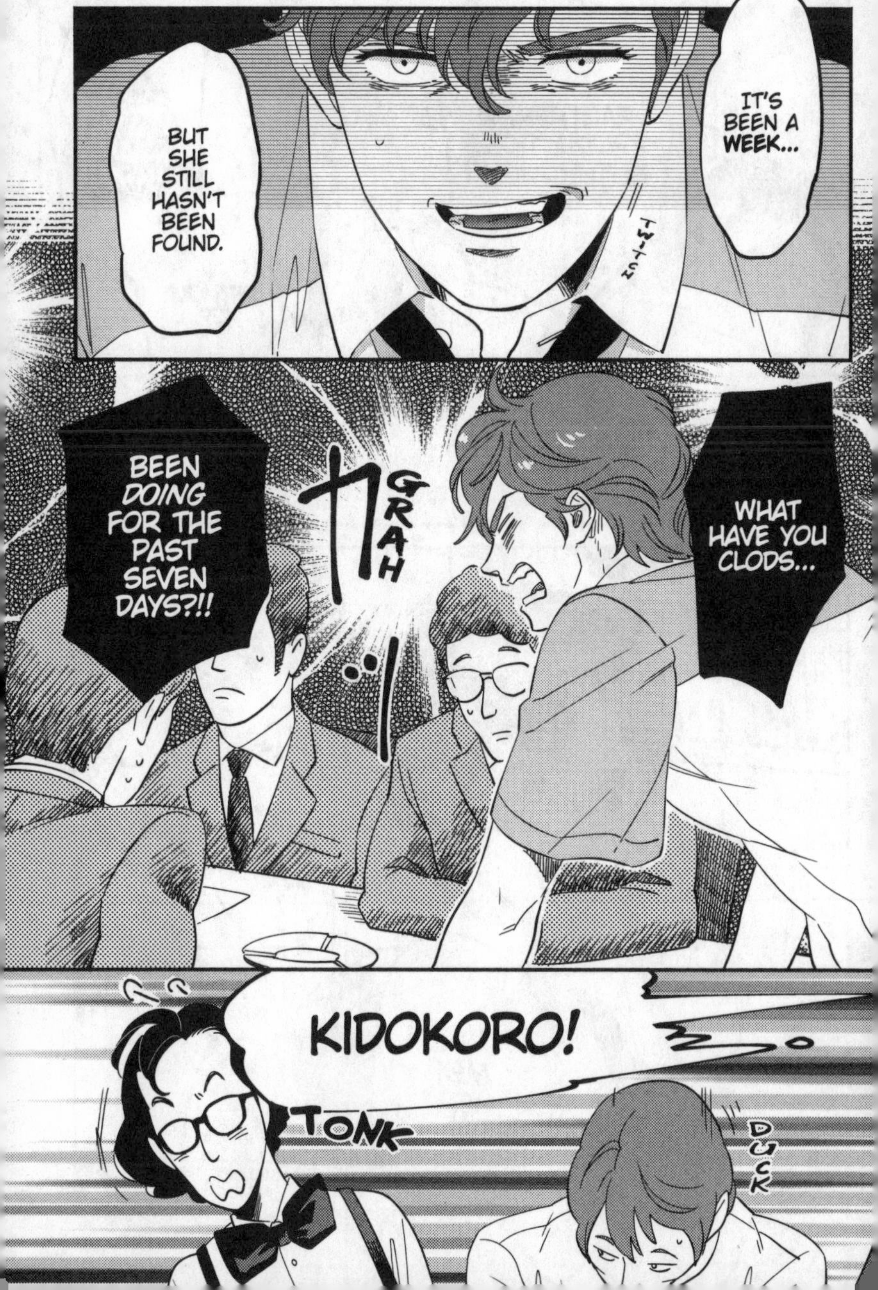
IT'S BEEN A WEEK...
TWITCH
BUT SHE STILL HASN'T BEEN FOUND.
WHAT HAVE YOU CLODS...
GRAH
BEEN *DOING* FOR THE PAST SEVEN DAYS?!!
KIDOKORO!
DUCK
TONK

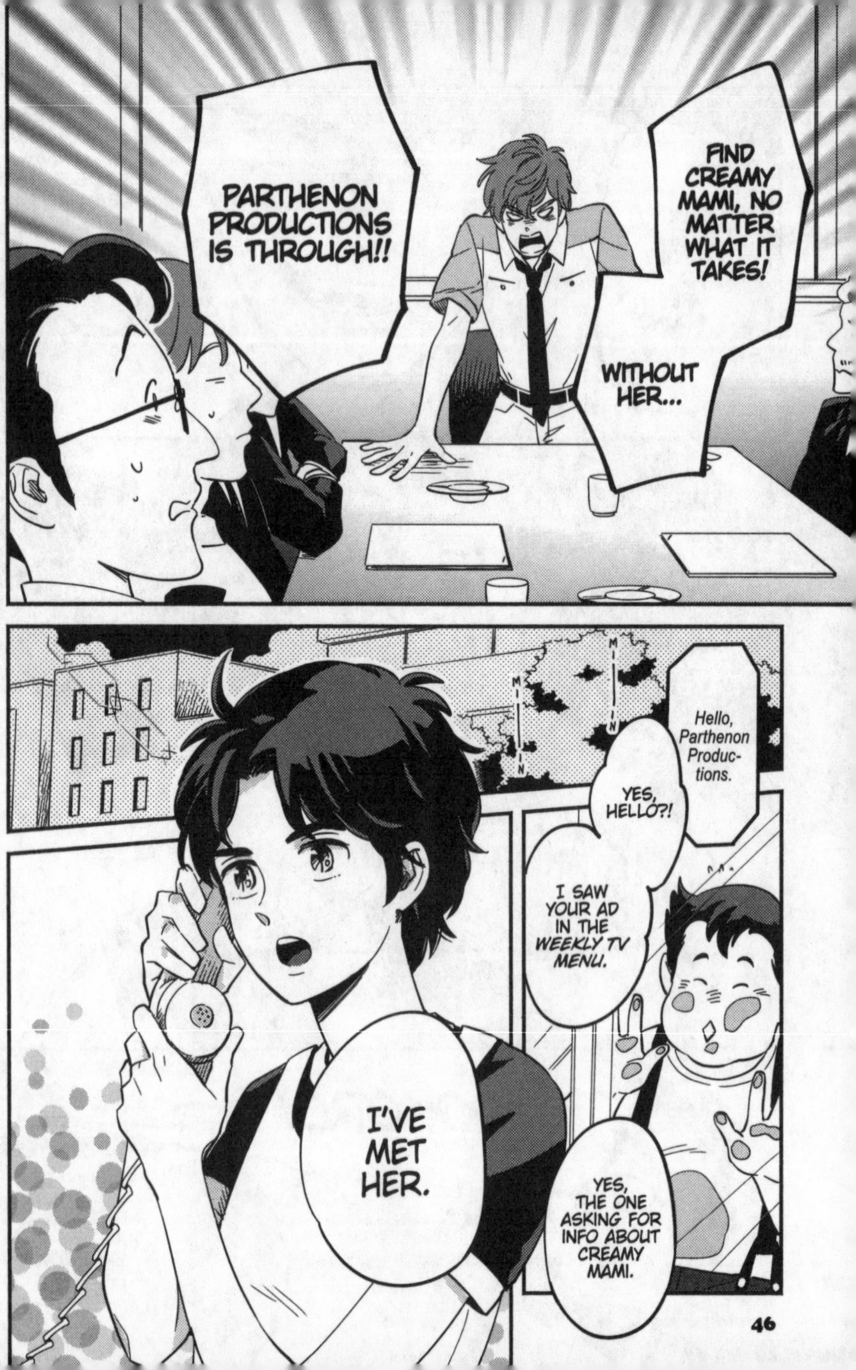
FIND CREAMY MAMI, NO MATTER WHAT IT TAKES!
WITHOUT HER...
PARTHENON PRODUCTIONS IS THROUGH!!
MIN
MIN
Hello, Parthenon Productions.
YES, HELLO?!
I SAW YOUR AD IN THE *WEEKLY TV MENU*.
YES, THE ONE ASKING FOR INFO ABOUT CREAMY MAMI.
I'VE MET HER.

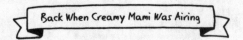

Back When Creamy Mami Was Airing

1982: The introduction of the five-hundred-yen coin.

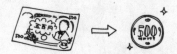

IT'S OBVIOUS THESE COINS ARE BETTER! THEY'RE SHINY, HEAVY, NEW, AND MADE OF METAL! THEY'RE THE BEST!!
BILLS ARE BETTER! I CAN CARRY MORE MONEY WITH THEM!!

Those who like new currency.

Those who collect things like notched ten yen coins or five yen coins with the old script on them.

Magical Angel
Creamy Mami
and the
Spoiled Princess

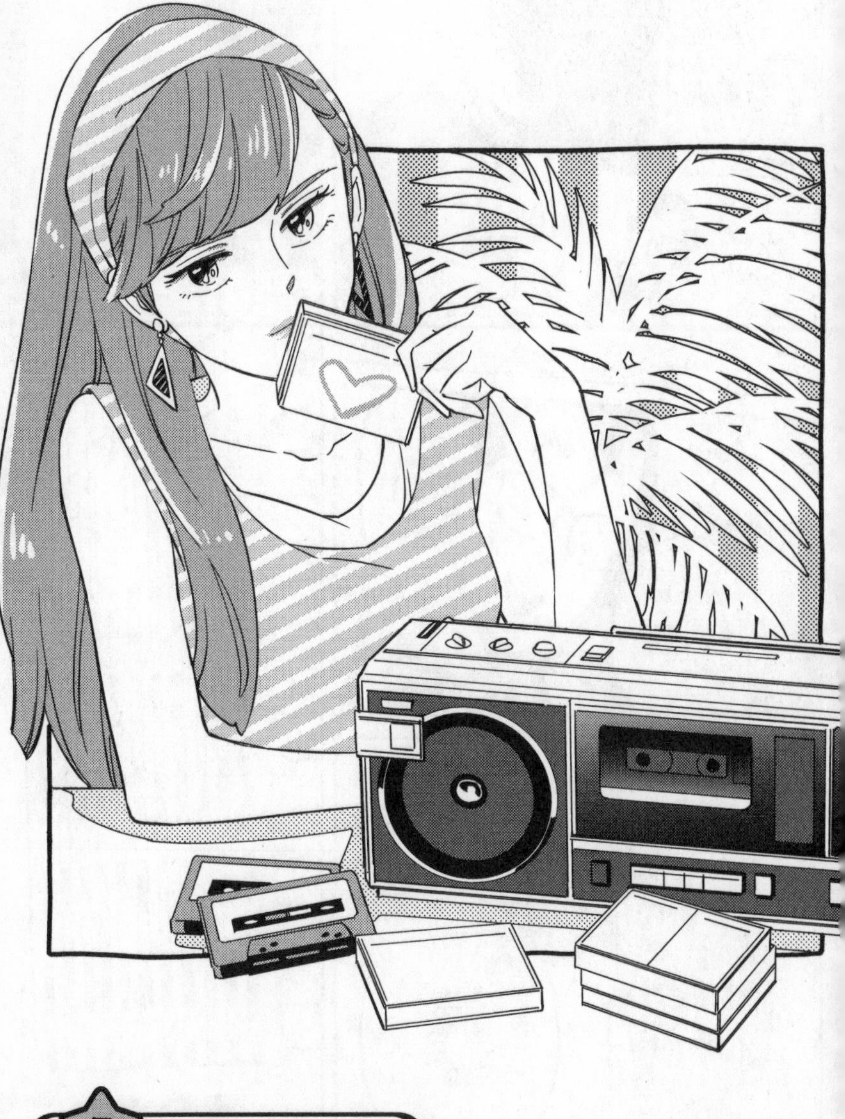

3 No Longer on Top

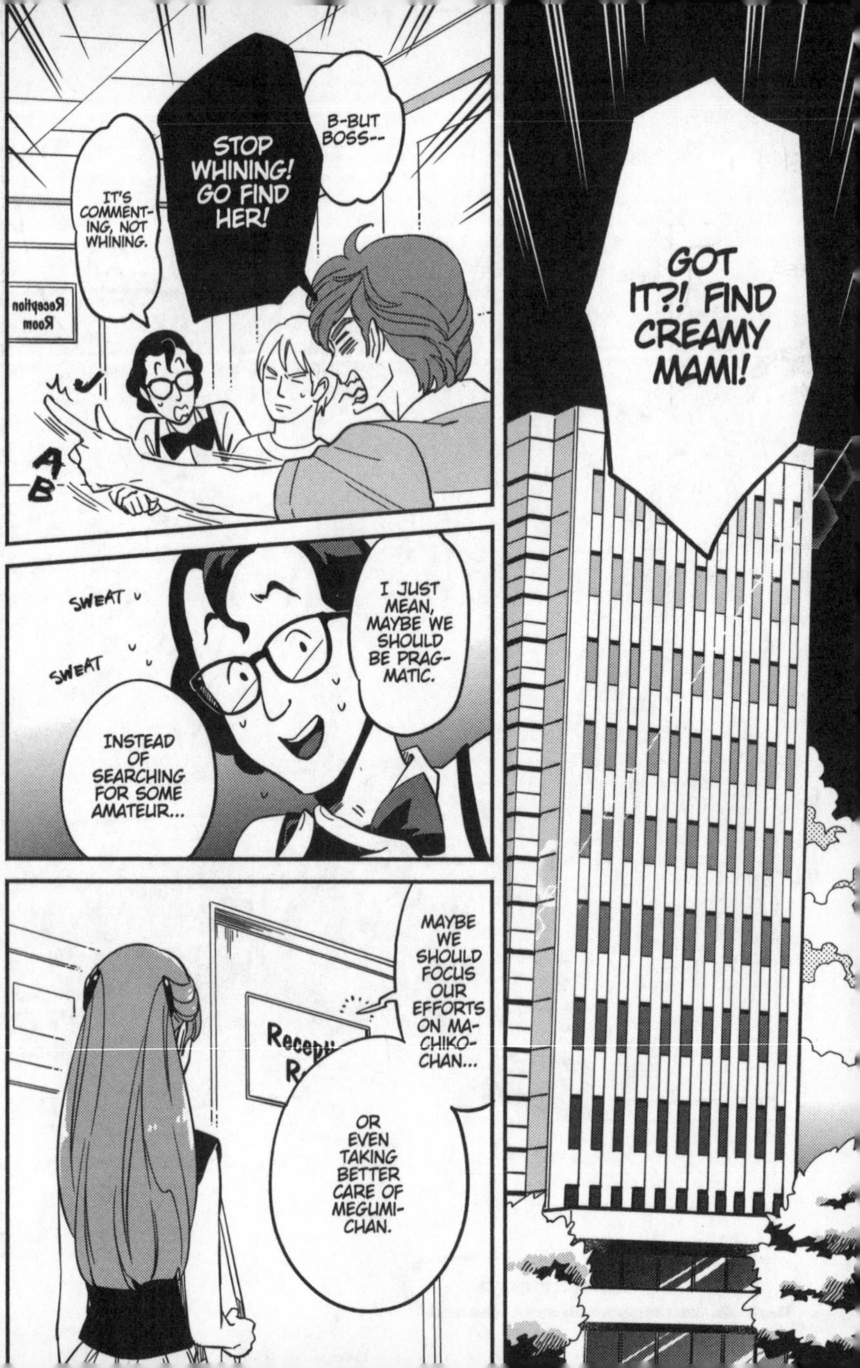
GOT IT?! FIND CREAMY MAMI!
B-BUT BOSS--
STOP WHINING! GO FIND HER!
IT'S COMMENTING, NOT WHINING.
Reception Room
AB
I JUST MEAN, MAYBE WE SHOULD BE PRAGMATIC.
SWEAT
SWEAT
INSTEAD OF SEARCHING FOR SOME AMATEUR...
MAYBE WE SHOULD FOCUS OUR EFFORTS ON MACHIKO-CHAN...
OR EVEN TAKING BETTER CARE OF MEGUMI-CHAN.

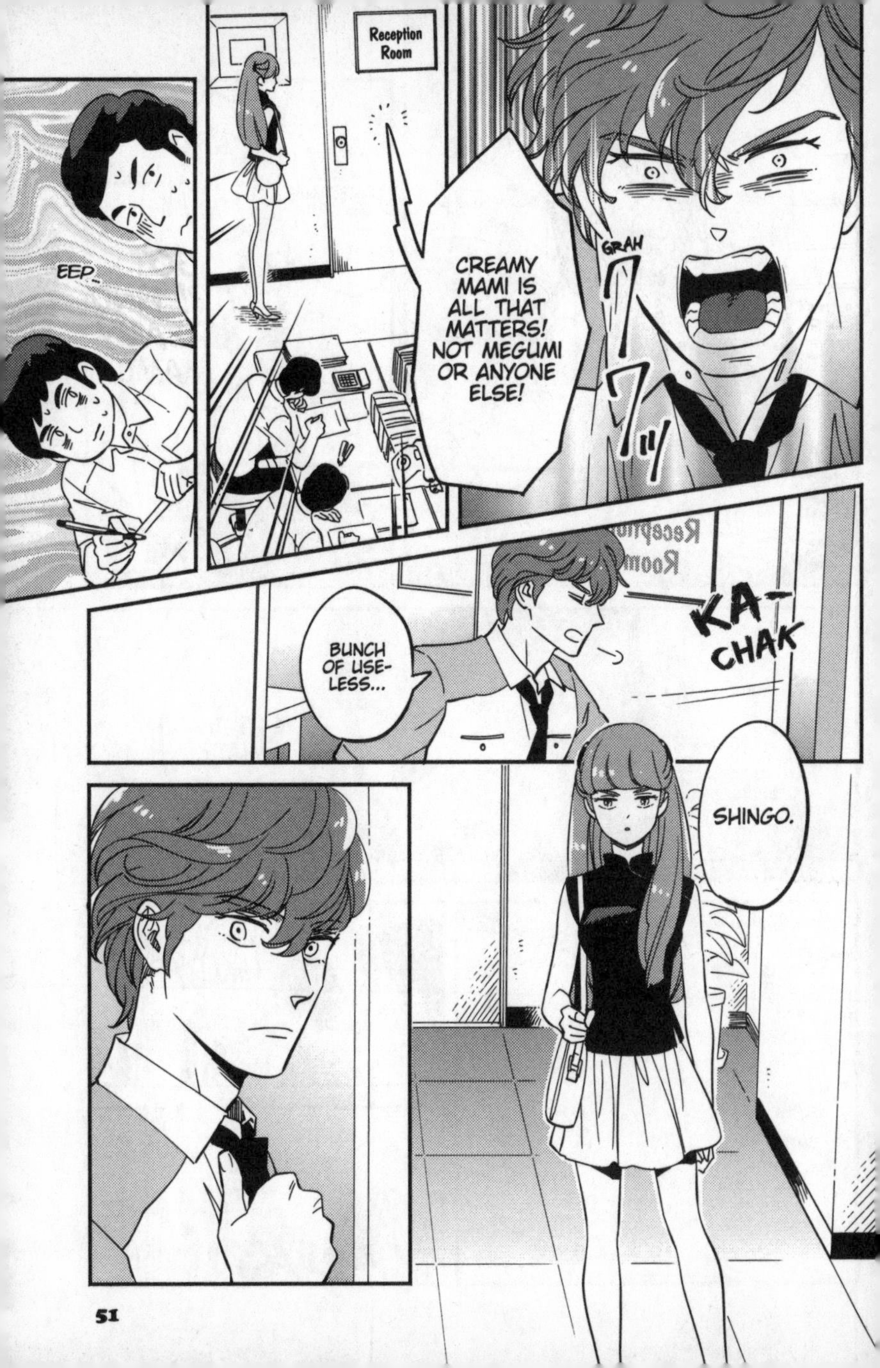
CREAMY MAMI IS ALL THAT MATTERS! NOT MEGUMI OR ANYONE ELSE!
GRAH
Reception Room
EEP...
KA-CHAK
BUNCH OF USE-LESS...
SHINGO.

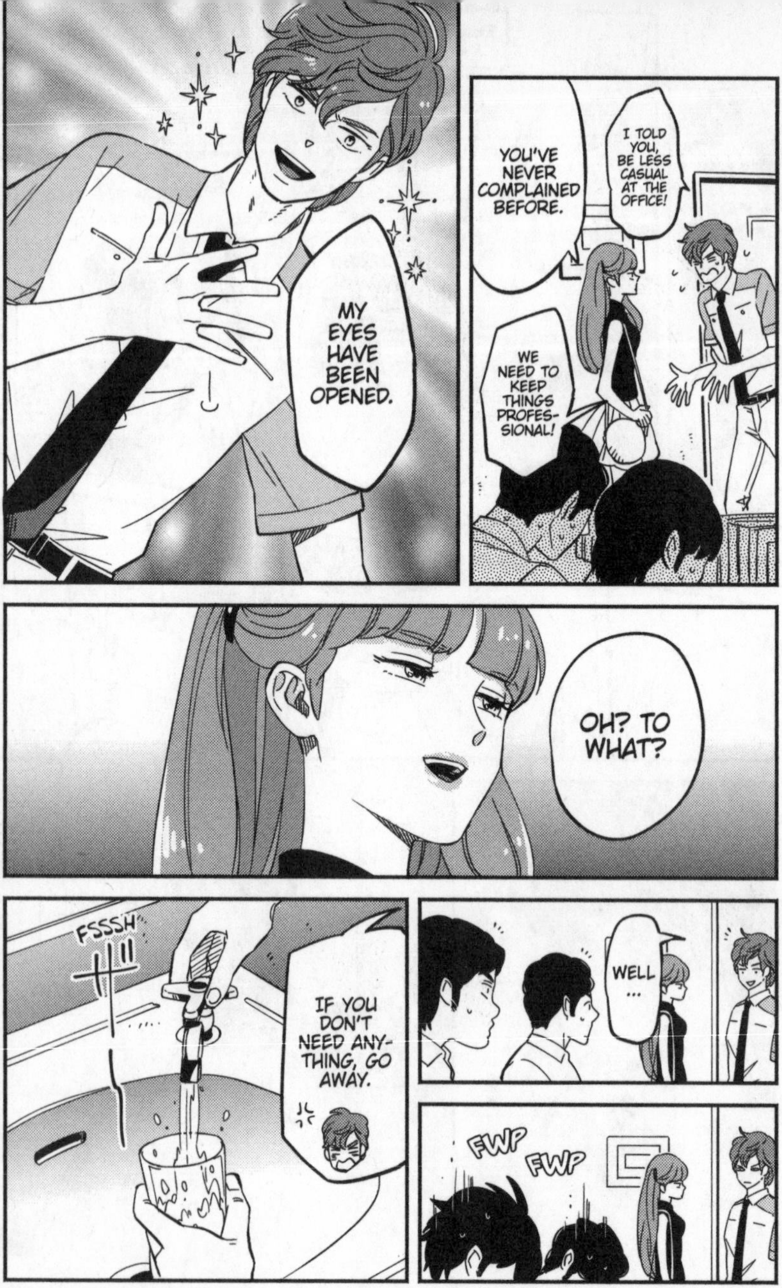
I TOLD YOU, BE LESS CASUAL AT THE OFFICE!
YOU'VE NEVER COMPLAINED BEFORE.
WE NEED TO KEEP THINGS PROFES-SIONAL!
MY EYES HAVE BEEN OPENED.
OH? TO WHAT?
WELL ...
FWP
FWP
FSSSH
IF YOU DON'T NEED ANY-THING, GO AWAY.

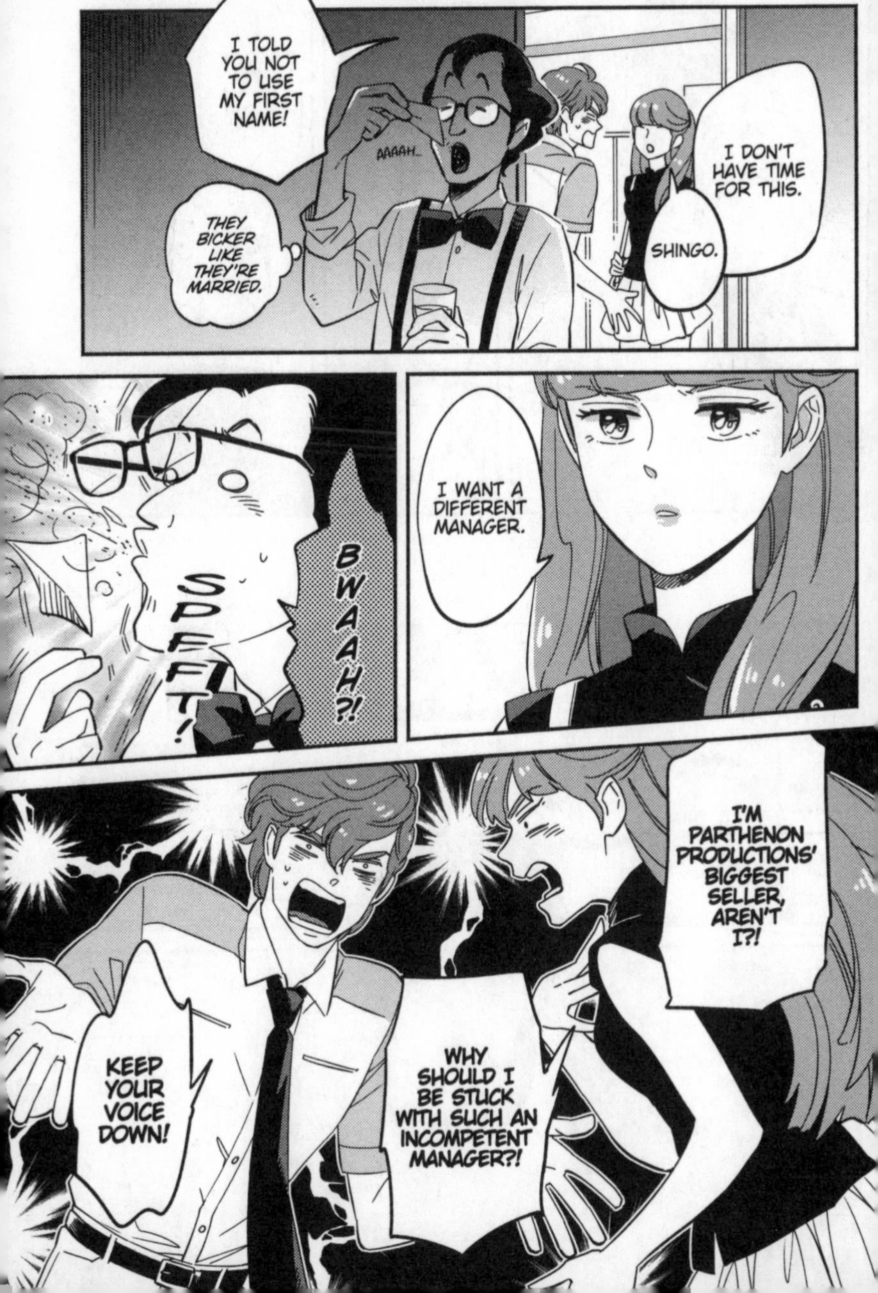
I DON'T HAVE TIME FOR THIS.
SHINGO.
I TOLD YOU NOT TO USE MY FIRST NAME!
AAAAH...
THEY BICKER LIKE THEY'RE MARRIED.
I WANT A DIFFERENT MANAGER.
BWAAAH?!
SPFFT!
I'M PARTHENON PRODUCTIONS' BIGGEST SELLER, AREN'T I?!
WHY SHOULD I BE STUCK WITH SUCH AN INCOMPETENT MANAGER?!
KEEP YOUR VOICE DOWN!

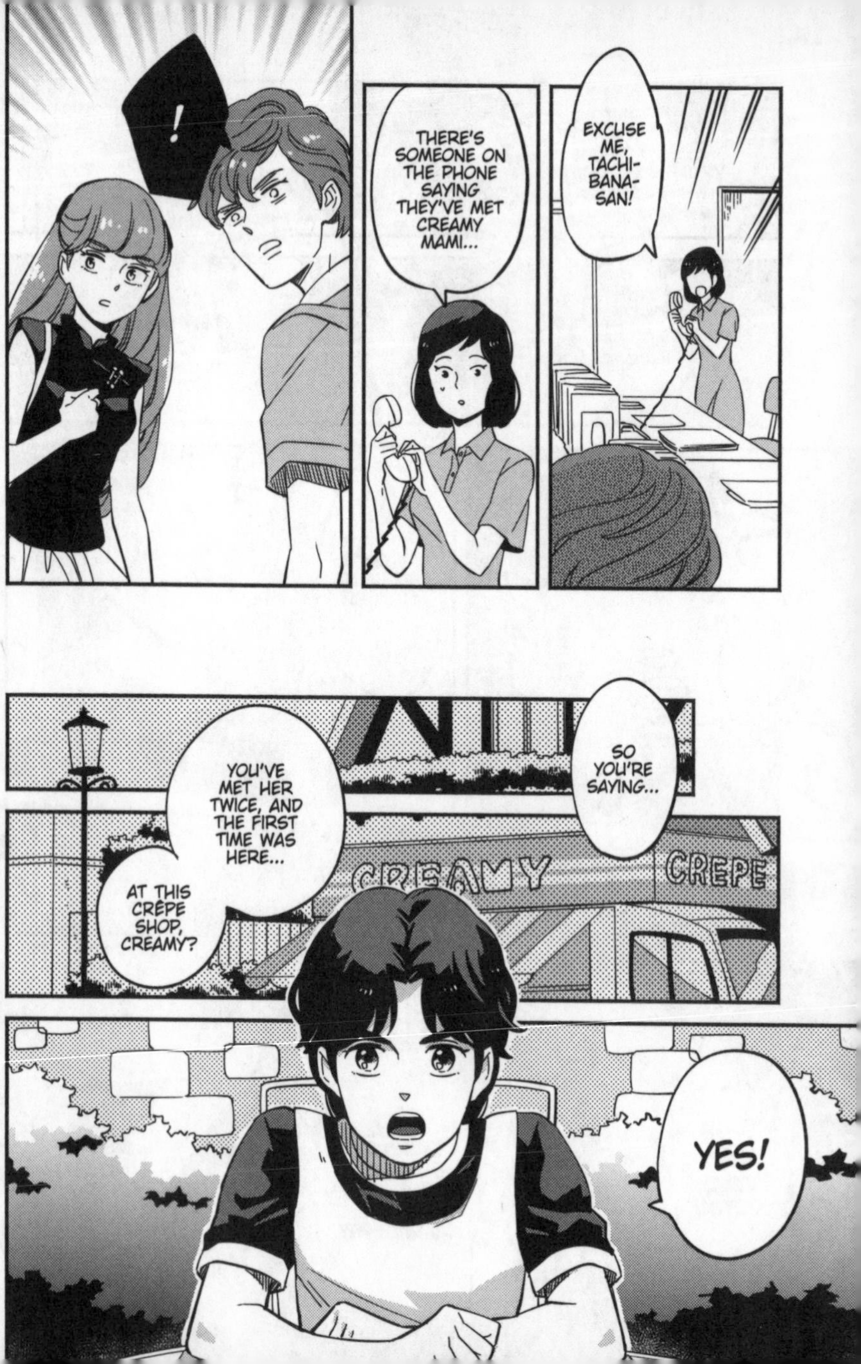
EXCUSE ME, TACHIBANA-SAN!
THERE'S SOMEONE ON THE PHONE SAYING THEY'VE MET CREAMY MAMI...
!
SO YOU'RE SAYING...
YOU'VE MET HER TWICE, AND THE FIRST TIME WAS HERE...
AT THIS CRÊPE SHOP, CREAMY?
CREAMY
CREPE
YES!

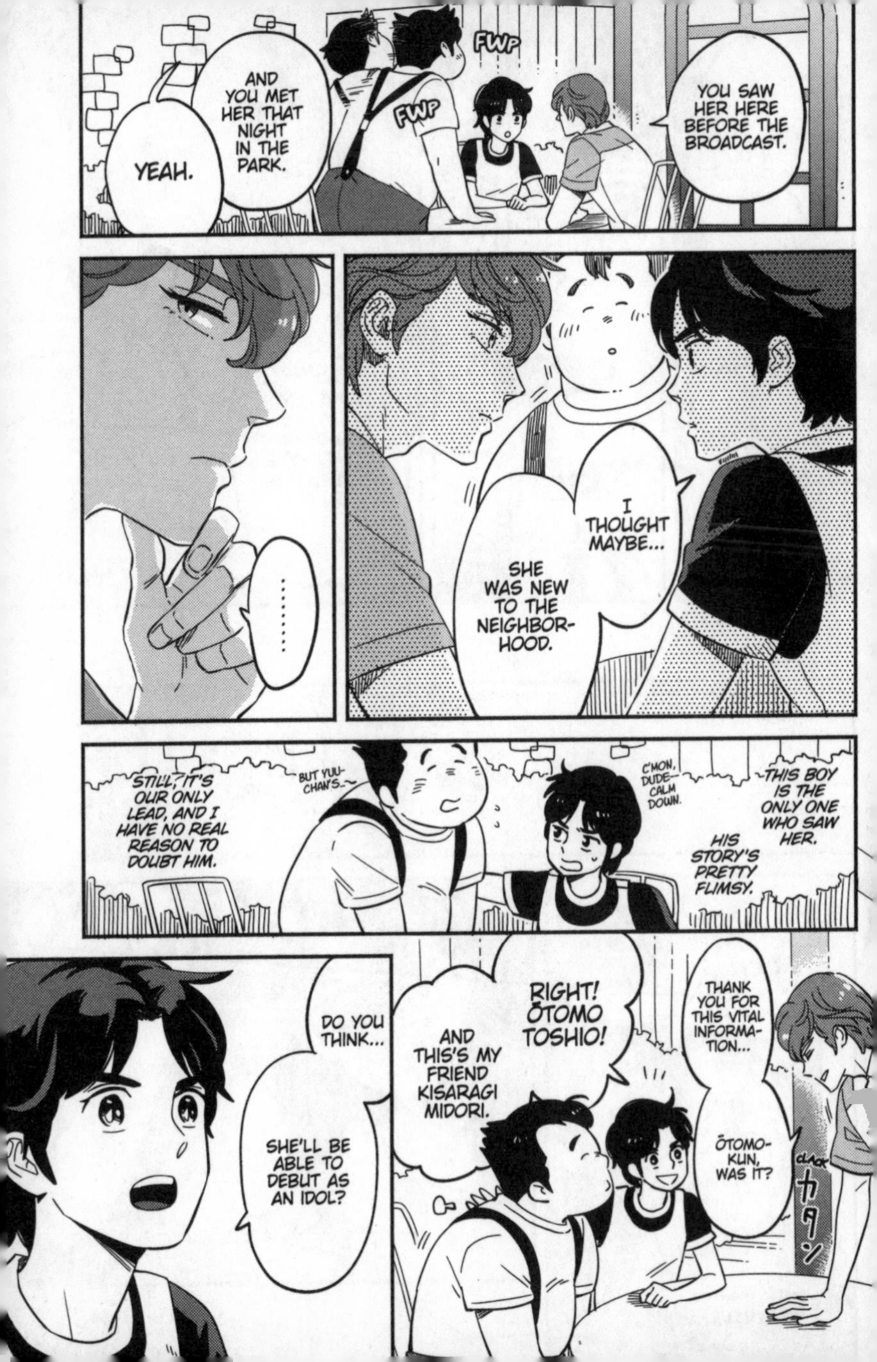
FWP
FWP
YOU SAW HER HERE BEFORE THE BROADCAST.
AND YOU MET HER THAT NIGHT IN THE PARK.
YEAH.
I THOUGHT MAYBE...
SHE WAS NEW TO THE NEIGHBORHOOD.
......
THIS BOY IS THE ONLY ONE WHO SAW HER.
HIS STORY'S PRETTY FLIMSY.
C'MON, DUDE—CALM DOWN.
BUT YUU-CHAN'S~
STILL, IT'S OUR ONLY LEAD, AND I HAVE NO REAL REASON TO DOUBT HIM.
CLACK
カタン
THANK YOU FOR THIS VITAL INFORMATION...
ŌTOMO-KUN, WAS IT?
RIGHT! ŌTOMO TOSHIO!
AND THIS'S MY FRIEND KISARAGI MIDORI.
DO YOU THINK...
SHE'LL BE ABLE TO DEBUT AS AN IDOL?

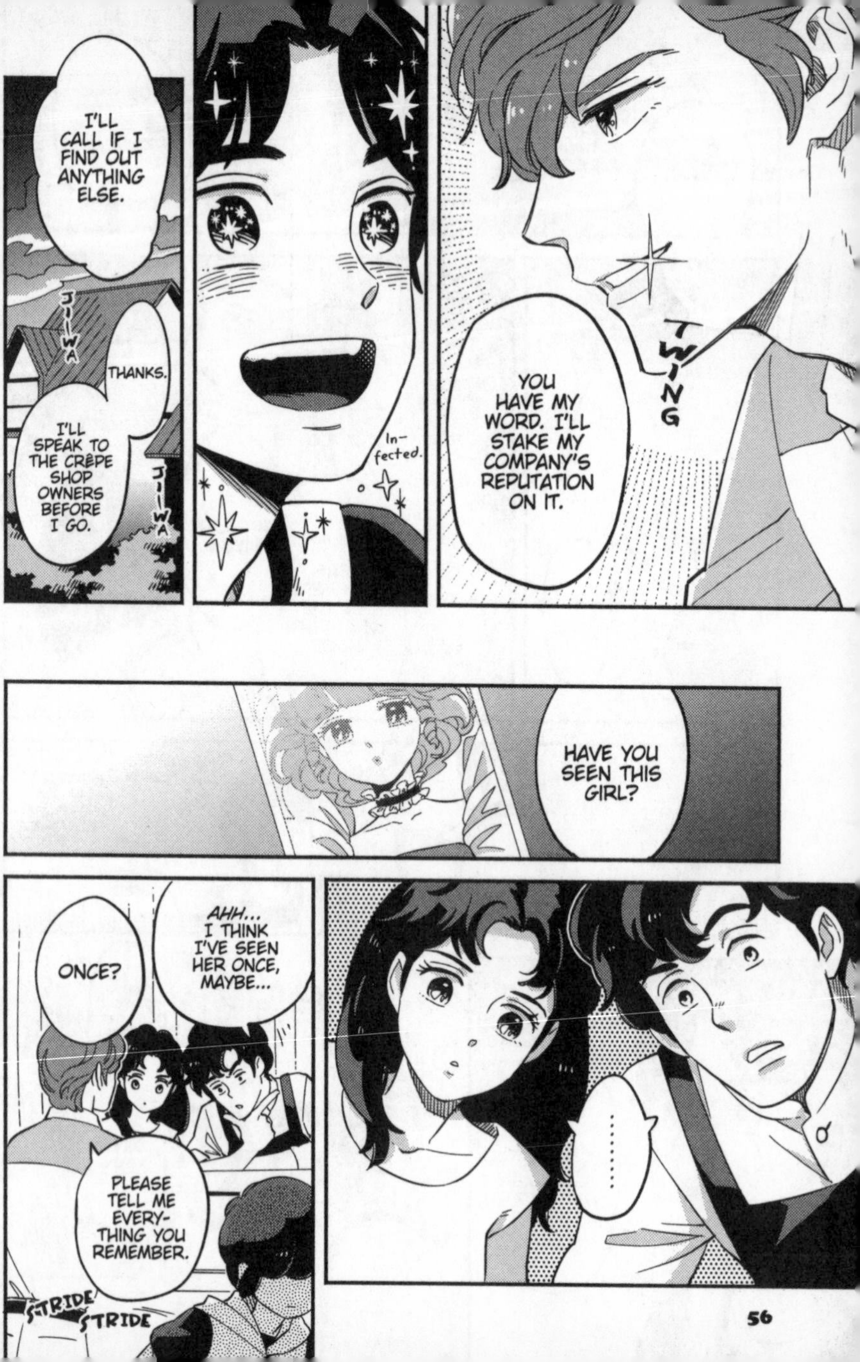
YOU HAVE MY WORD. I'LL STAKE MY COMPANY'S REPUTATION ON IT.
TWING
In-fected.
I'LL CALL IF I FIND OUT ANYTHING ELSE.
JI-WA
THANKS.
I'LL SPEAK TO THE CRÊPE SHOP OWNERS BEFORE I GO.
JI-WA
HAVE YOU SEEN THIS GIRL?
......
AHH... I THINK I'VE SEEN HER ONCE, MAYBE...
ONCE?
PLEASE TELL ME EVERY-THING YOU REMEMBER.
STRIDE
STRIDE

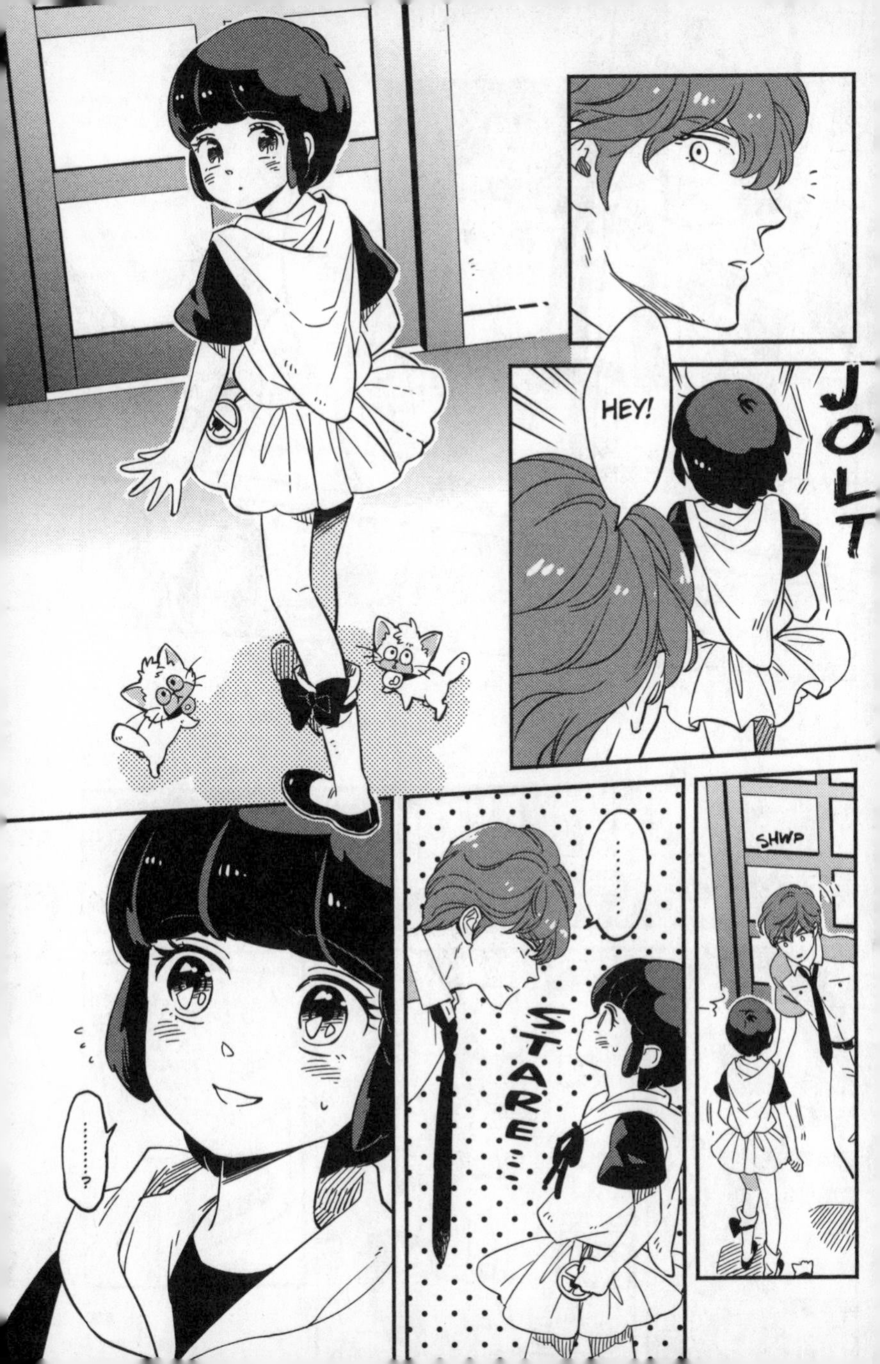
HEY!
JOLT
SHWP
......
STARE...
......?

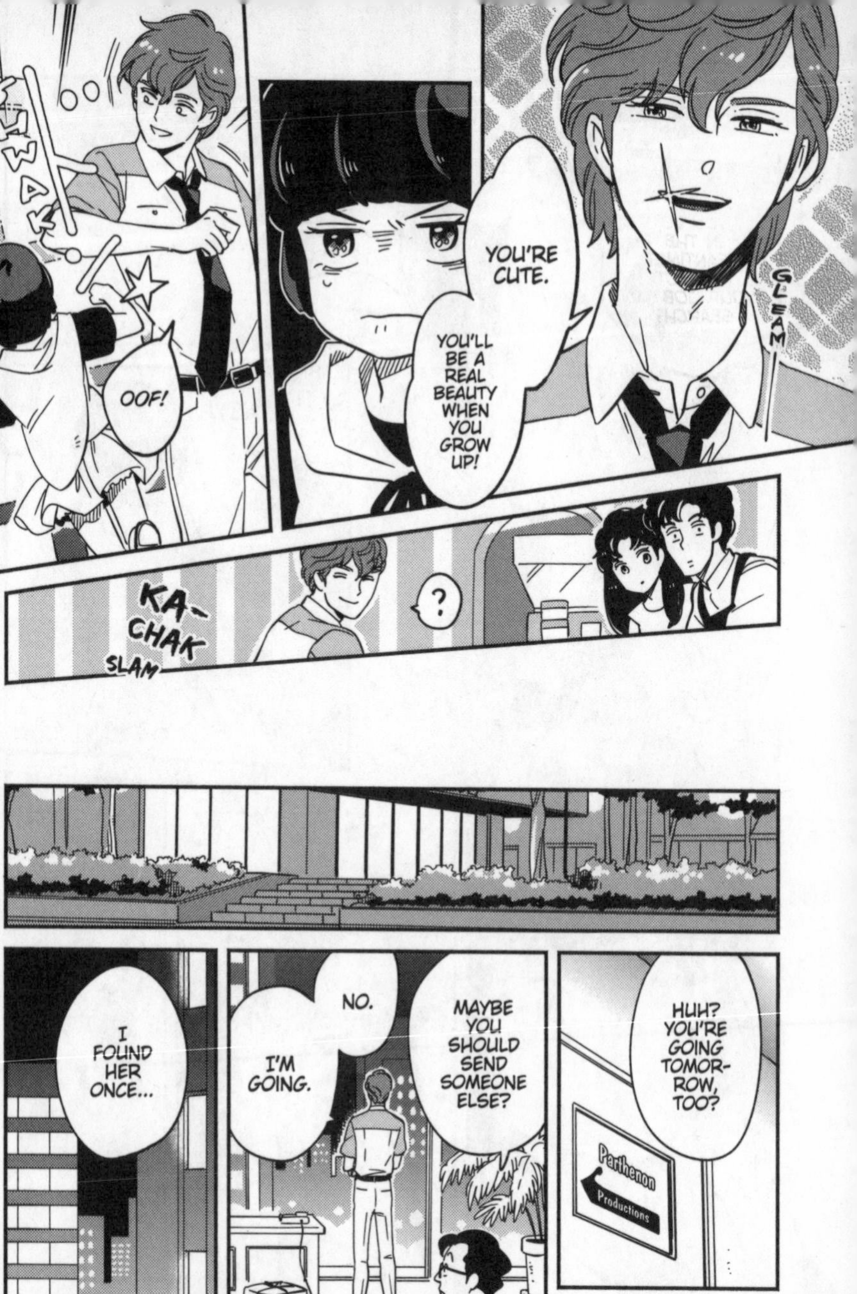
YOU'RE CUTE.
YOU'LL BE A REAL BEAUTY WHEN YOU GROW UP!
GLEAM
SHWAK
OOF!
?
KA-CHAK
SLAM
HUH? YOU'RE GOING TOMOR-ROW, TOO?
Parthenon Productions
MAYBE YOU SHOULD SEND SOMEONE ELSE?
NO.
I'M GOING.
I FOUND HER ONCE...

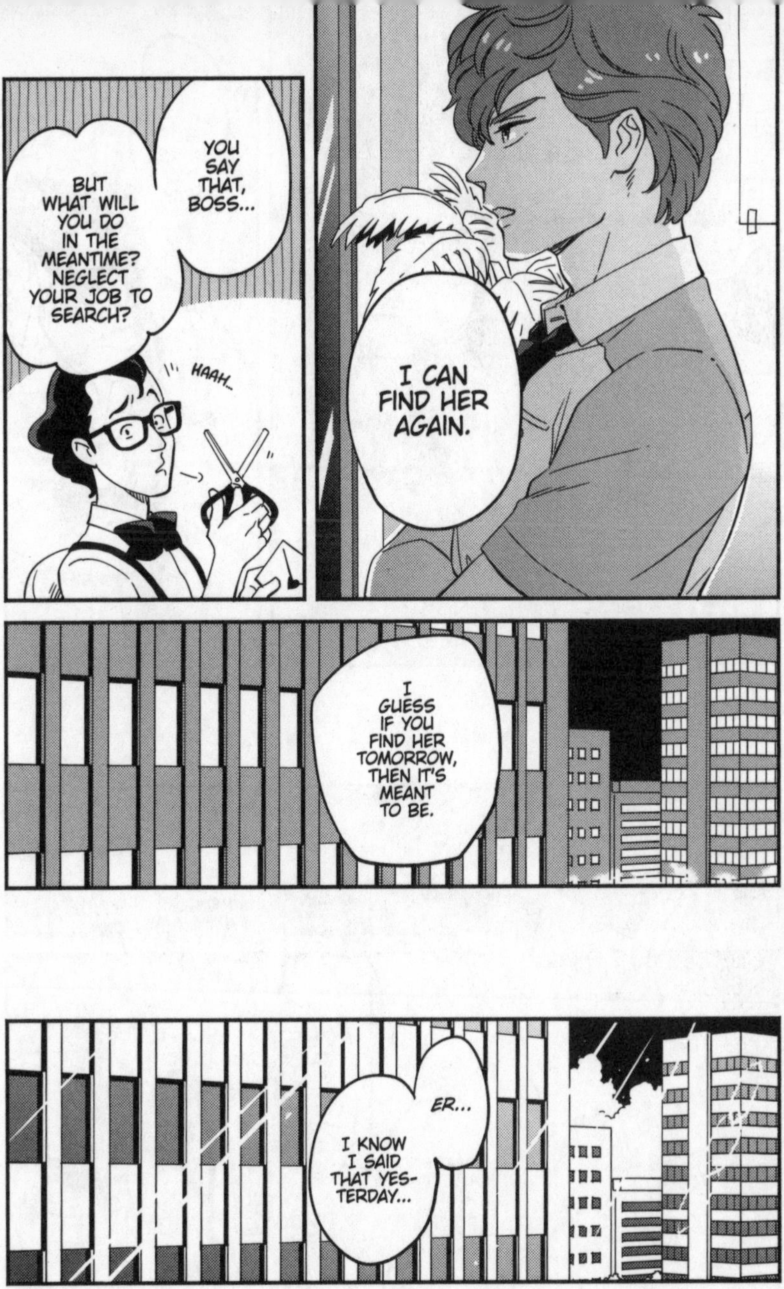
I CAN FIND HER AGAIN.
YOU SAY THAT, BOSS...
BUT WHAT WILL YOU DO IN THE MEANTIME? NEGLECT YOUR JOB TO SEARCH?
HAAH..
I GUESS IF YOU FIND HER TOMORROW, THEN IT'S MEANT TO BE.
ER...
I KNOW I SAID THAT YES-TERDAY...

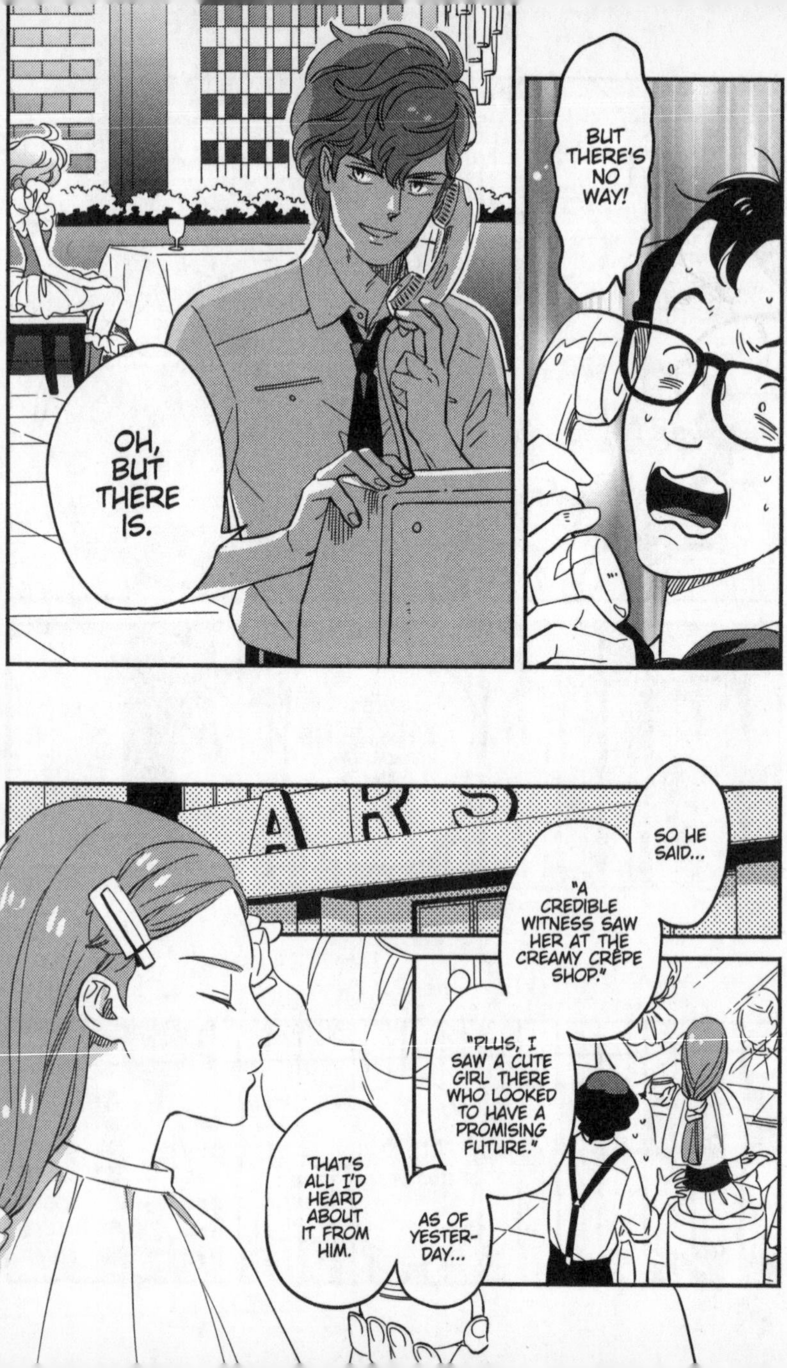
BUT THERE'S NO WAY!
OH, BUT THERE IS.
SO HE SAID...
"A CREDIBLE WITNESS SAW HER AT THE CREAMY CRÊPE SHOP."
"PLUS, I SAW A CUTE GIRL THERE WHO LOOKED TO HAVE A PROMISING FUTURE."
AS OF YESTER-DAY...
THAT'S ALL I'D HEARD ABOUT IT FROM HIM.

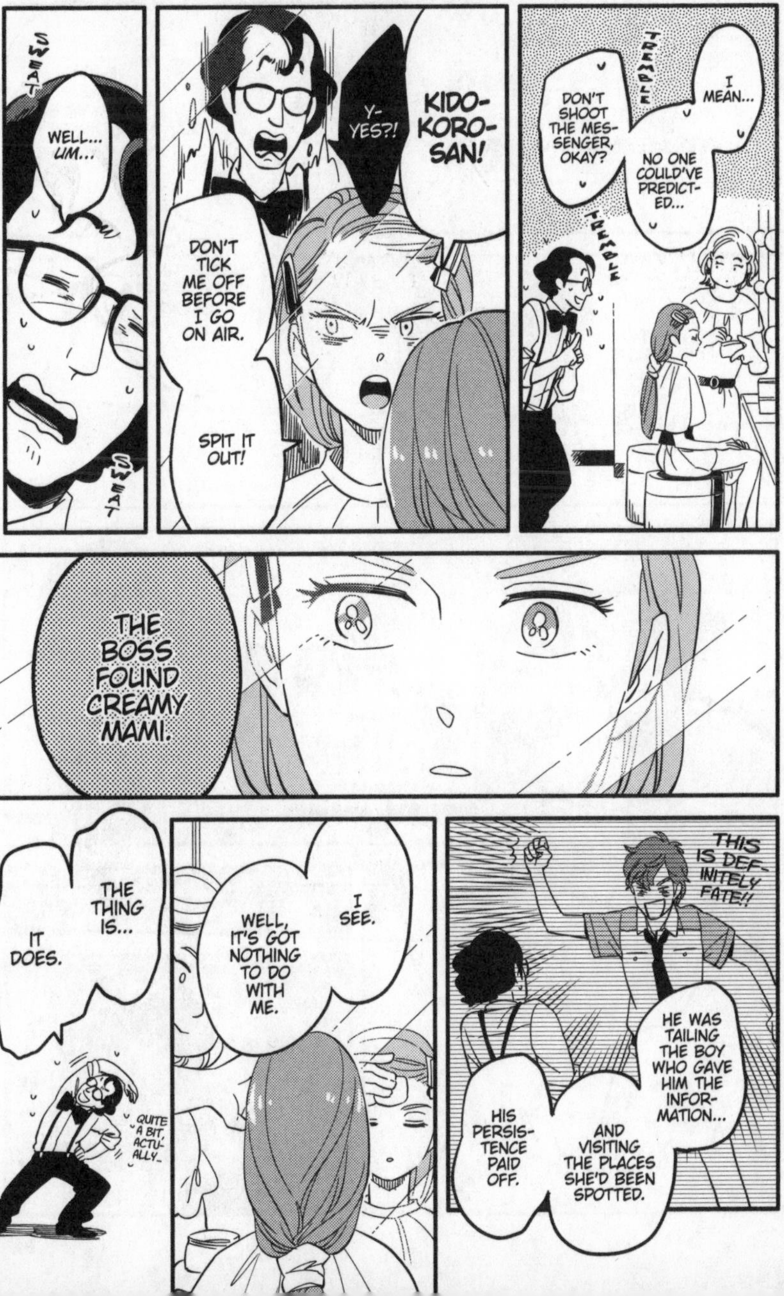
I MEAN...
TREMBLE
DON'T SHOOT THE MES-SENGER, OKAY?
NO ONE COULD'VE PREDICT-ED...
TREMBLE
KIDO-KORO-SAN!
Y-YES?!
DON'T TICK ME OFF BEFORE I GO ON AIR.
SPIT IT OUT!
SWEAT
WELL... UM...
SWEAT
THE BOSS FOUND CREAMY MAMI.
THIS IS DEF-INITELY FATE!!
HE WAS TAILING THE BOY WHO GAVE HIM THE INFOR-MATION...
AND VISITING THE PLACES SHE'D BEEN SPOTTED.
HIS PERSIS-TENCE PAID OFF.
I SEE.
WELL, IT'S GOT NOTHING TO DO WITH ME.
THE THING IS...
IT DOES.
QUITE A BIT, ACTU-ALLY...

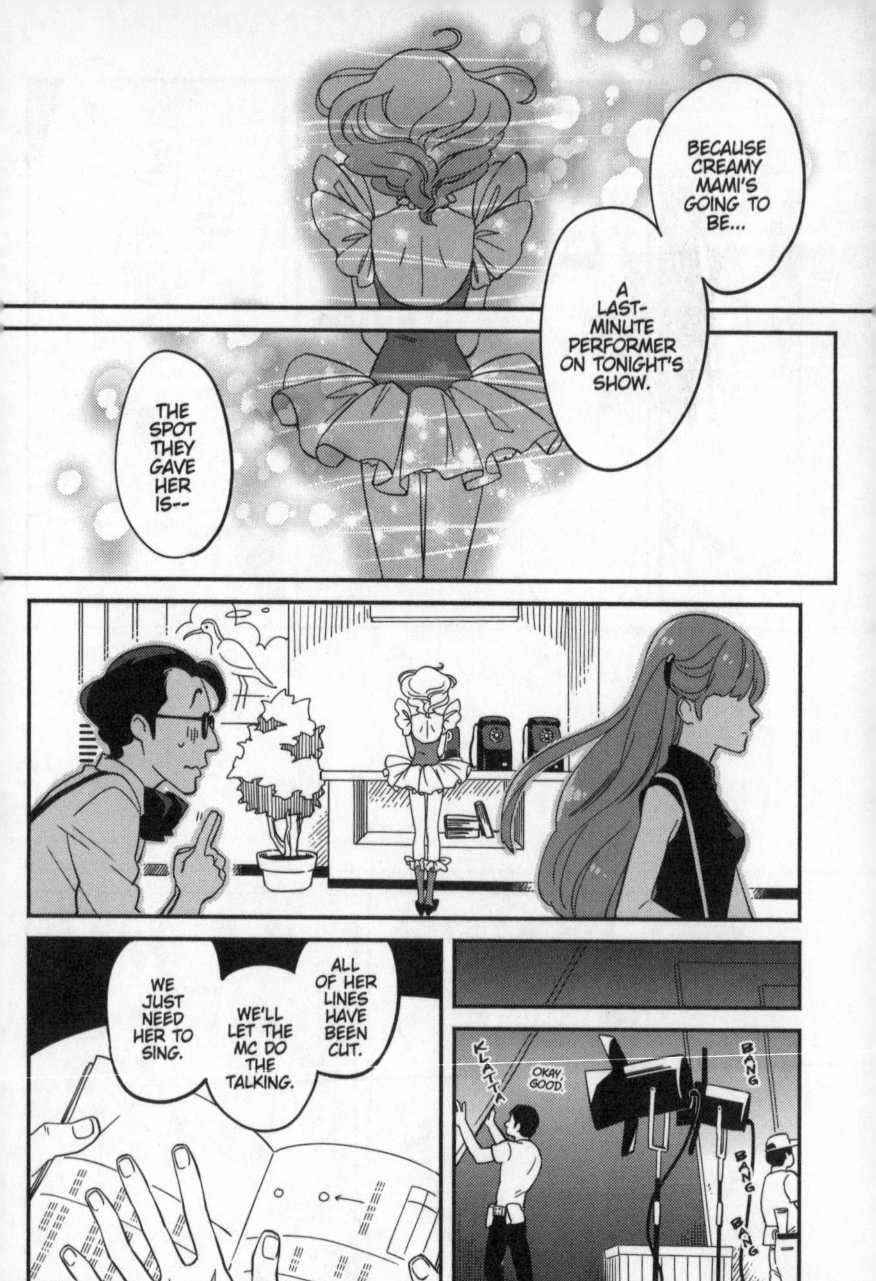
BECAUSE CREAMY MAMI'S GOING TO BE...
A LAST-MINUTE PERFORMER ON TONIGHT'S SHOW.
THE SPOT THEY GAVE HER IS--
KLATTA
OKAY, GOOD.
BANG
BANG BANG BANG
ALL OF HER LINES HAVE BEEN CUT.
WE'LL LET THE MC DO THE TALKING.
WE JUST NEED HER TO SING.

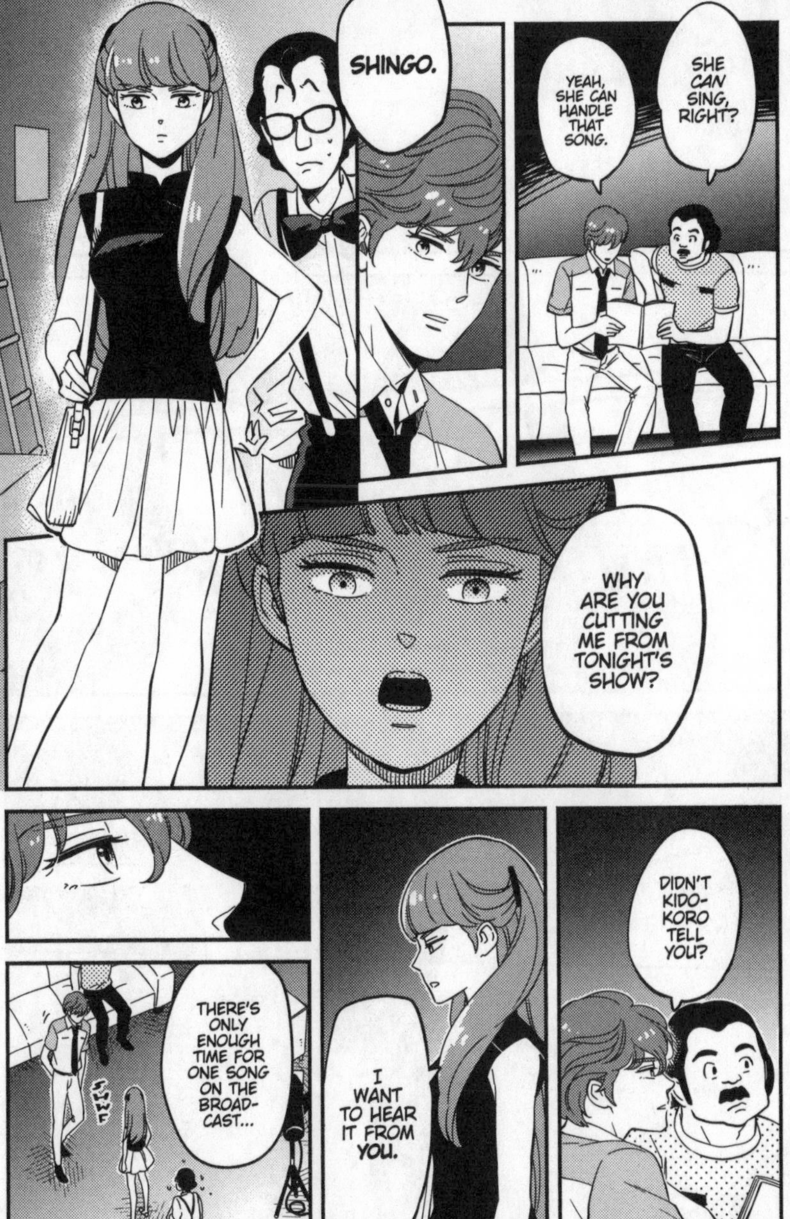
SHE CAN SING, RIGHT?
YEAH, SHE CAN HANDLE THAT SONG.
SHINGO.
WHY ARE YOU CUTTING ME FROM TONIGHT'S SHOW?
DIDN'T KIDO-KORO TELL YOU?
I WANT TO HEAR IT FROM YOU.
THERE'S ONLY ENOUGH TIME FOR ONE SONG ON THE BROAD-CAST...

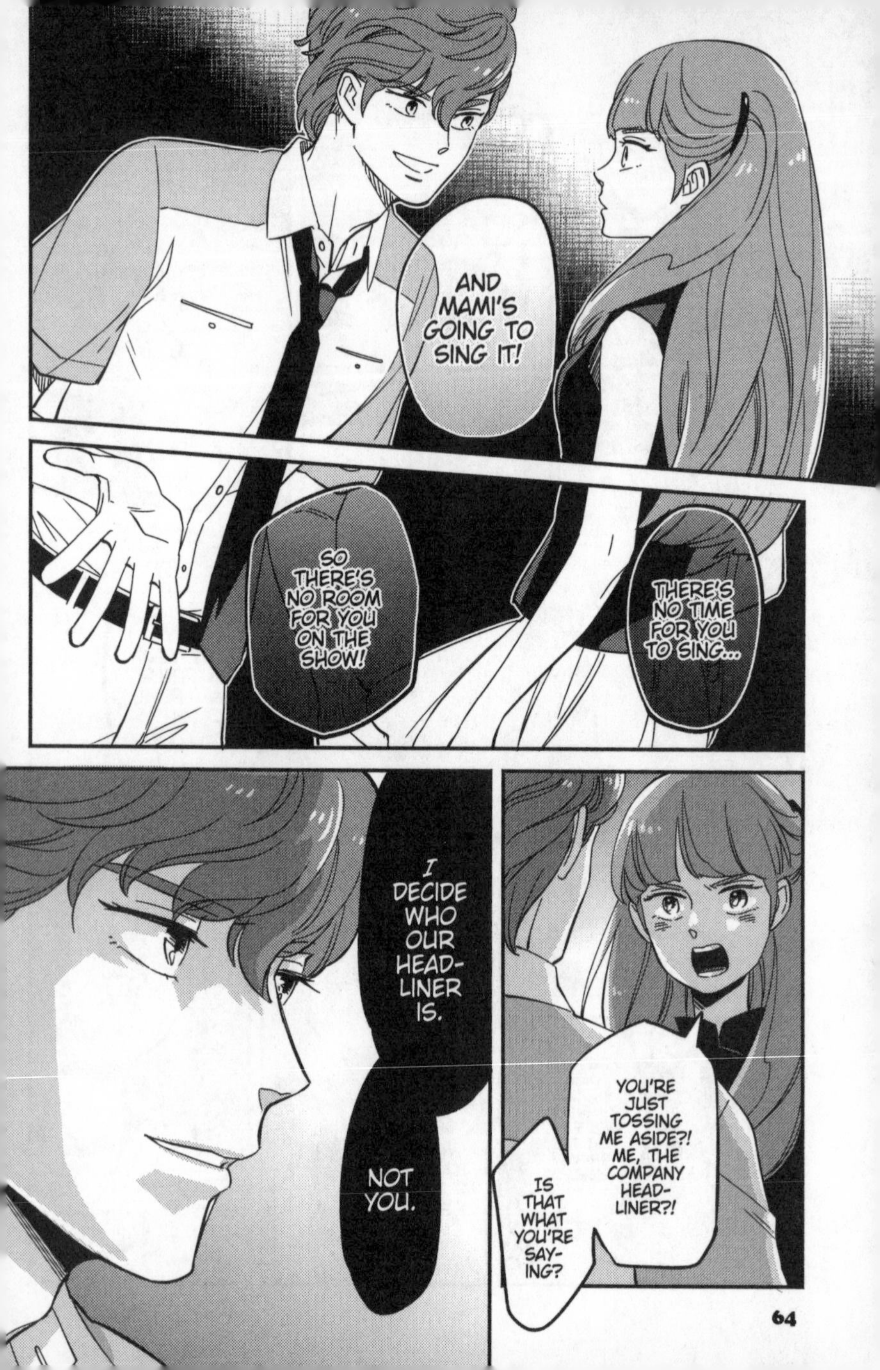
AND MAMI'S GOING TO SING IT!
THERE'S NO TIME FOR YOU TO SING...
SO THERE'S NO ROOM FOR YOU ON THE SHOW!
YOU'RE JUST TOSSING ME ASIDE?! ME, THE COMPANY HEAD-LINER?!
IS THAT WHAT YOU'RE SAY-ING?
I DECIDE WHO OUR HEAD-LINER IS.
NOT YOU.

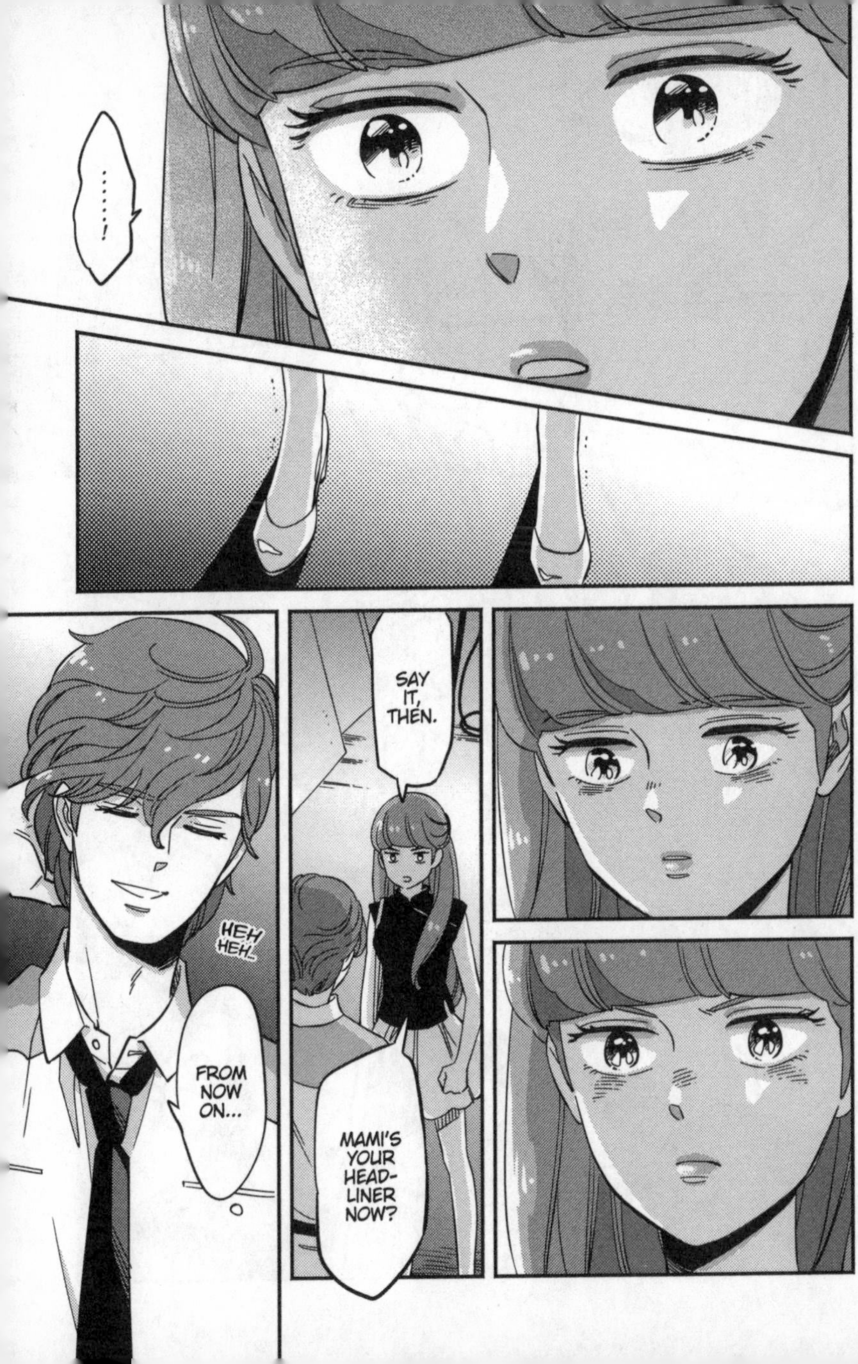
……!
SAY IT, THEN.
MAMI'S YOUR HEADLINER NOW?
HEH HEH...
FROM NOW ON...

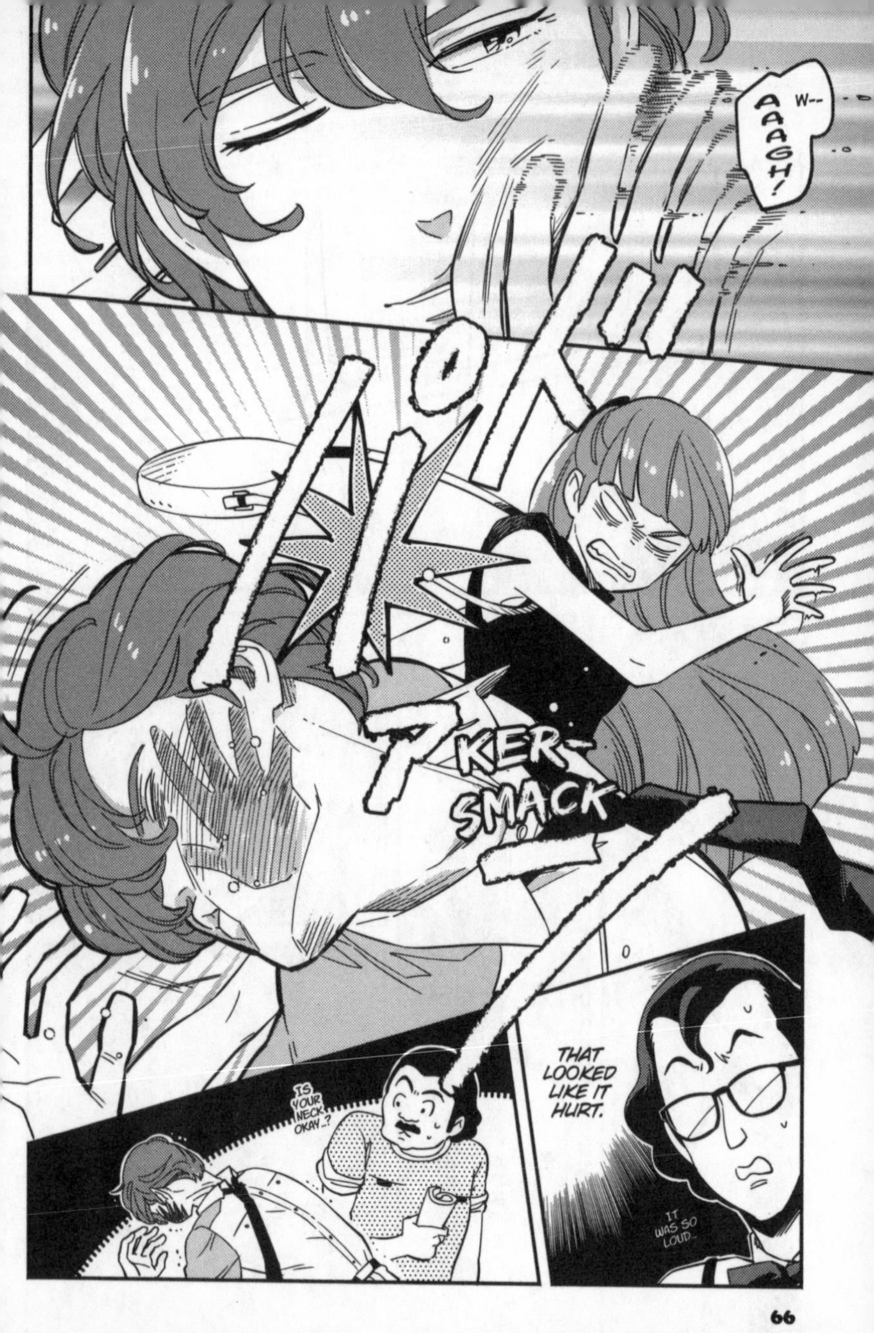
W--
AAAGH!
KER-SMACK
THAT LOOKED LIKE IT HURT.
IT WAS SO LOUD...
IS YOUR NECK OKAY...?

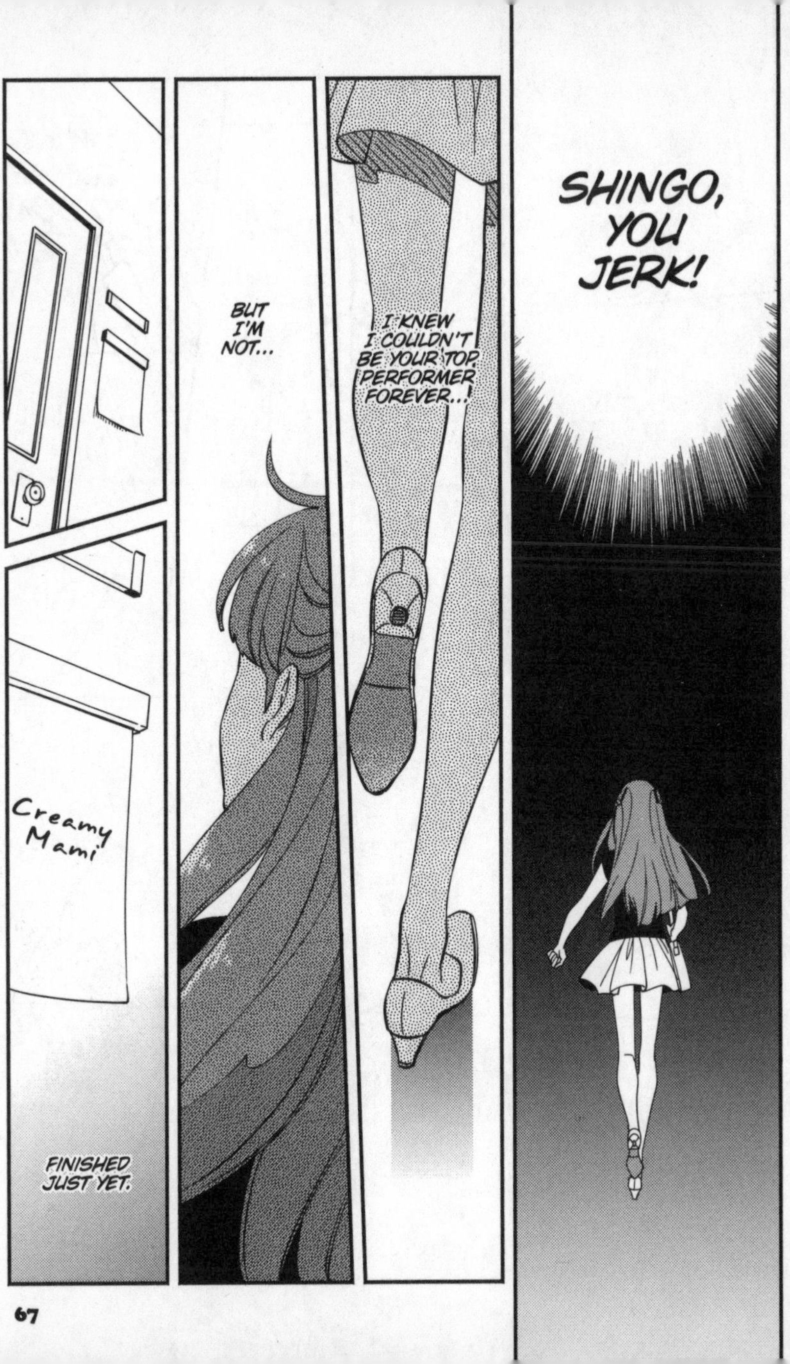
SHINGO, YOU JERK!
I KNEW I COULDN'T BE YOUR TOP PERFORMER FOREVER...!
BUT I'M NOT...
Creamy Mami
FINISHED JUST YET.

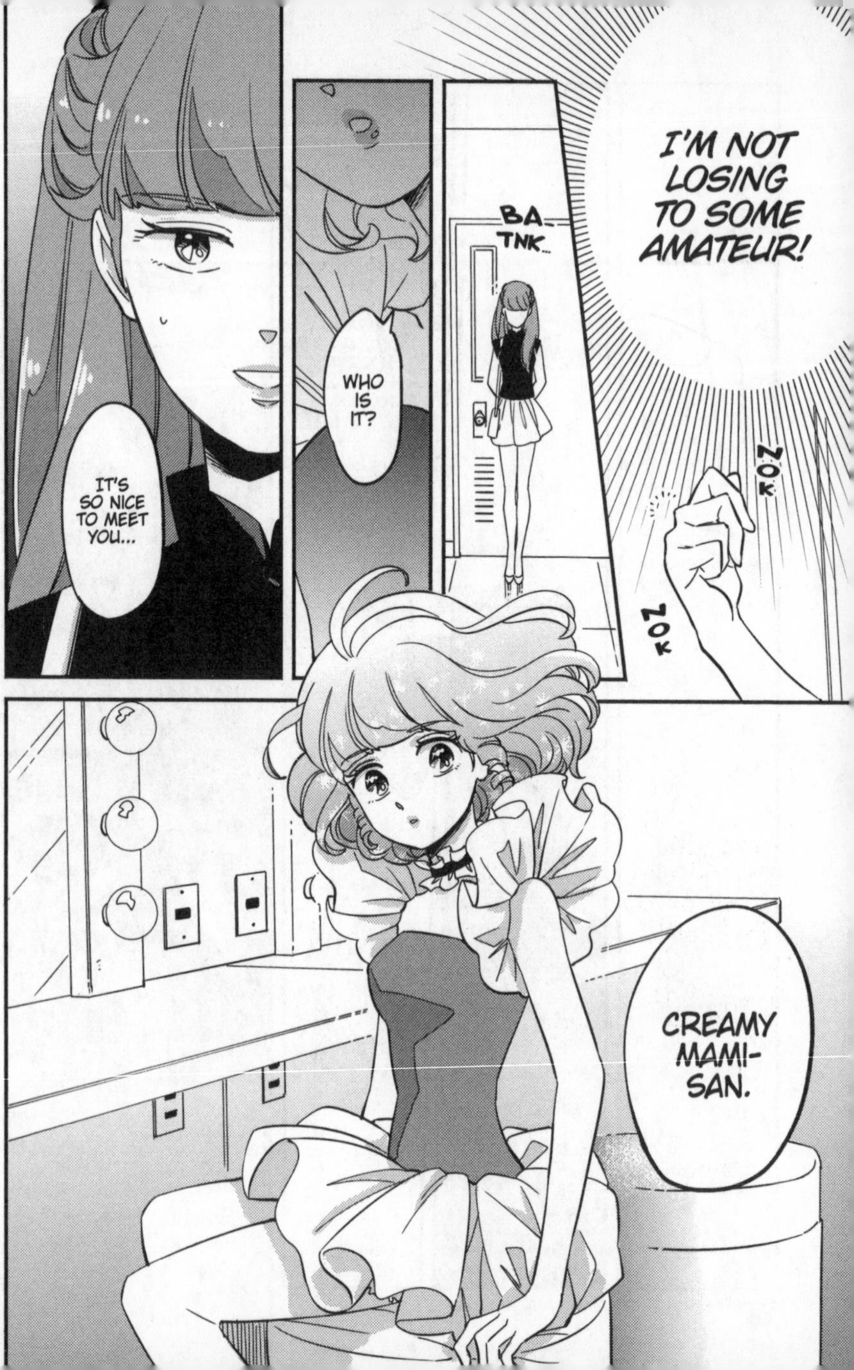
I'M NOT LOSING TO SOME AMATEUR!
ZOK
ZOK
BA-TNK...
WHO IS IT?
IT'S SO NICE TO MEET YOU...
CREAMY MAMI-SAN.

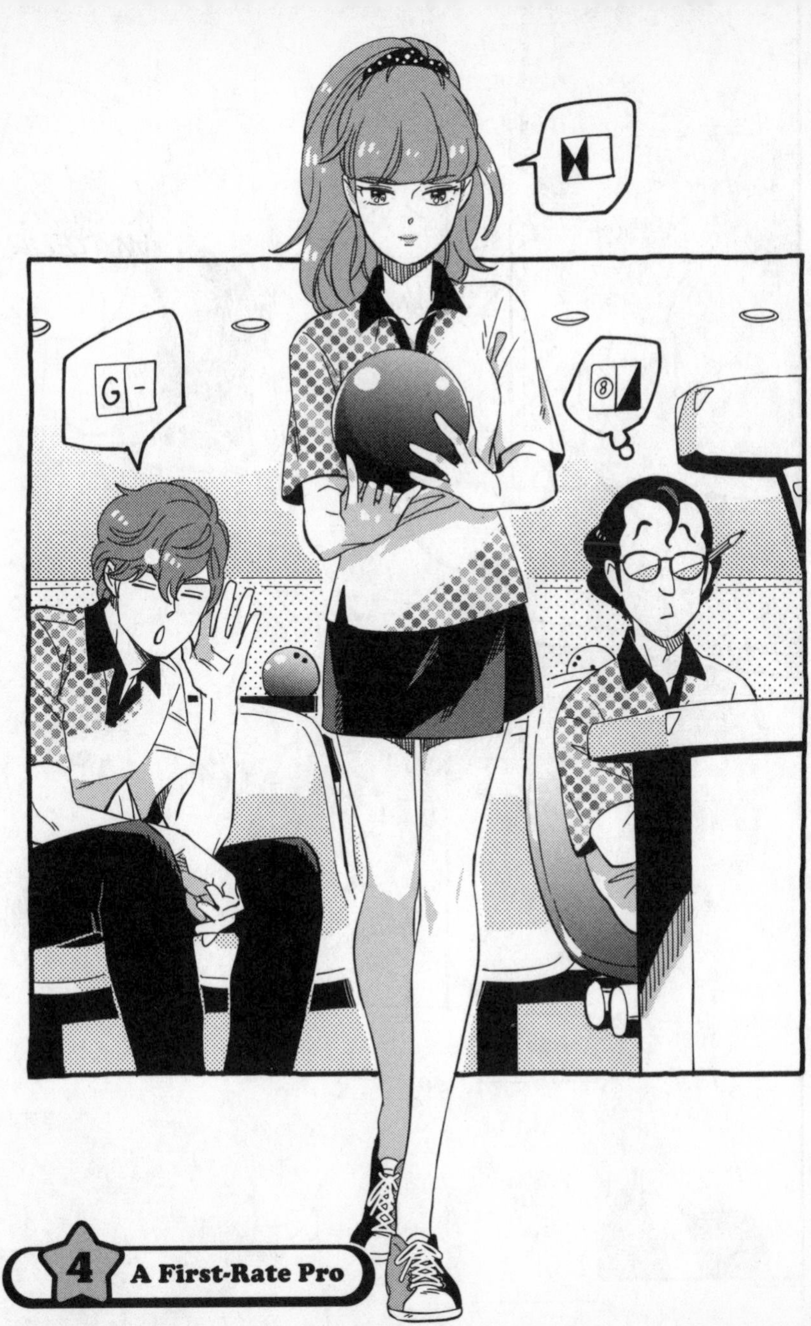
8
G -

4 A First-Rate Pro

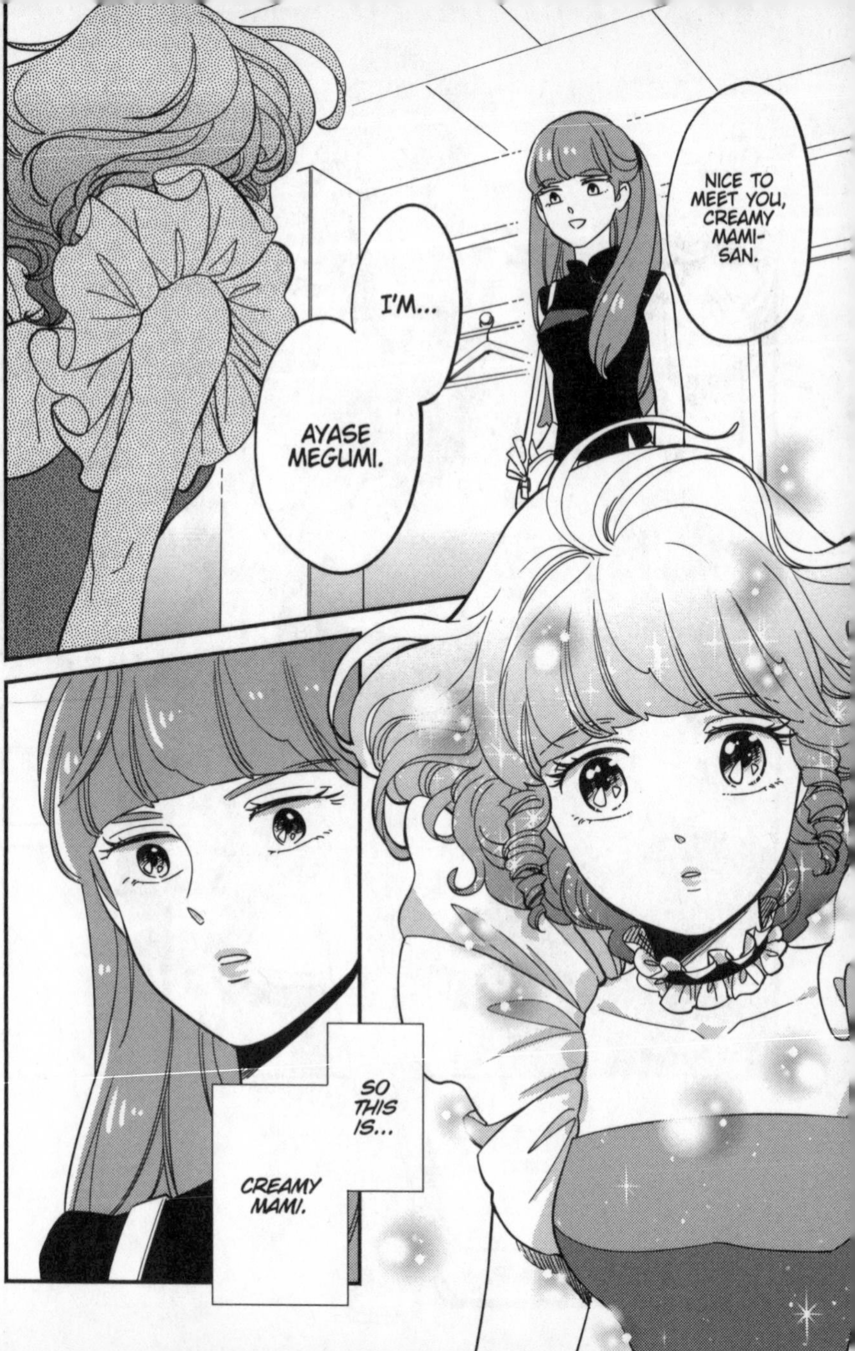
NICE TO MEET YOU, CREAMY MAMI-SAN.
I'M...
AYASE MEGUMI.
SO THIS IS...
CREAMY MAMI.

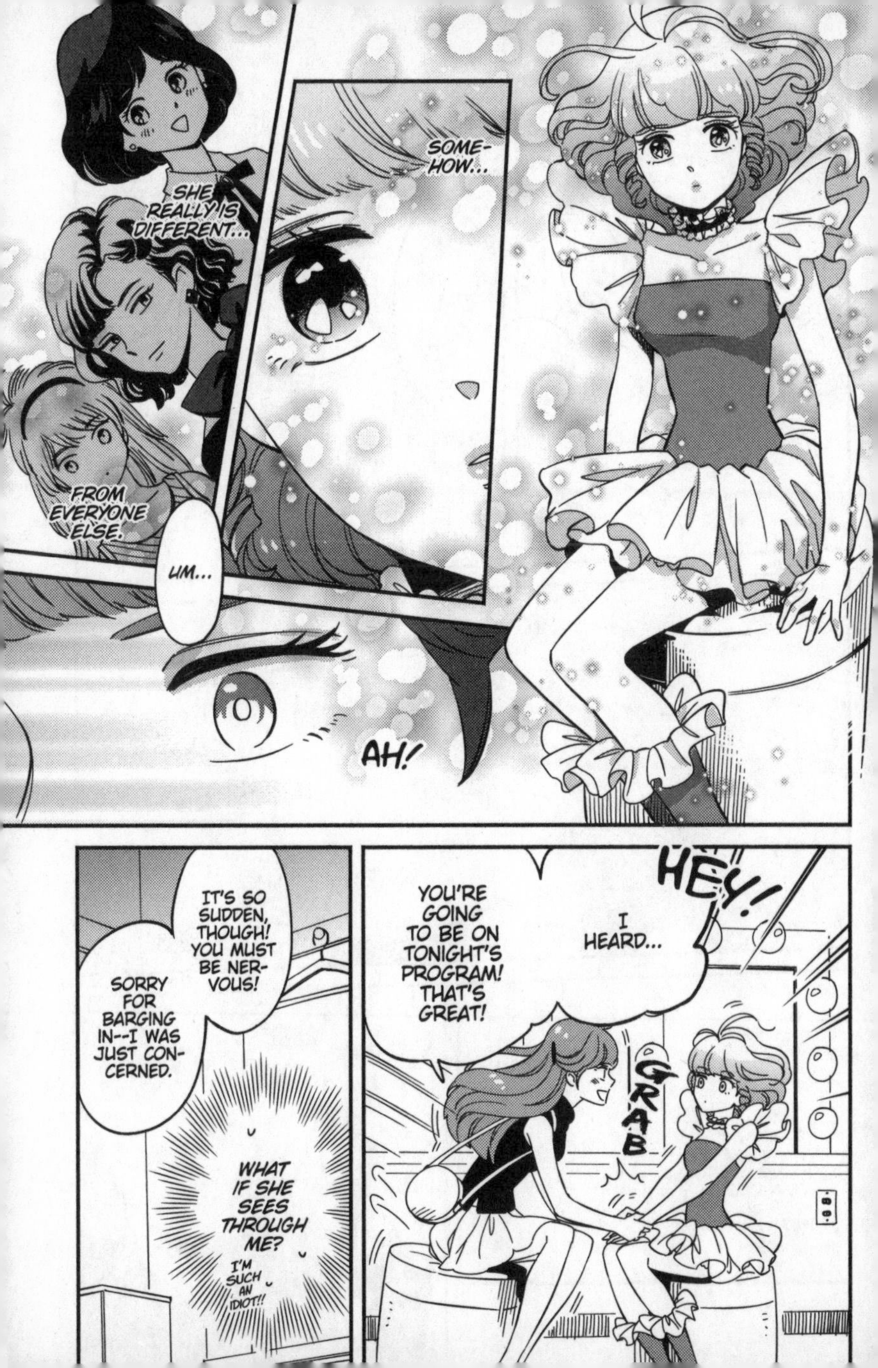
SOME-HOW...
SHE REALLY IS DIFFERENT...
FROM EVERYONE ELSE.
UM...
AH!
HEY!
I HEARD...
YOU'RE GOING TO BE ON TONIGHT'S PROGRAM! THAT'S GREAT!
GRAB
IT'S SO SUDDEN, THOUGH! YOU MUST BE NER-VOUS!
SORRY FOR BARGING IN--I WAS JUST CON-CERNED.
WHAT IF SHE SEES THROUGH ME?
I'M SUCH AN IDIOT!!

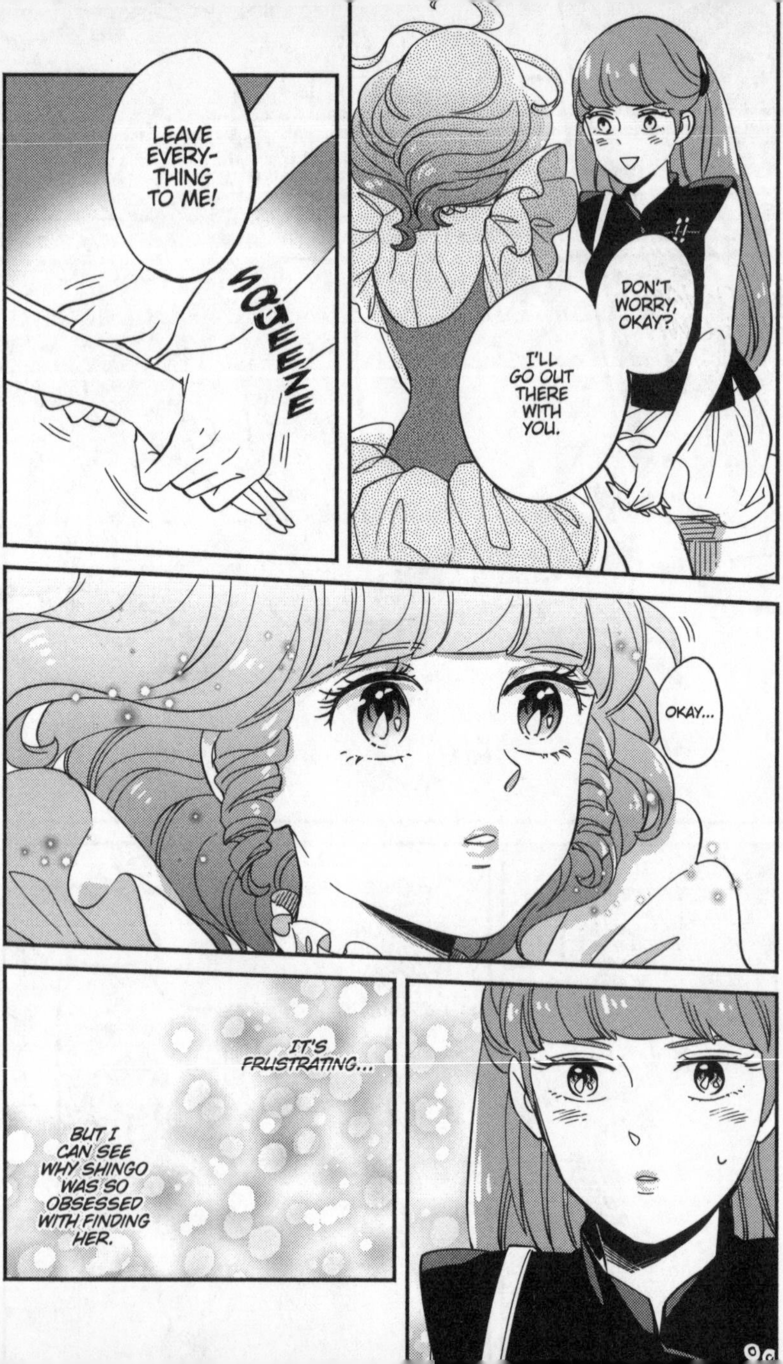
DON'T WORRY, OKAY?
I'LL GO OUT THERE WITH YOU.
LEAVE EVERY-THING TO ME!
SQUEEZE
OKAY...
IT'S FRUSTRATING...
BUT I CAN SEE WHY SHINGO WAS SO OBSESSED WITH FINDING HER.

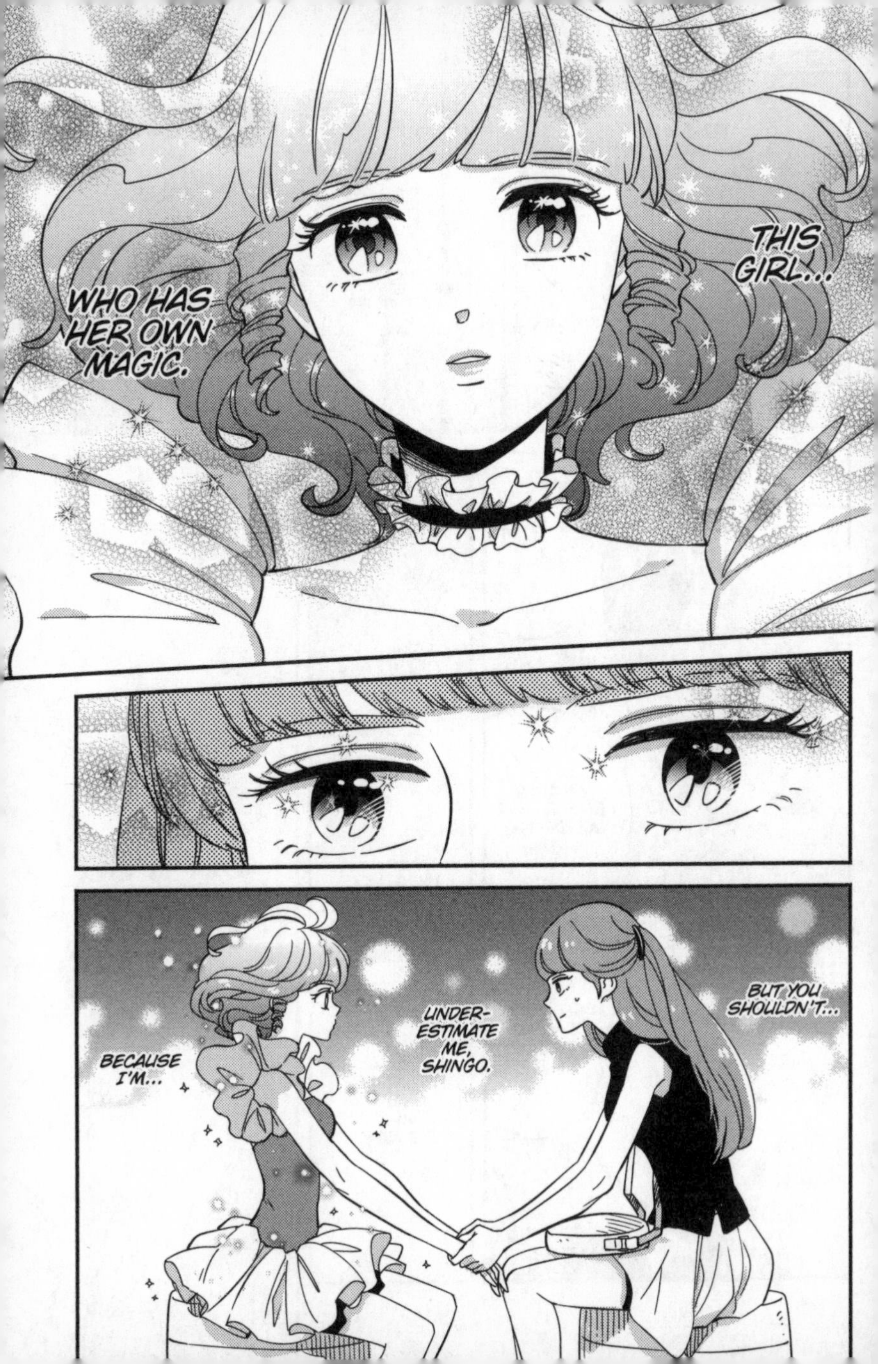
THIS GIRL...
WHO HAS HER OWN MAGIC.
BUT YOU SHOULDN'T...
UNDER-ESTIMATE ME, SHINGO.
BECAUSE I'M...

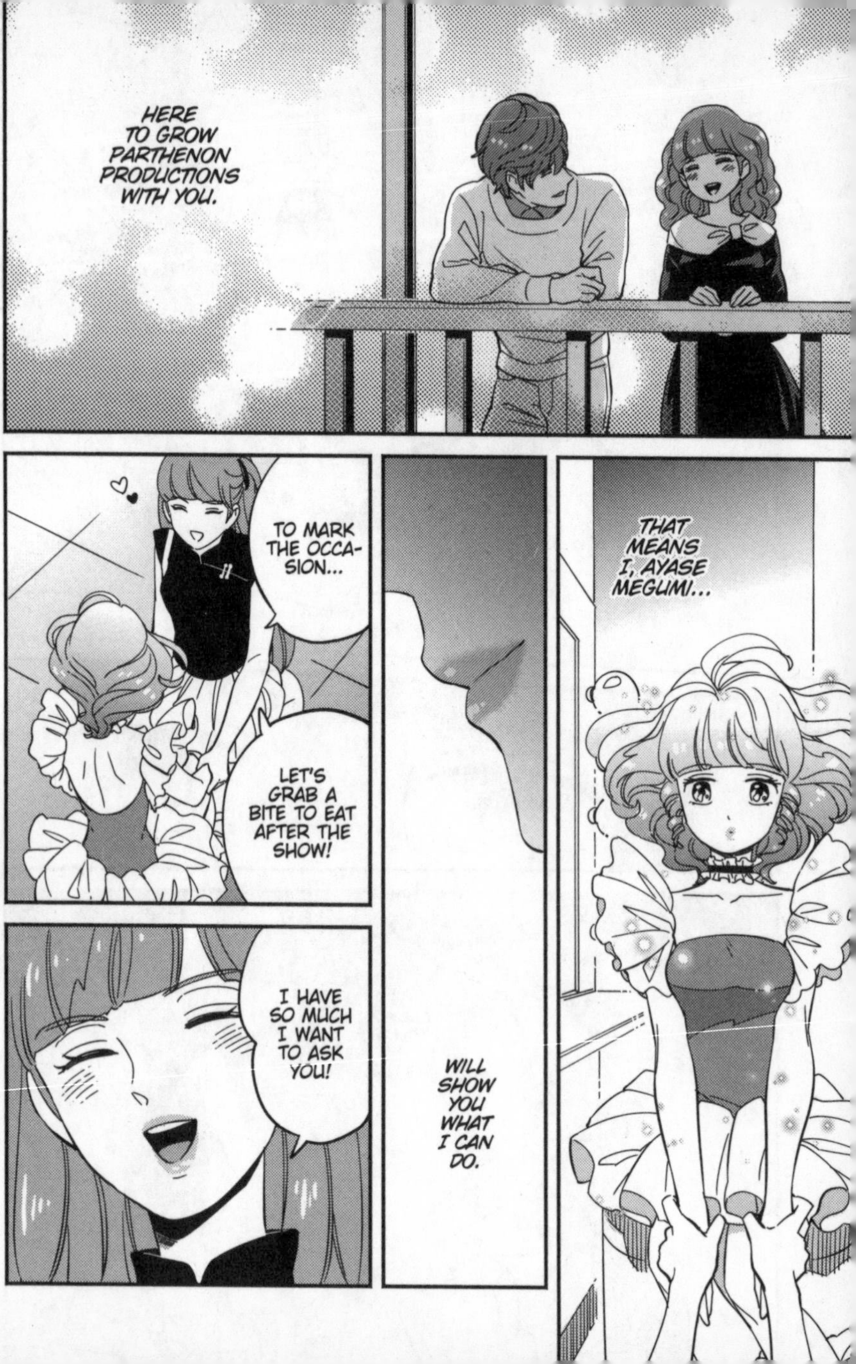
HERE TO GROW PARTHENON PRODUCTIONS WITH YOU.
THAT MEANS I, AYASE MEGUMI...
WILL SHOW YOU WHAT I CAN DO.
TO MARK THE OCCA-SION...
LET'S GRAB A BITE TO EAT AFTER THE SHOW!
I HAVE SO MUCH I WANT TO ASK YOU!

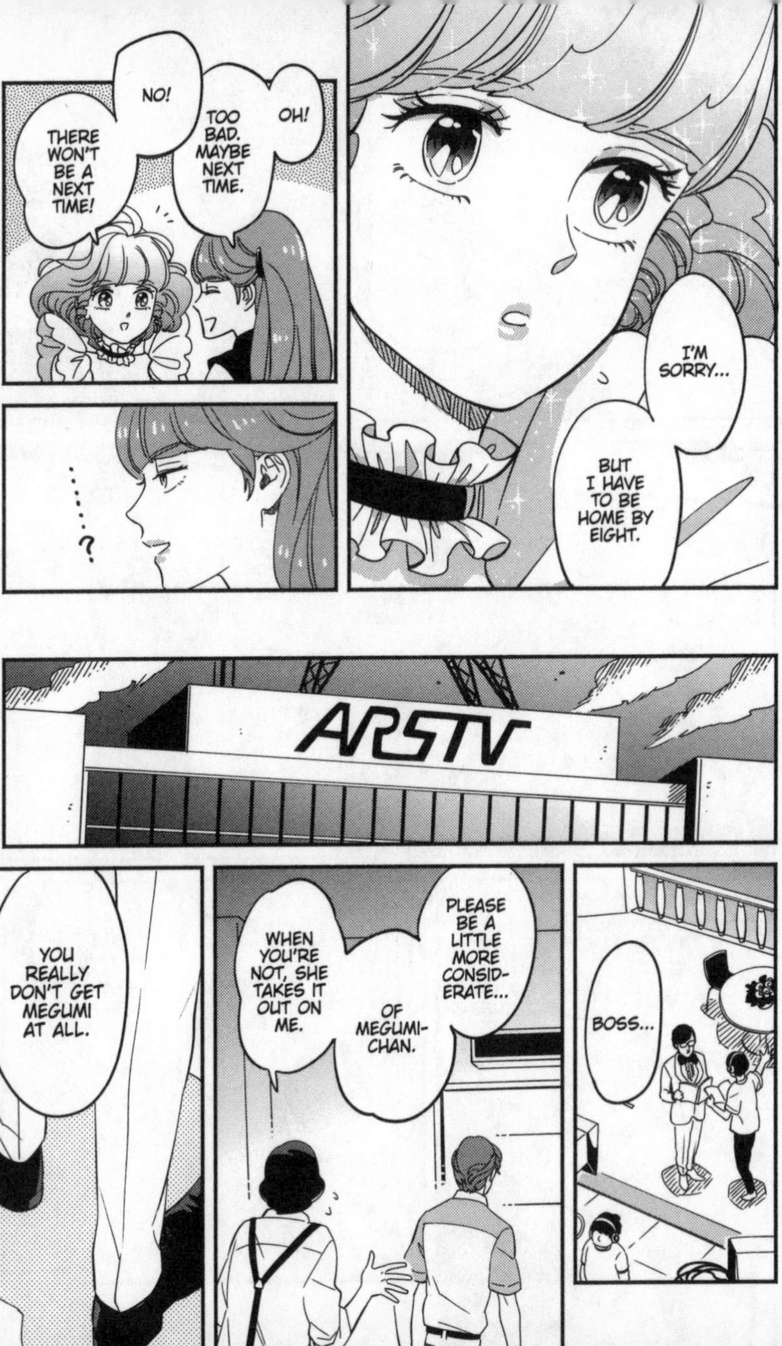
I'M SORRY...
BUT I HAVE TO BE HOME BY EIGHT.
OH!
TOO BAD. MAYBE NEXT TIME.
NO!
THERE WON'T BE A NEXT TIME!
.....?
ARSTV
BOSS...
PLEASE BE A LITTLE MORE CONSIDERATE...
OF MEGUMI-CHAN.
WHEN YOU'RE NOT, SHE TAKES IT OUT ON ME.
YOU REALLY DON'T GET MEGUMI AT ALL.

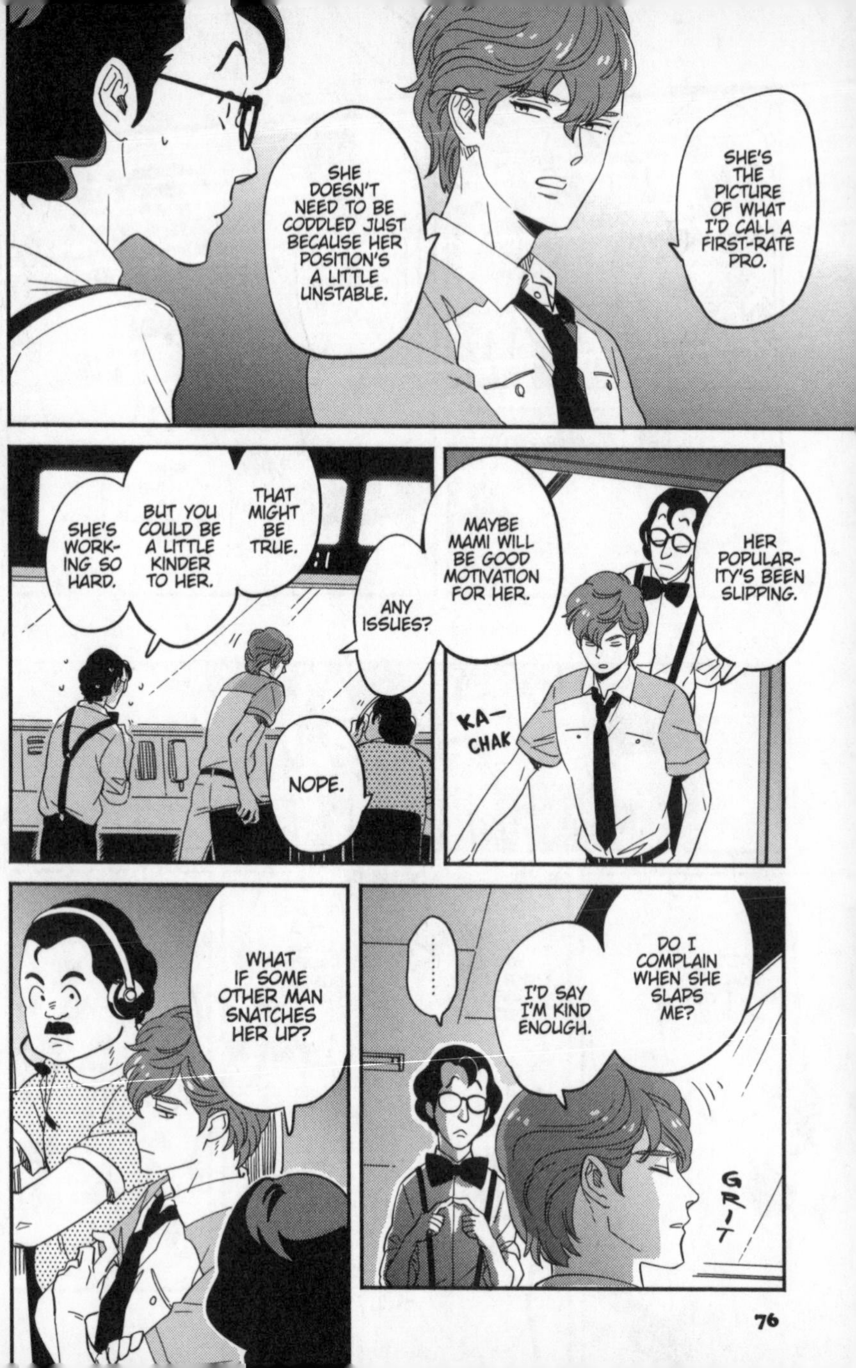
SHE'S THE PICTURE OF WHAT I'D CALL A FIRST-RATE PRO.
SHE DOESN'T NEED TO BE CODDLED JUST BECAUSE HER POSITION'S A LITTLE UNSTABLE.
HER POPULAR-ITY'S BEEN SLIPPING.
KA-CHAK
MAYBE MAMI WILL BE GOOD MOTIVATION FOR HER.
THAT MIGHT BE TRUE.
BUT YOU COULD BE A LITTLE KINDER TO HER.
SHE'S WORK-ING SO HARD.
ANY ISSUES?
NOPE.
DO I COMPLAIN WHEN SHE SLAPS ME?
I'D SAY I'M KIND ENOUGH.
......
GRIT
WHAT IF SOME OTHER MAN SNATCHES HER UP?

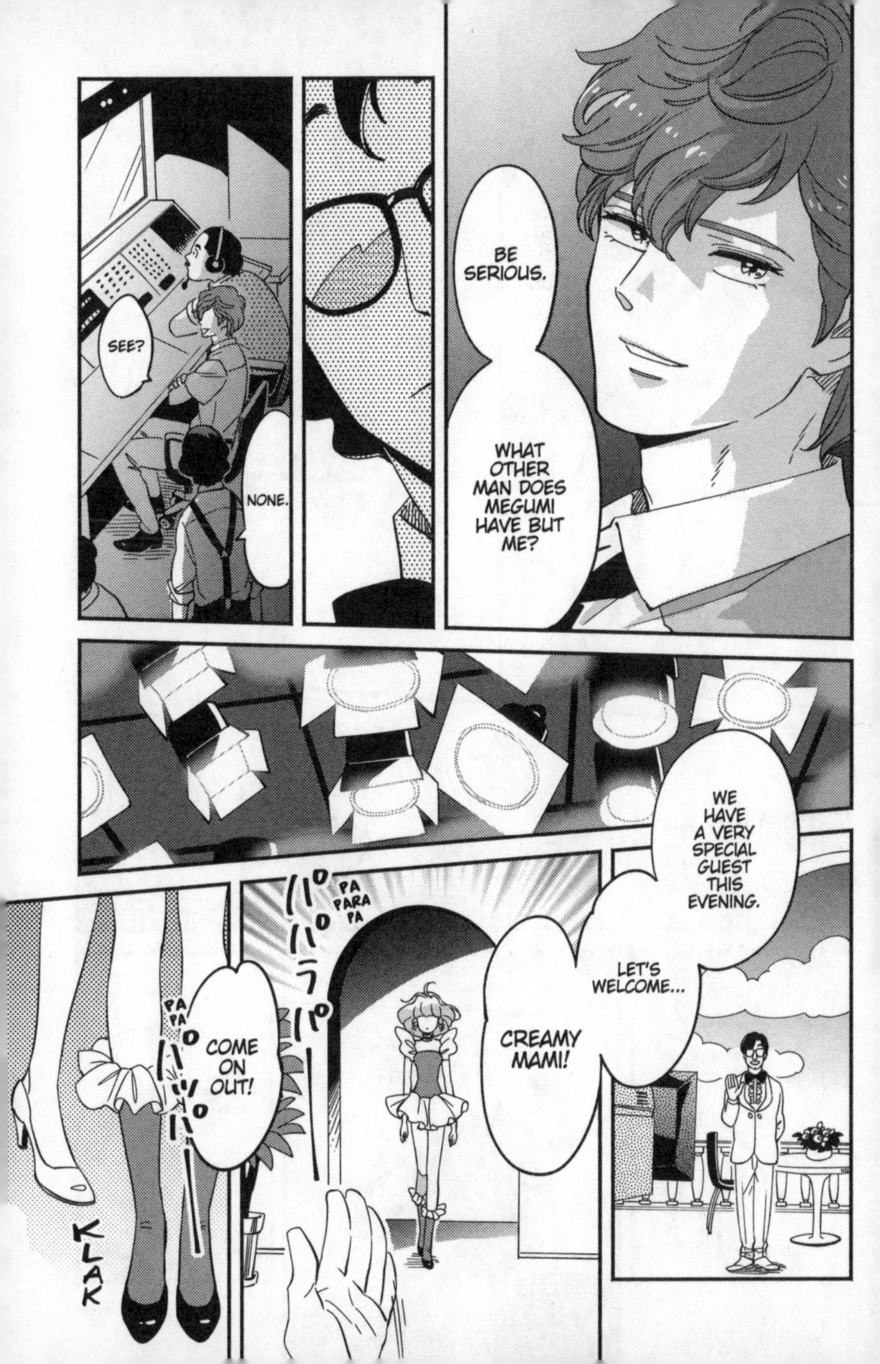
BE SERIOUS.
WHAT OTHER MAN DOES MEGUMI HAVE BUT ME?
NONE.
SEE?
WE HAVE A VERY SPECIAL GUEST THIS EVENING.
LET'S WELCOME...
CREAMY MAMI!
PA PARA PA
COME ON OUT!
PA PA
KLAK

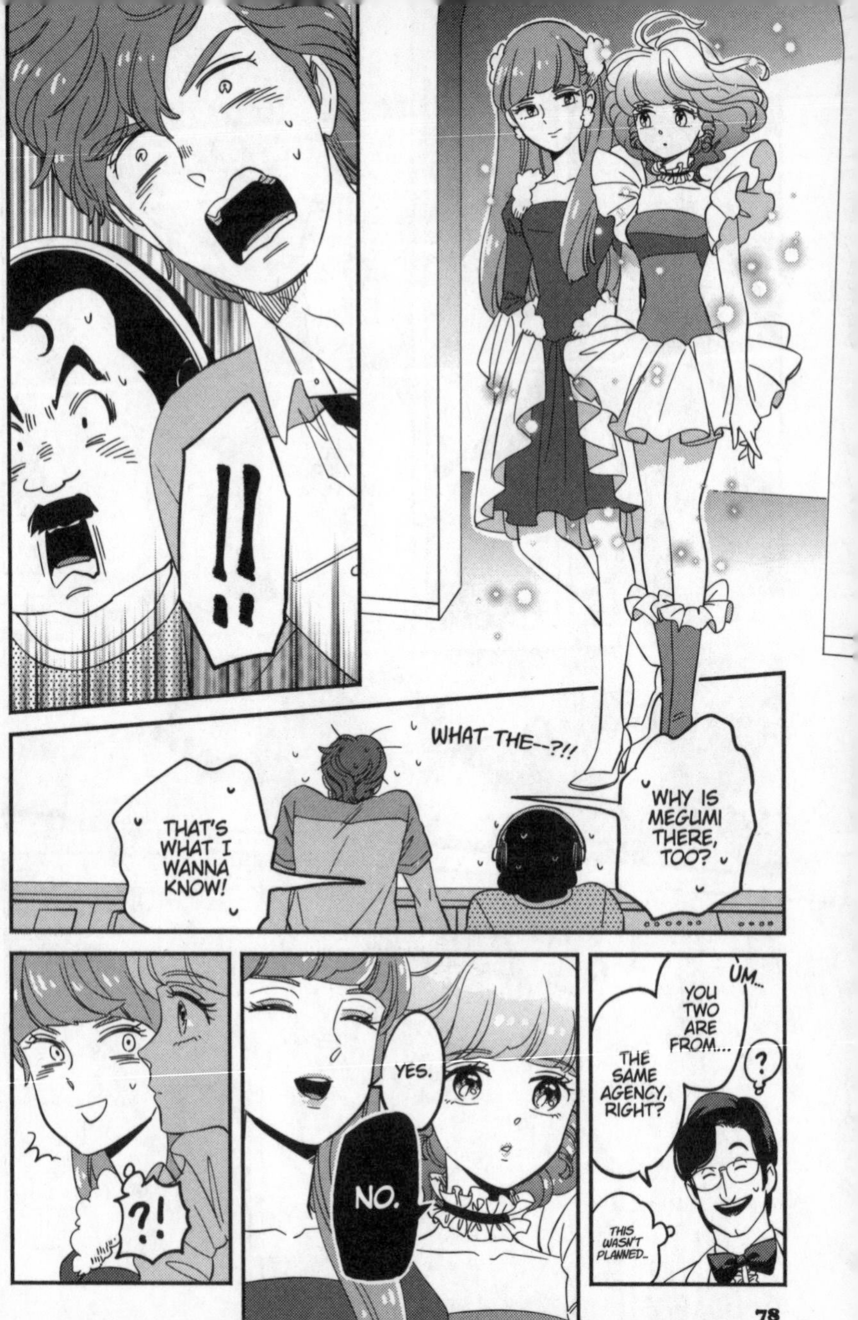
!!
WHAT THE--?!!
WHY IS MEGUMI THERE, TOO?
THAT'S WHAT I WANNA KNOW!
UM...
YOU TWO ARE FROM...
THE SAME AGENCY, RIGHT?
?
THIS WASN'T PLANNED...
YES.
NO.
?!

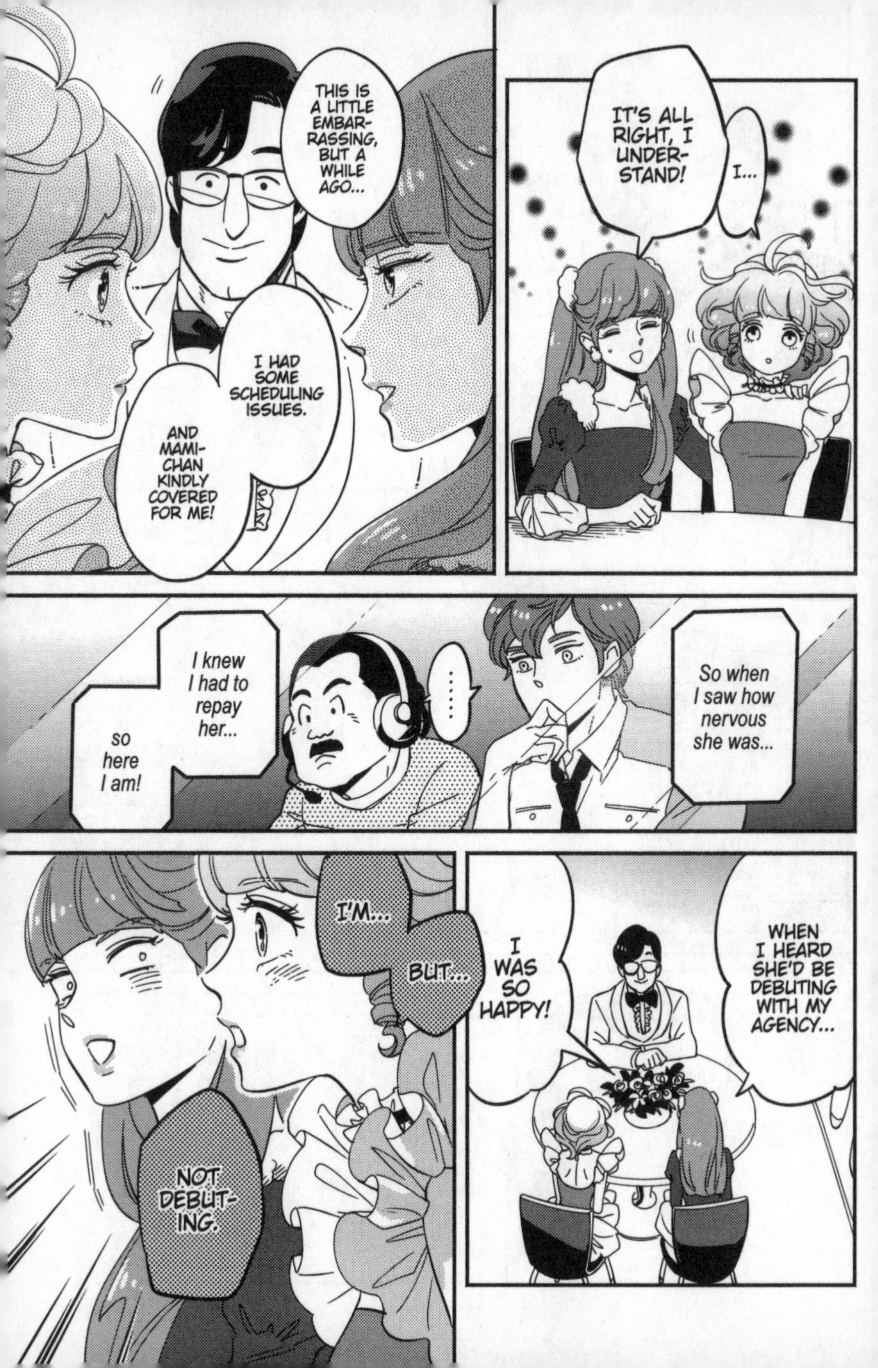
I...
IT'S ALL RIGHT, I UNDER-STAND!
THIS IS A LITTLE EMBAR-RASSING, BUT A WHILE AGO...
I HAD SOME SCHEDULING ISSUES.
AND MAMI-CHAN KINDLY COVERED FOR ME!
So when I saw how nervous she was...
......
I knew I had to repay her...
so here I am!
WHEN I HEARD SHE'D BE DEBUTING WITH MY AGENCY...
I WAS SO HAPPY!
I'M...
BUT...
NOT DEBUT-ING.

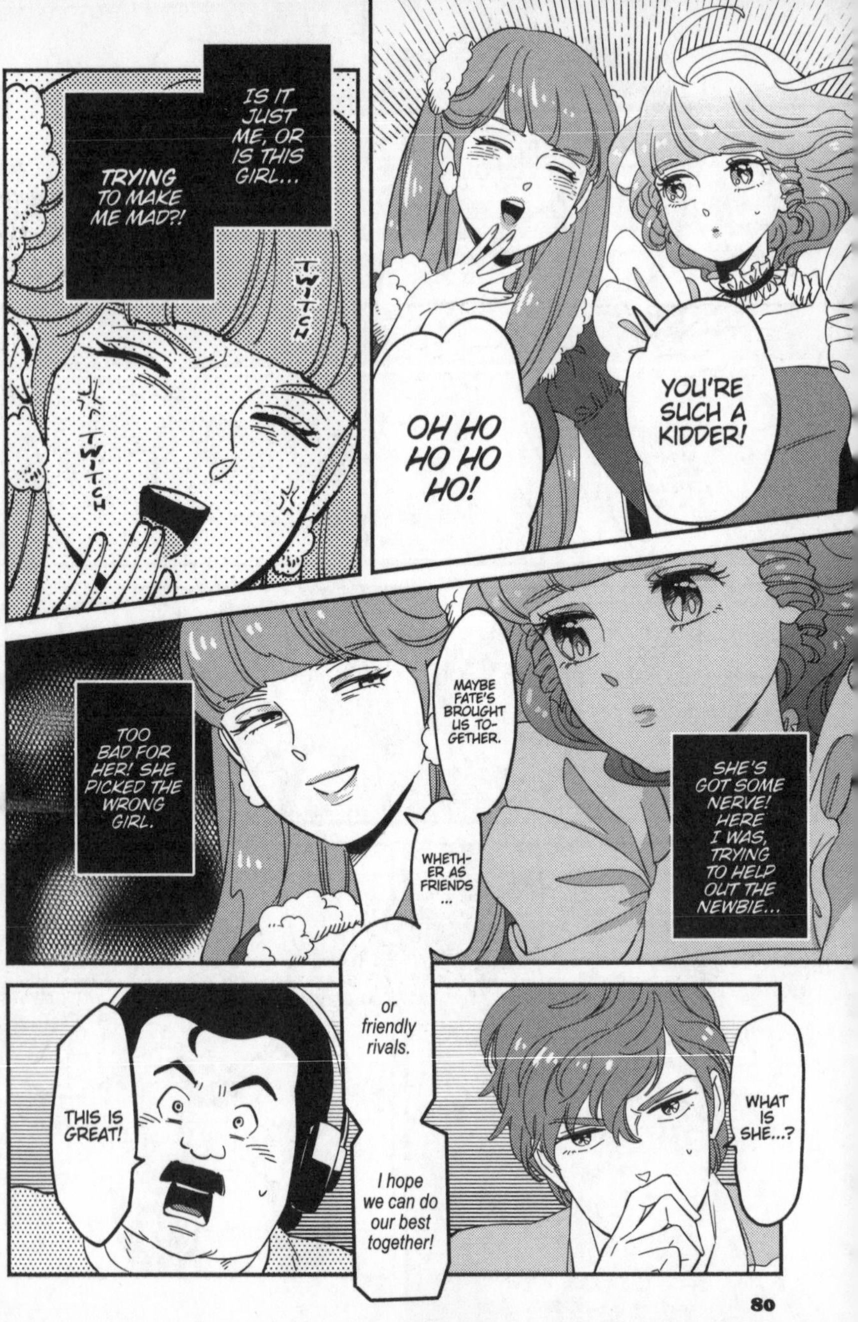
YOU'RE SUCH A KIDDER!
OH HO HO HO HO!
IS IT JUST ME, OR IS THIS GIRL...
TRYING TO MAKE ME MAD?!
TWITCH
TWITCH
SHE'S GOT SOME NERVE! HERE I WAS, TRYING TO HELP OUT THE NEWBIE...
MAYBE FATE'S BROUGHT US TO-GETHER.
WHETH-ER AS FRIENDS...
TOO BAD FOR HER! SHE PICKED THE WRONG GIRL.
WHAT IS SHE...?
or friendly rivals.
I hope we can do our best together!
THIS IS GREAT!

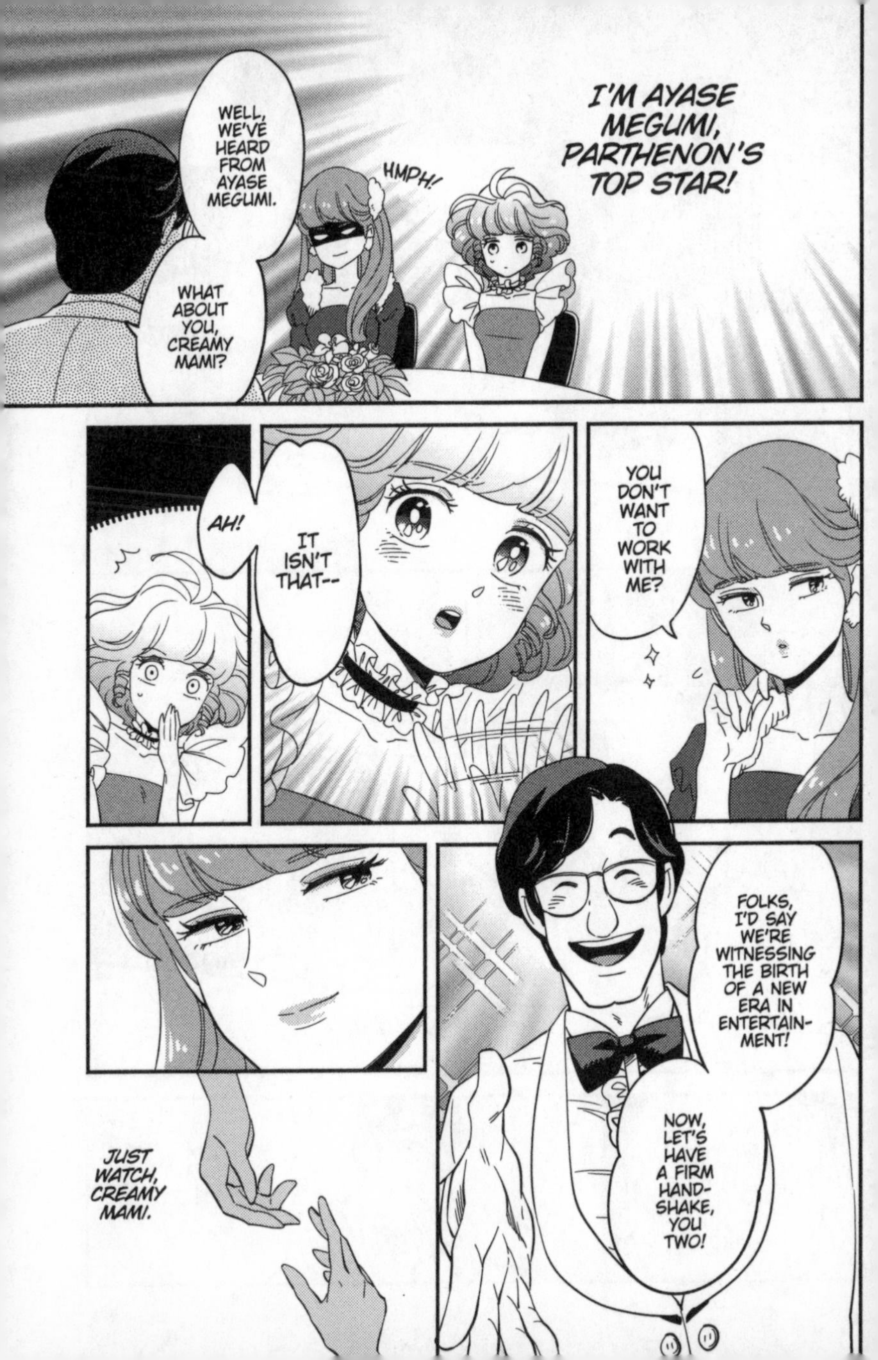
I'M AYASE MEGUMI, PARTHENON'S TOP STAR!
HMPH!
WELL, WE'VE HEARD FROM AYASE MEGUMI.
WHAT ABOUT YOU, CREAMY MAMI?
YOU DON'T WANT TO WORK WITH ME?
IT ISN'T THAT--
AH!
FOLKS, I'D SAY WE'RE WITNESSING THE BIRTH OF A NEW ERA IN ENTERTAIN-MENT!
NOW, LET'S HAVE A FIRM HAND-SHAKE, YOU TWO!
JUST WATCH, CREAMY MAMI.

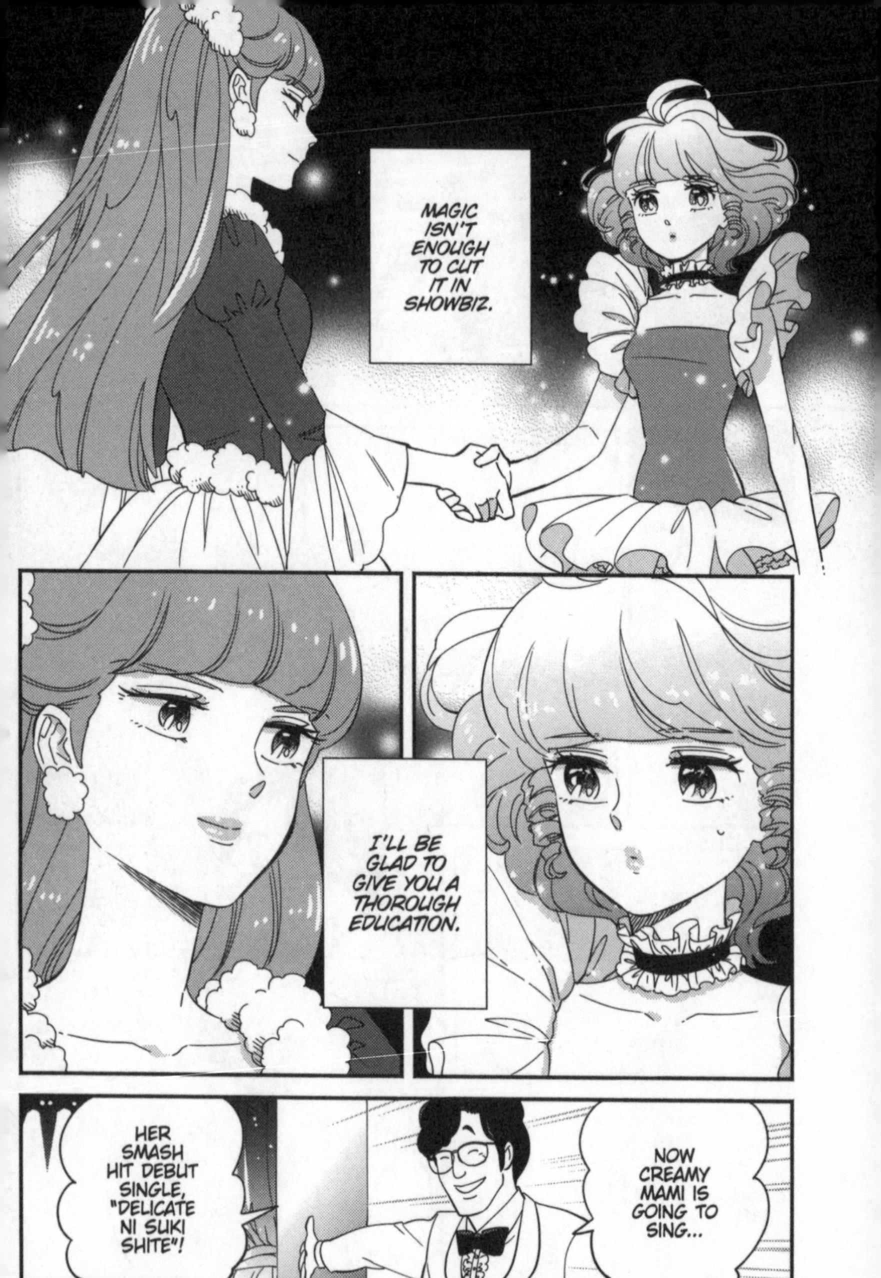
MAGIC ISN'T ENOUGH TO CUT IT IN SHOWBIZ.
I'LL BE GLAD TO GIVE YOU A THOROUGH EDUCATION.
NOW CREAMY MAMI IS GOING TO SING...
HER SMASH HIT DEBUT SINGLE, "DELICATE NI SUKI SHITE"!

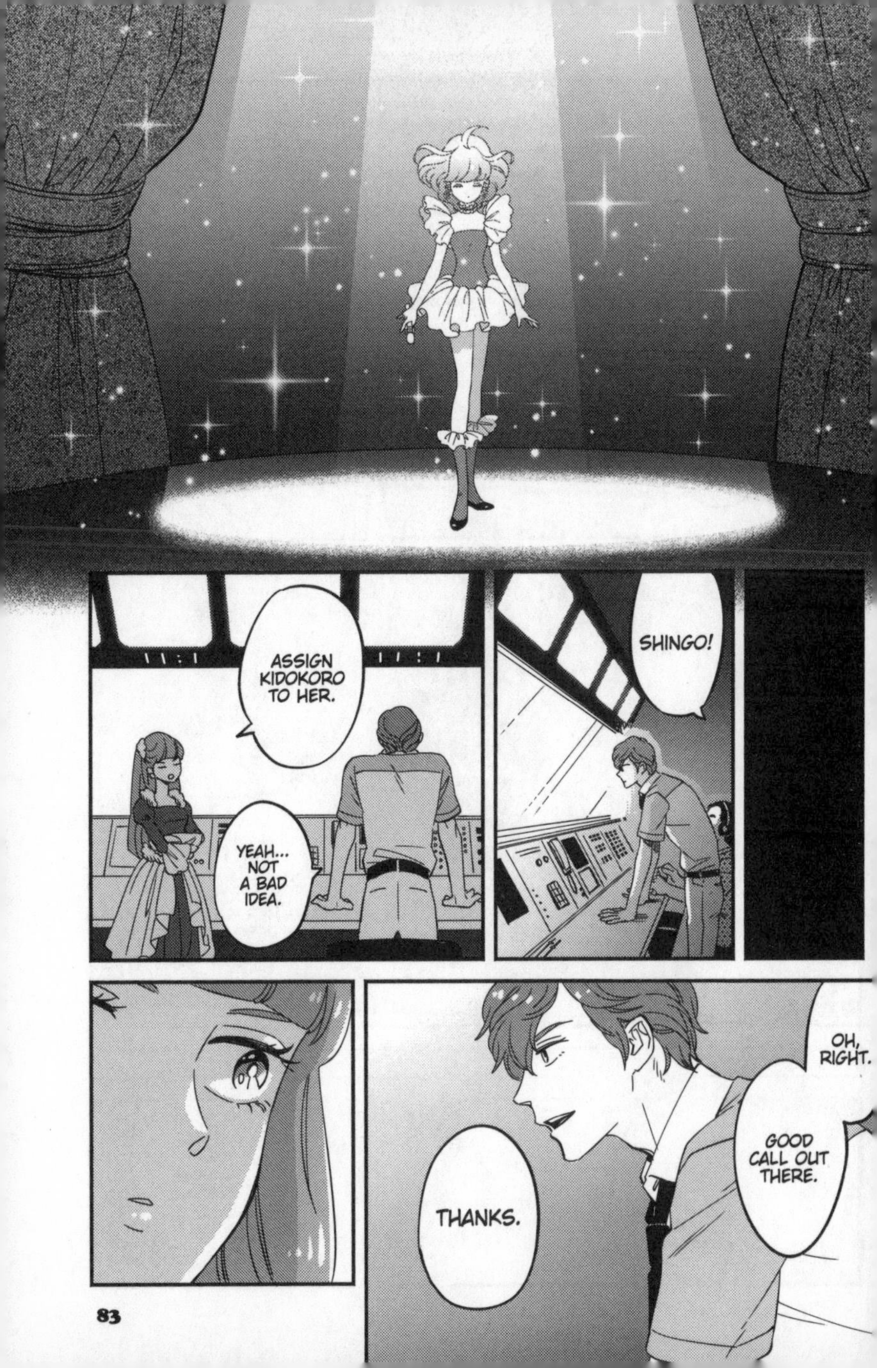
SHINGO!
ASSIGN KIDOKORO TO HER.
YEAH... NOT A BAD IDEA.
OH, RIGHT.
GOOD CALL OUT THERE.
THANKS.

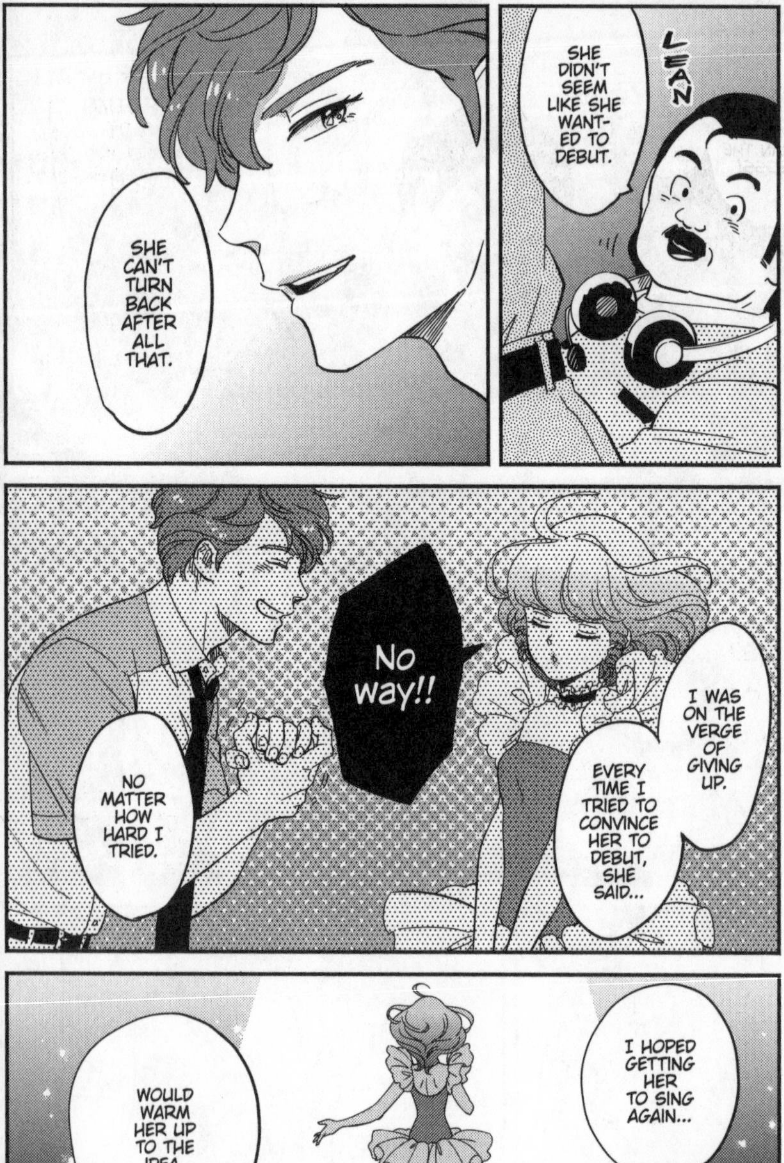
LEAN
SHE DIDN'T SEEM LIKE SHE WANT-ED TO DEBUT.
SHE CAN'T TURN BACK AFTER ALL THAT.
I WAS ON THE VERGE OF GIVING UP.
EVERY TIME I TRIED TO CONVINCE HER TO DEBUT, SHE SAID...
No way!!
NO MATTER HOW HARD I TRIED.
I HOPED GETTING HER TO SING AGAIN...
WOULD WARM HER UP TO THE IDEA.

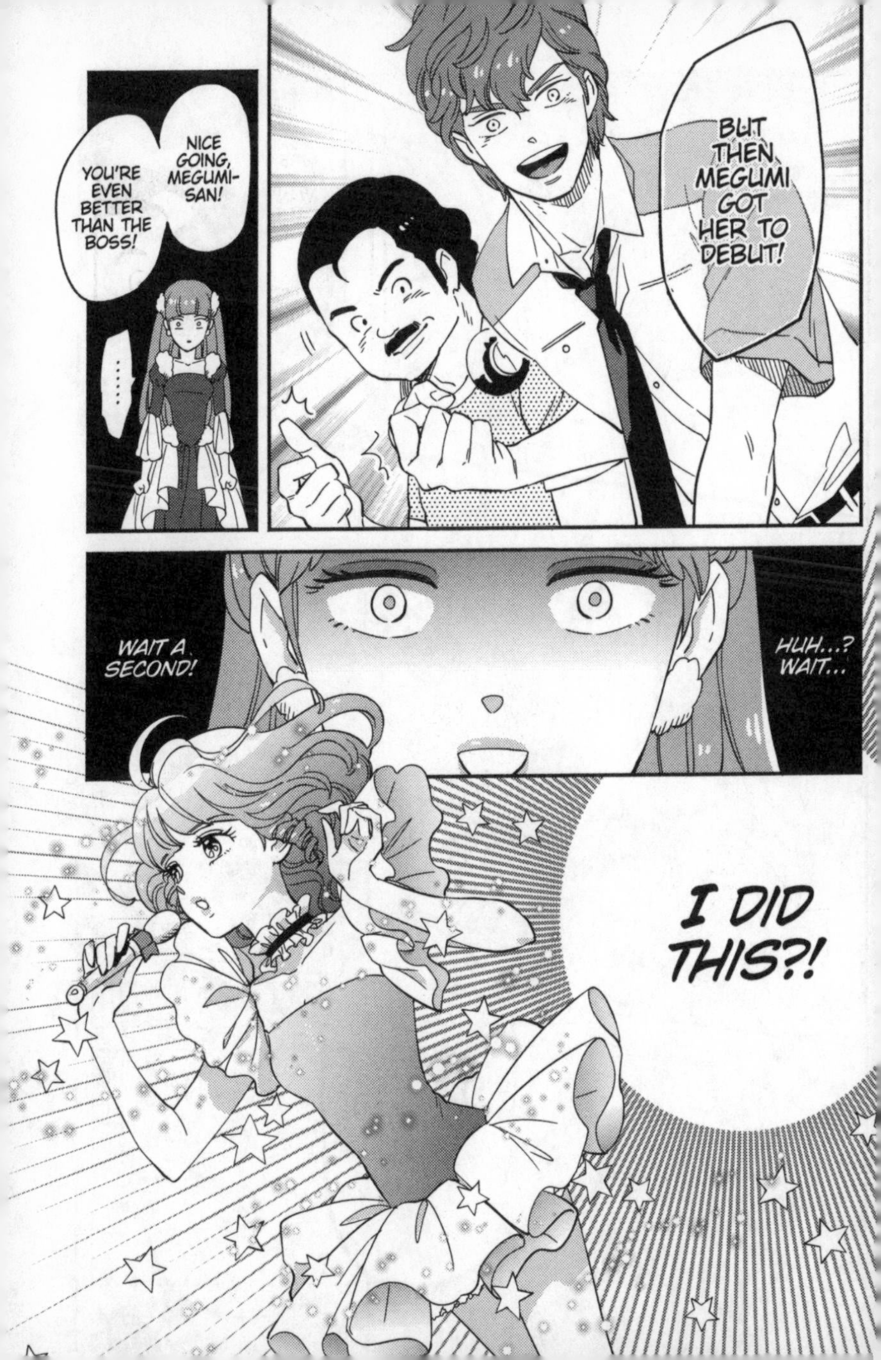
BUT THEN MEGUMI GOT HER TO DEBUT!
NICE GOING, MEGUMI-SAN!
YOU'RE EVEN BETTER THAN THE BOSS!
......
HUH...? WAIT...
WAIT A SECOND!
I DID THIS?!

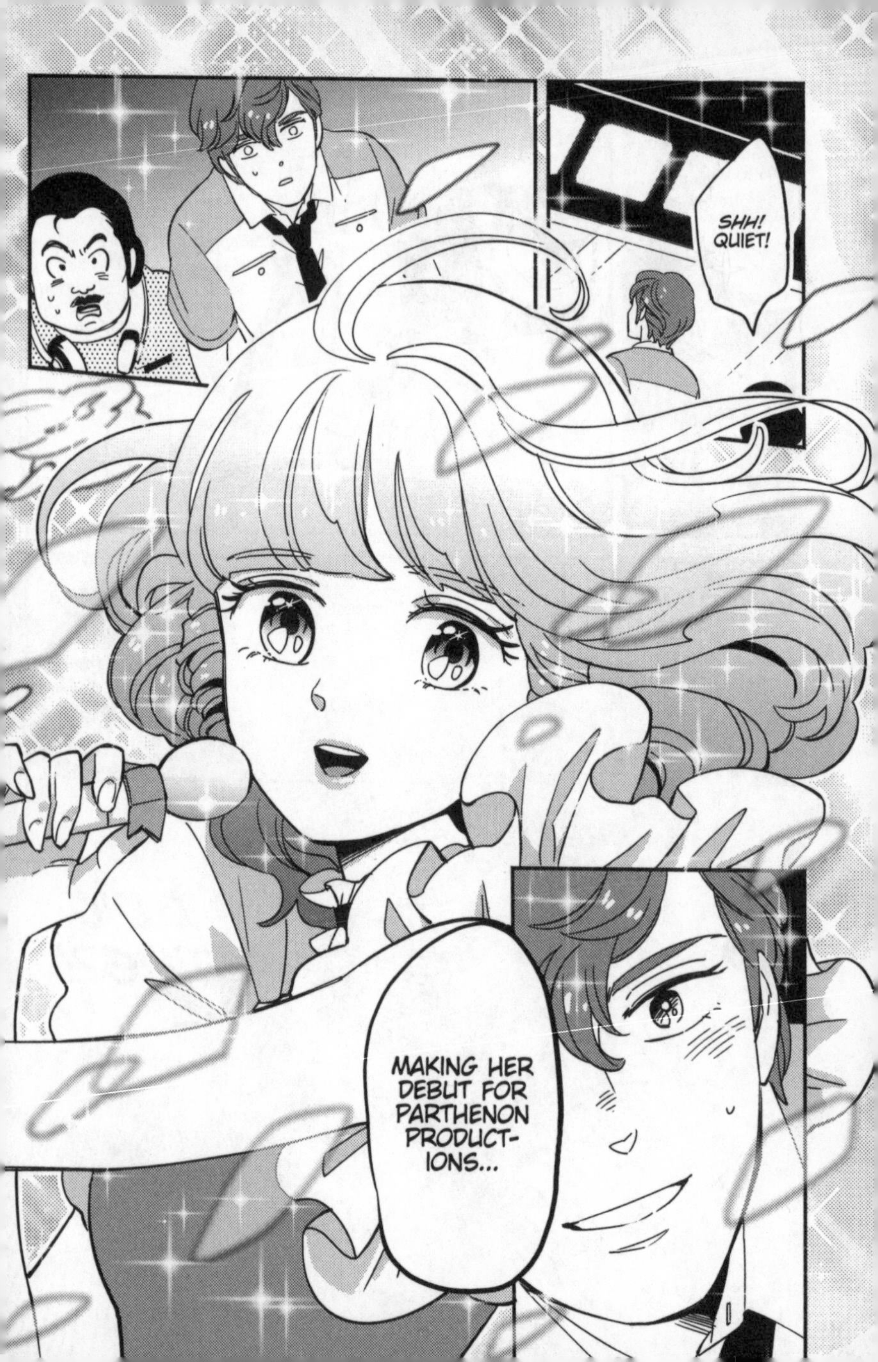
SHH! QUIET!
MAKING HER DEBUT FOR PARTHENON PRODUCT- IONS...

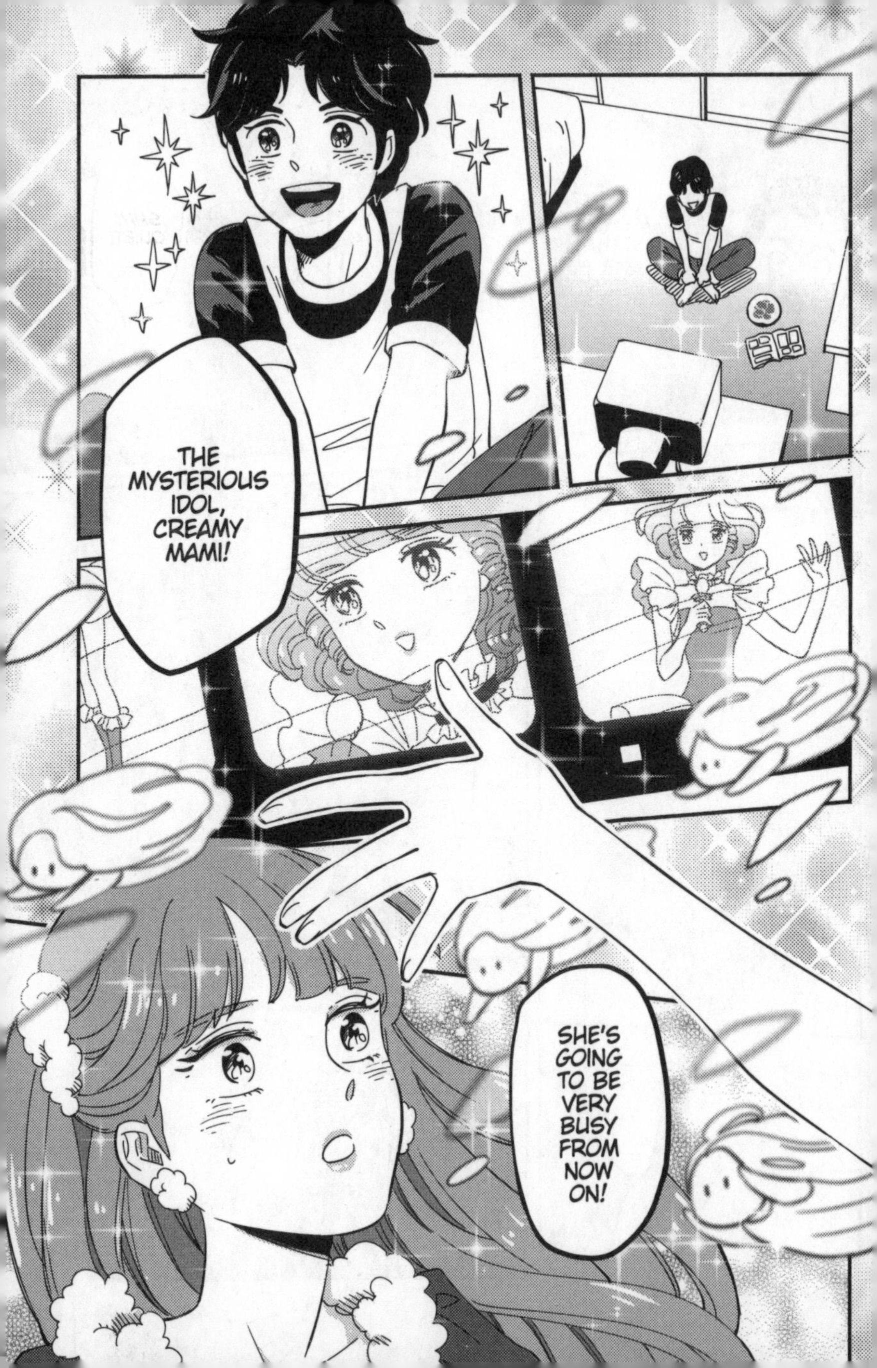
THE MYSTERIOUS IDOL, CREAMY MAMI!
SHE'S GOING TO BE VERY BUSY FROM NOW ON!

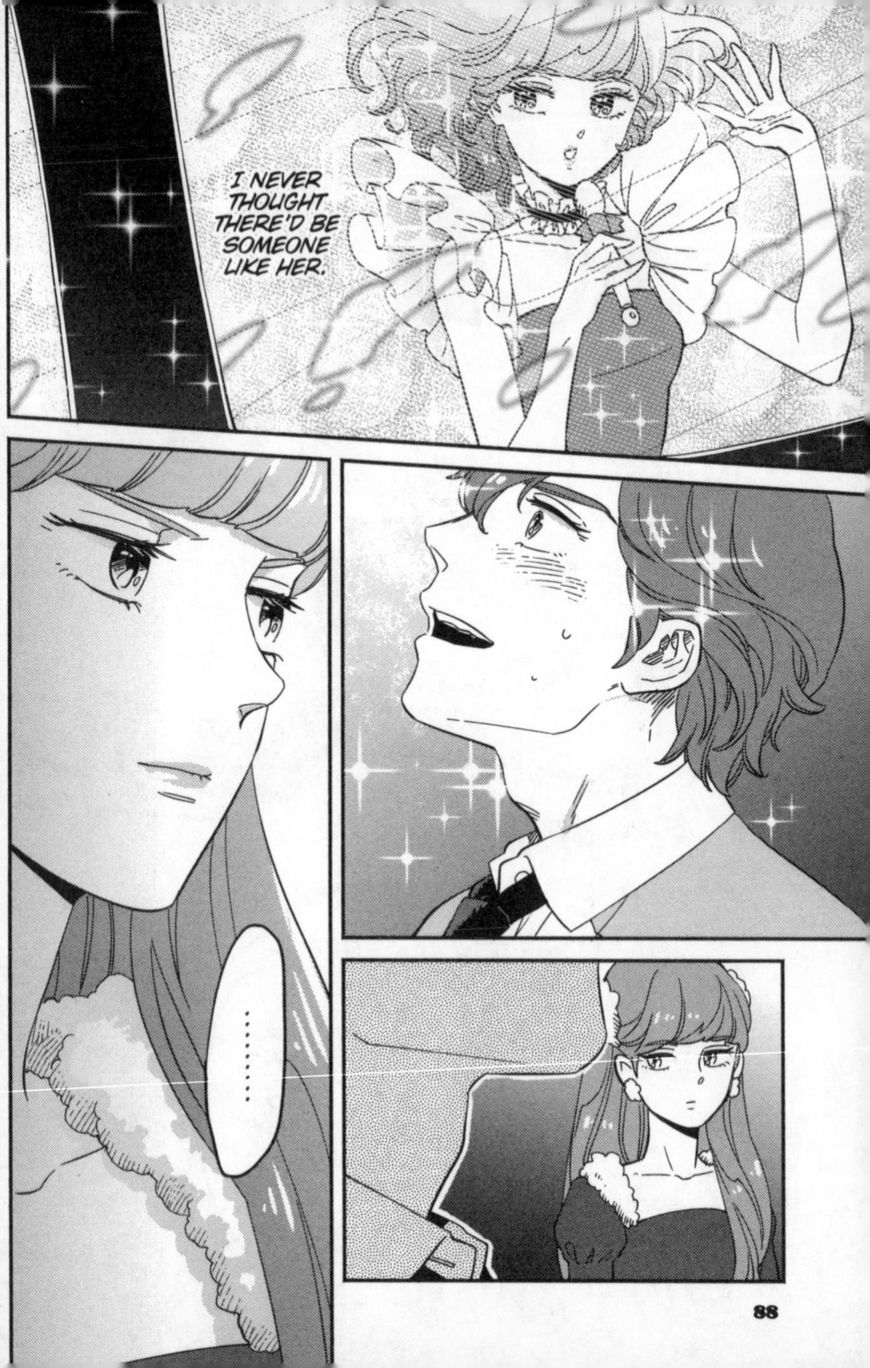
I NEVER THOUGHT THERE'D BE SOMEONE LIKE HER.
......

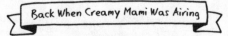

Back When Creamy Mami Was Airing

1983 The Nintendo Famicom Disk System goes on sale.

THE GAME & WATCH IS SO OUTDATED! NOW EVERYONE'LL BE PLAYING ON THEIR TVS!!

Game & Watch 1980

I STILL LIKE PLAYING WITH THESE!

Rubik's Cube 1981: Released in Japan

Magical Angel

CreamyMami

and the
Spoiled Princess

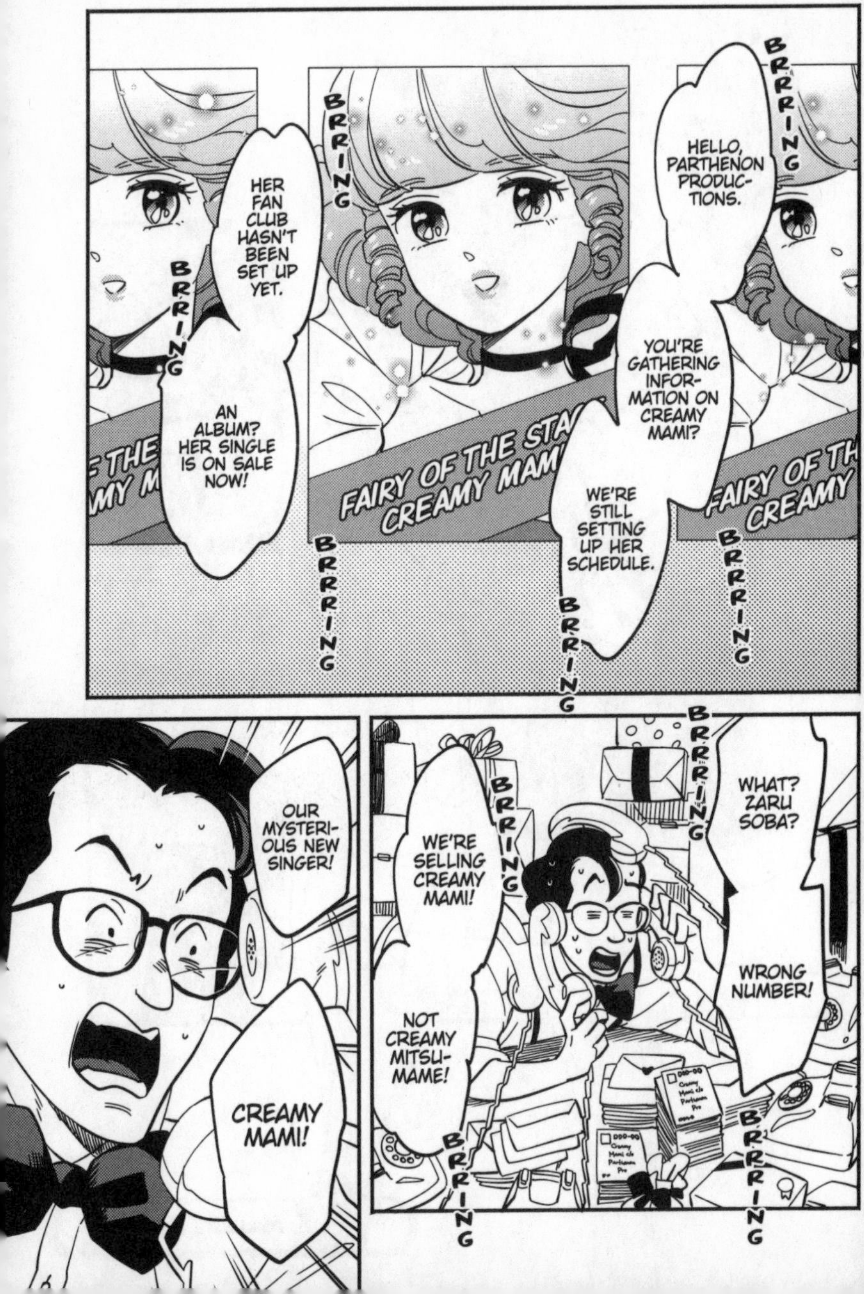
BRRRING
HELLO, PARTHENON PRODUCTIONS.
YOU'RE GATHERING INFORMATION ON CREAMY MAMI?
BRRRING
WE'RE STILL SETTING UP HER SCHEDULE.
BRRING
BRRING
HER FAN CLUB HASN'T BEEN SET UP YET.
BRRRING
BRRING
AN ALBUM? HER SINGLE IS ON SALE NOW!
BRRRING
WHAT? ZARU SOBA?
WRONG NUMBER!
BRRRING
BRRING
WE'RE SELLING CREAMY MAMI!
NOT CREAMY MITSU-MAME!
BRRING
OUR MYSTERIOUS NEW SINGER!
CREAMY MAMI!

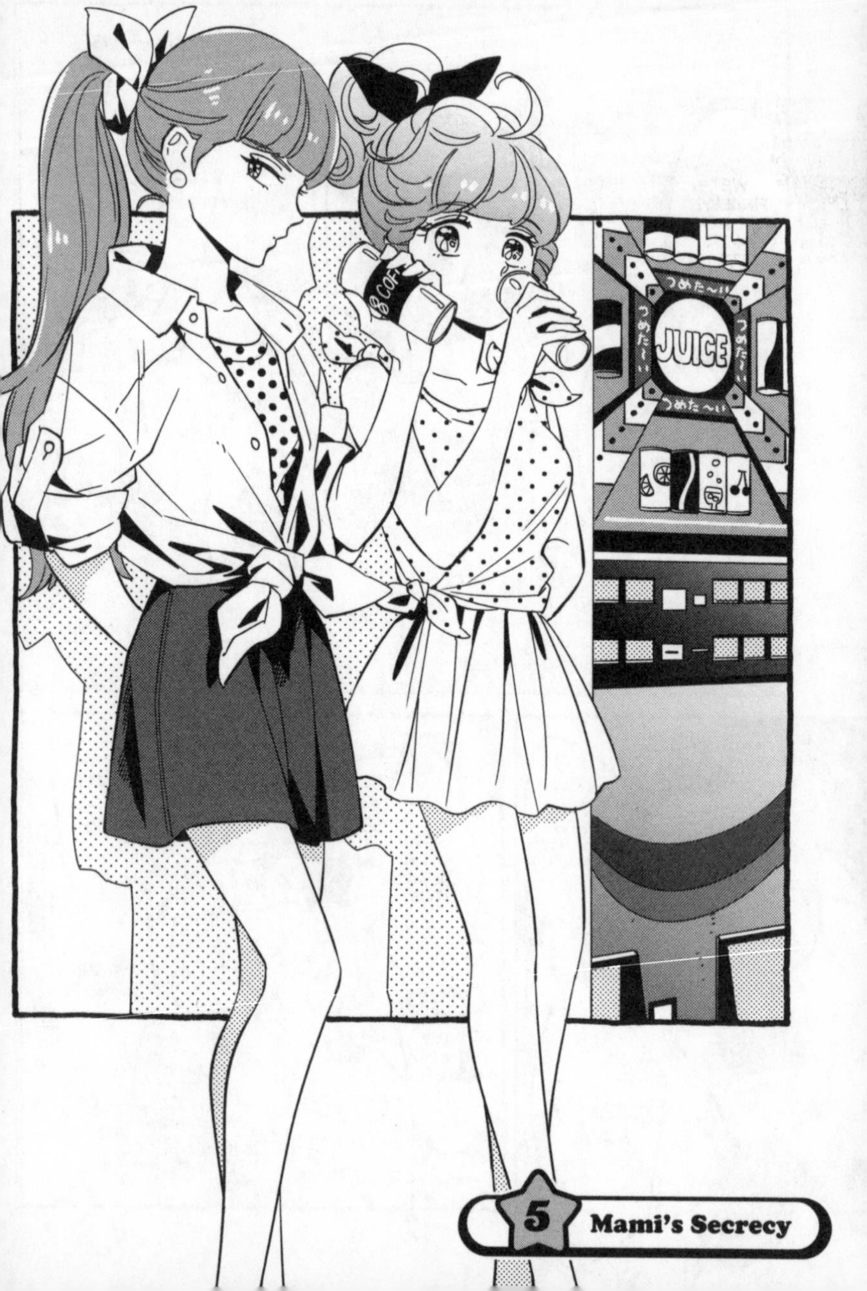
JUICE
つめた～い
つめた～い
つめた～い
つめた～い

5 Mami's Secrecy

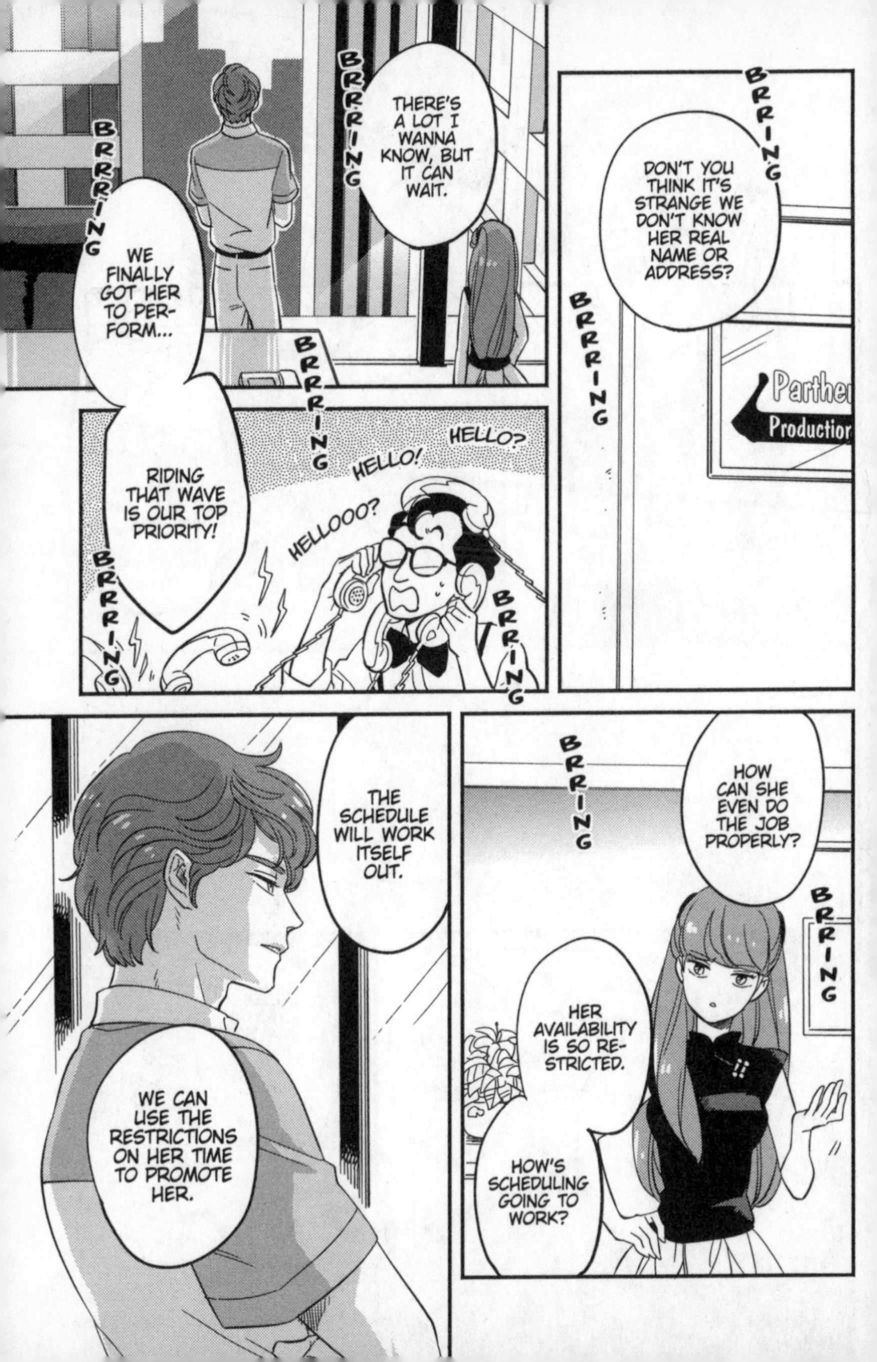
BRRING
DON'T YOU THINK IT'S STRANGE WE DON'T KNOW HER REAL NAME OR ADDRESS?
BRRRING
BRRRING
THERE'S A LOT I WANNA KNOW, BUT IT CAN WAIT.
BRRRING
WE FINALLY GOT HER TO PERFORM...
BRRRING
RIDING THAT WAVE IS OUR TOP PRIORITY!
HELLO?
HELLO!
HELLOOO?
BRRING
BRRRING
BRRING
HOW CAN SHE EVEN DO THE JOB PROPERLY?
BRRING
HER AVAILABILITY IS SO RESTRICTED.
HOW'S SCHEDULING GOING TO WORK?
THE SCHEDULE WILL WORK ITSELF OUT.
WE CAN USE THE RESTRICTIONS ON HER TIME TO PROMOTE HER.

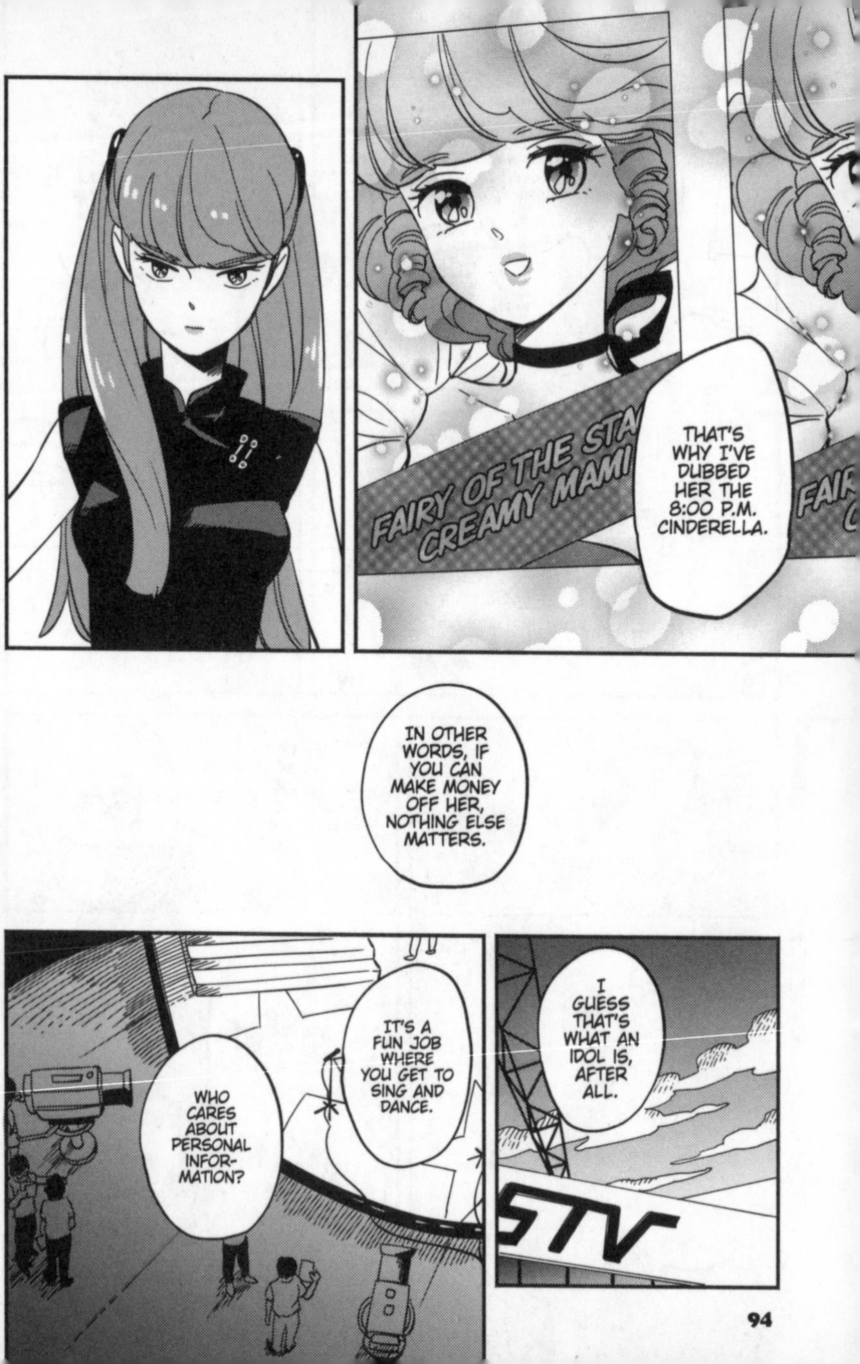
FAIRY OF THE
CREAMY MAMI
THAT'S WHY I'VE DUBBED HER THE 8:00 P.M. CINDERELLA.
IN OTHER WORDS, IF YOU CAN MAKE MONEY OFF HER, NOTHING ELSE MATTERS.
I GUESS THAT'S WHAT AN IDOL IS, AFTER ALL.
STV
IT'S A FUN JOB WHERE YOU GET TO SING AND DANCE.
WHO CARES ABOUT PERSONAL INFOR-MATION?

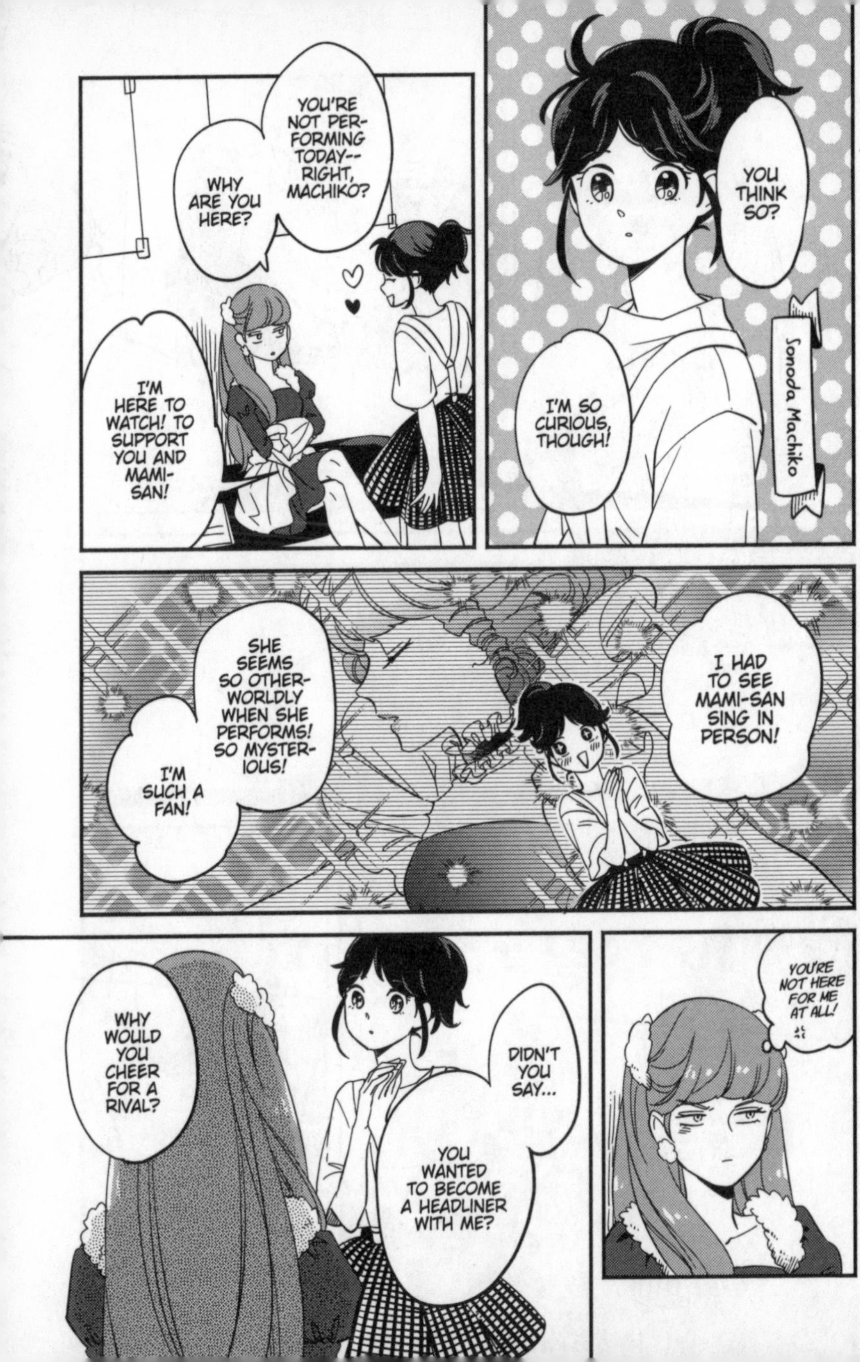
YOU THINK SO?
I'M SO CURIOUS, THOUGH!
Sonoda Machiko
YOU'RE NOT PER-FORMING TODAY--RIGHT, MACHIKO?
WHY ARE YOU HERE?
I'M HERE TO WATCH! TO SUPPORT YOU AND MAMI-SAN!
I HAD TO SEE MAMI-SAN SING IN PERSON!
SHE SEEMS SO OTHER-WORLDLY WHEN SHE PERFORMS! SO MYSTER-IOUS!
I'M SUCH A FAN!
YOU'RE NOT HERE FOR ME AT ALL!
WHY WOULD YOU CHEER FOR A RIVAL?
DIDN'T YOU SAY...
YOU WANTED TO BECOME A HEADLINER WITH ME?

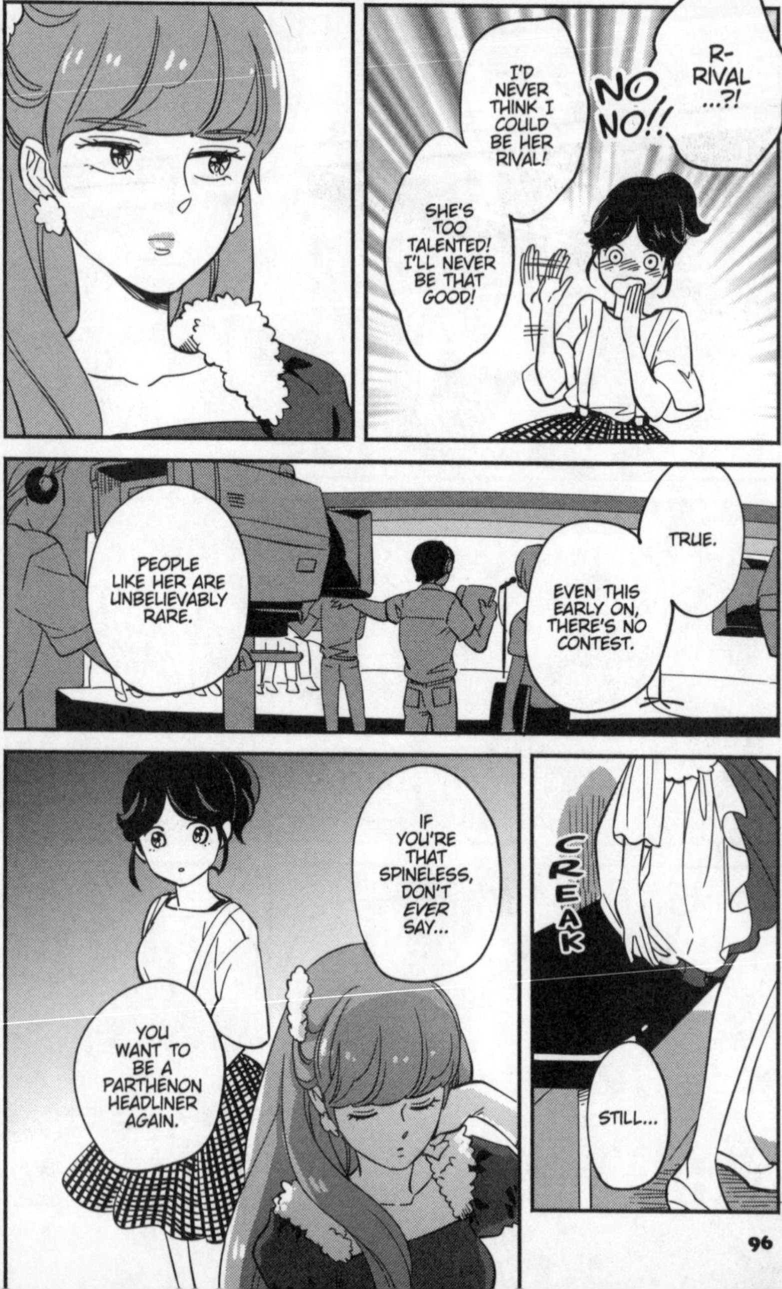
R-RIVAL...?!
NO NO!!
I'D NEVER THINK I COULD BE HER RIVAL!
SHE'S TOO TALENTED! I'LL NEVER BE THAT GOOD!
TRUE.
EVEN THIS EARLY ON, THERE'S NO CONTEST.
PEOPLE LIKE HER ARE UNBELIEVABLY RARE.
CREAK
STILL...
IF YOU'RE THAT SPINELESS, DON'T *EVER* SAY...
YOU WANT TO BE A PARTHENON HEADLINER AGAIN.

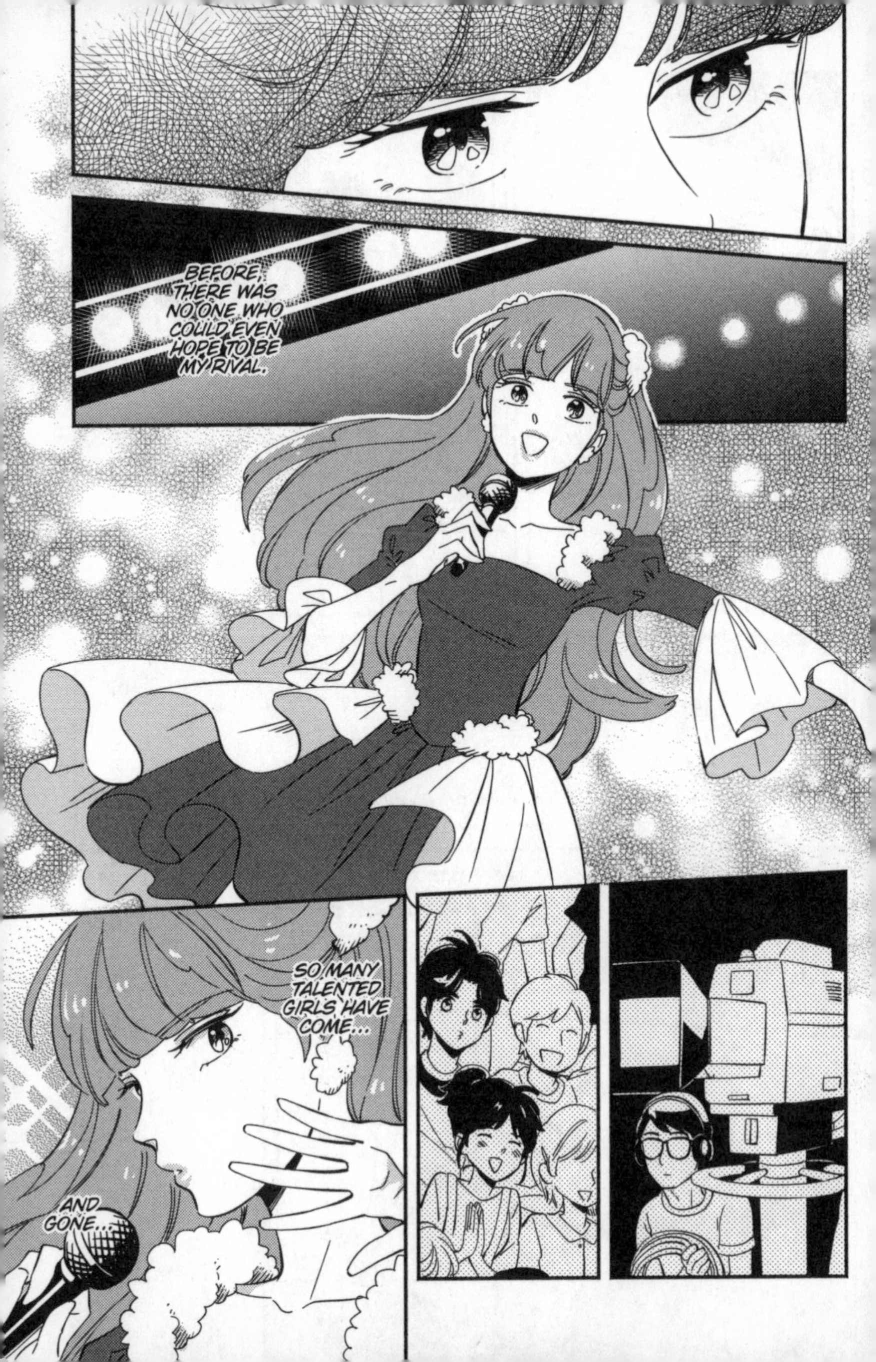
BEFORE, THERE WAS NO ONE WHO COULD EVEN HOPE TO BE MY RIVAL.
SO MANY TALENTED GIRLS HAVE COME...
AND GONE...

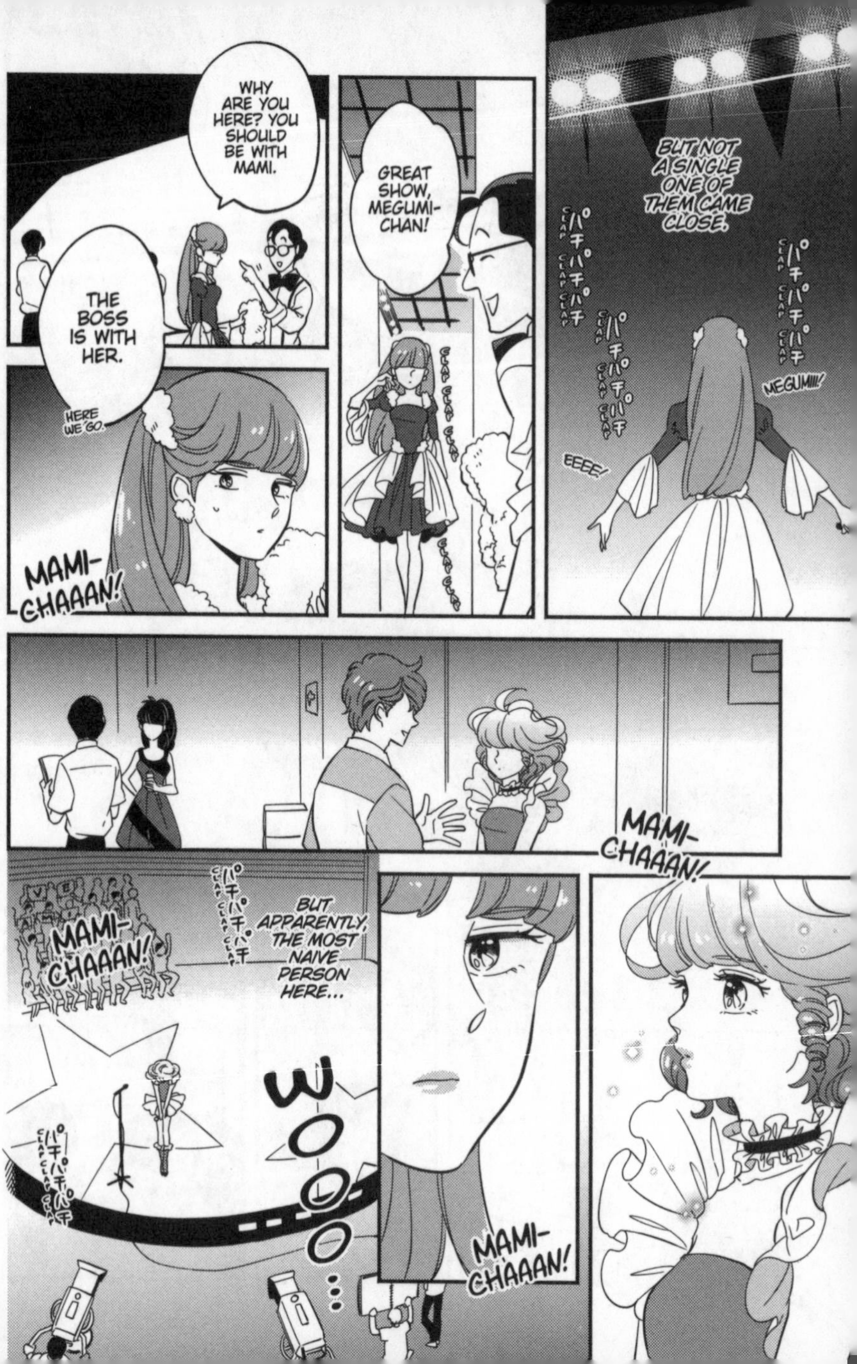
BUT NOT A SINGLE ONE OF THEM CAME CLOSE.
パチパチパチ
CLAP CLAP CLAP
パチパチパチ
CLAP CLAP CLAP
パチパチパチ
CLAP CLAP CLAP
MEGUMIII!
EEEE!
GREAT SHOW, MEGUMI-CHAN!
CLAP CLAP CLAP
CLAP CLAP
WHY ARE YOU HERE? YOU SHOULD BE WITH MAMI.
THE BOSS IS WITH HER.
HERE WE GO.
MAMI-CHAAAN!
MAMI-CHAAAN!
MAMI-CHAAAN!
BUT APPARENTLY, THE MOST NAIVE PERSON HERE...
パチパチパチ
CLAP CLAP CLAP
MAMI-CHAAAN!
WOOOO...
パチパチパチ
CLAP CLAP CLAP

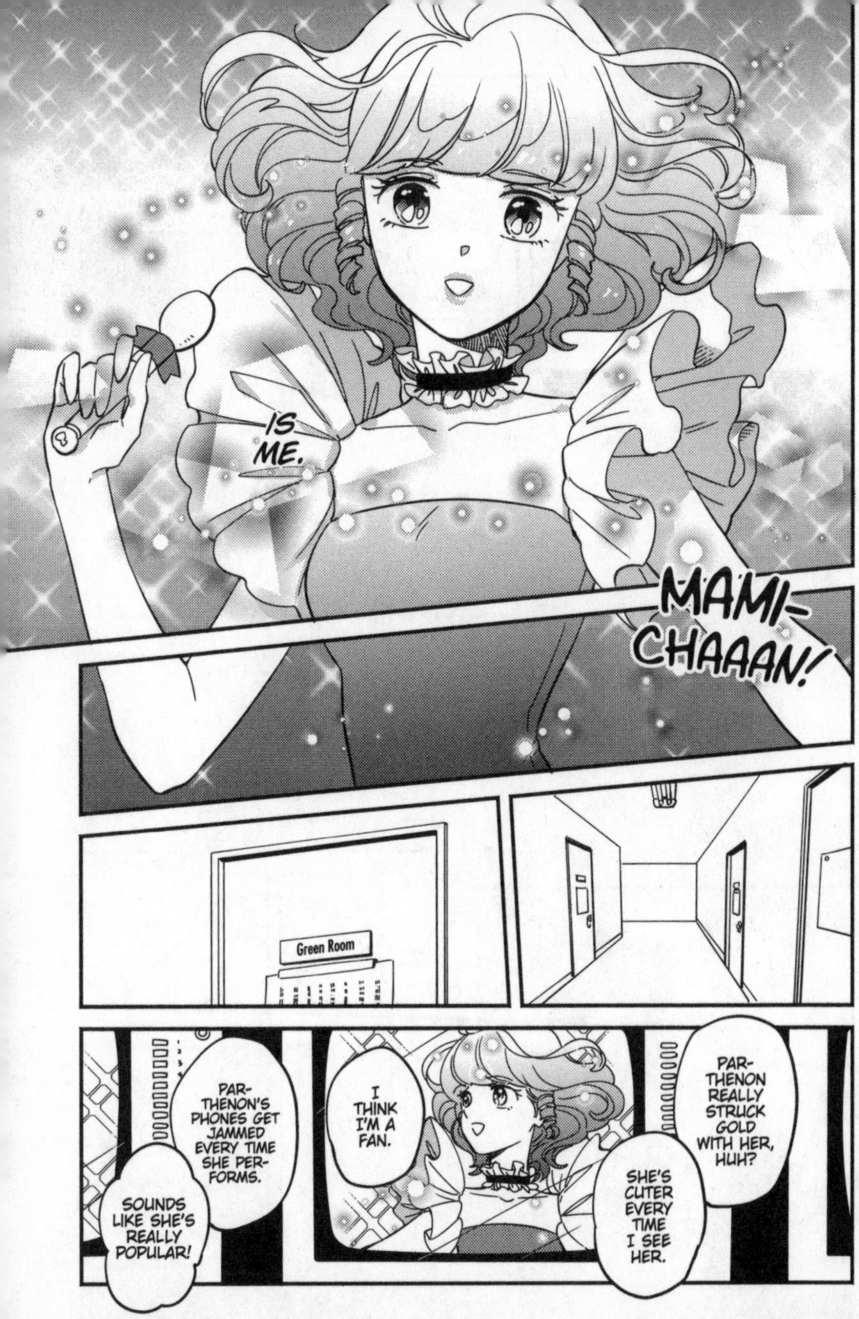
IS ME.
MAMI-CHAAAN!
Green Room
PARTHENON REALLY STRUCK GOLD WITH HER, HUH?
SHE'S CUTER EVERY TIME I SEE HER.
I THINK I'M A FAN.
PARTHENON'S PHONES GET JAMMED EVERY TIME SHE PERFORMS.
SOUNDS LIKE SHE'S REALLY POPULAR!

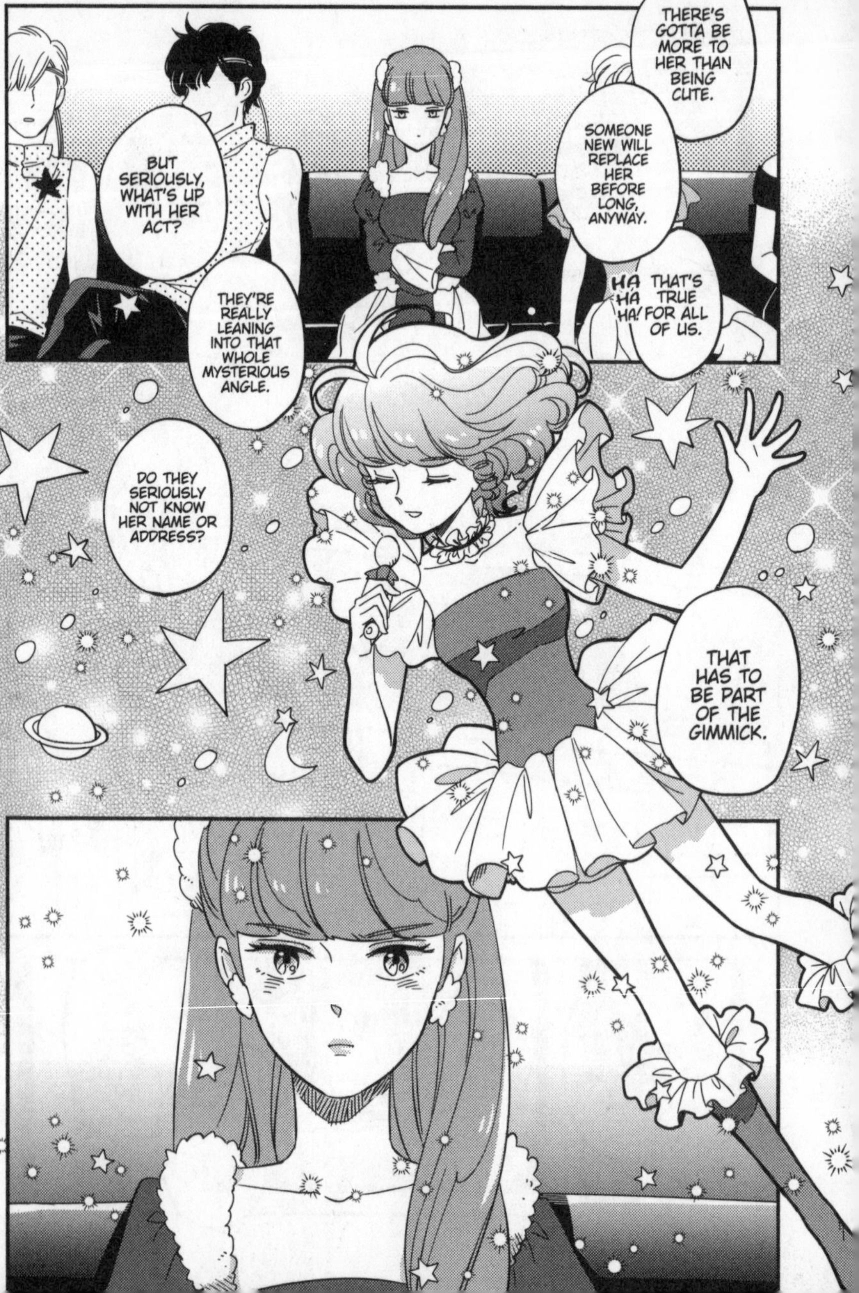
THERE'S GOTTA BE MORE TO HER THAN BEING CUTE.
SOMEONE NEW WILL REPLACE HER BEFORE LONG, ANYWAY.
HA HA HA!
THAT'S TRUE FOR ALL OF US.
BUT SERIOUSLY, WHAT'S UP WITH HER ACT?
THEY'RE REALLY LEANING INTO THAT WHOLE MYSTERIOUS ANGLE.
DO THEY SERIOUSLY NOT KNOW HER NAME OR ADDRESS?
THAT HAS TO BE PART OF THE GIMMICK.

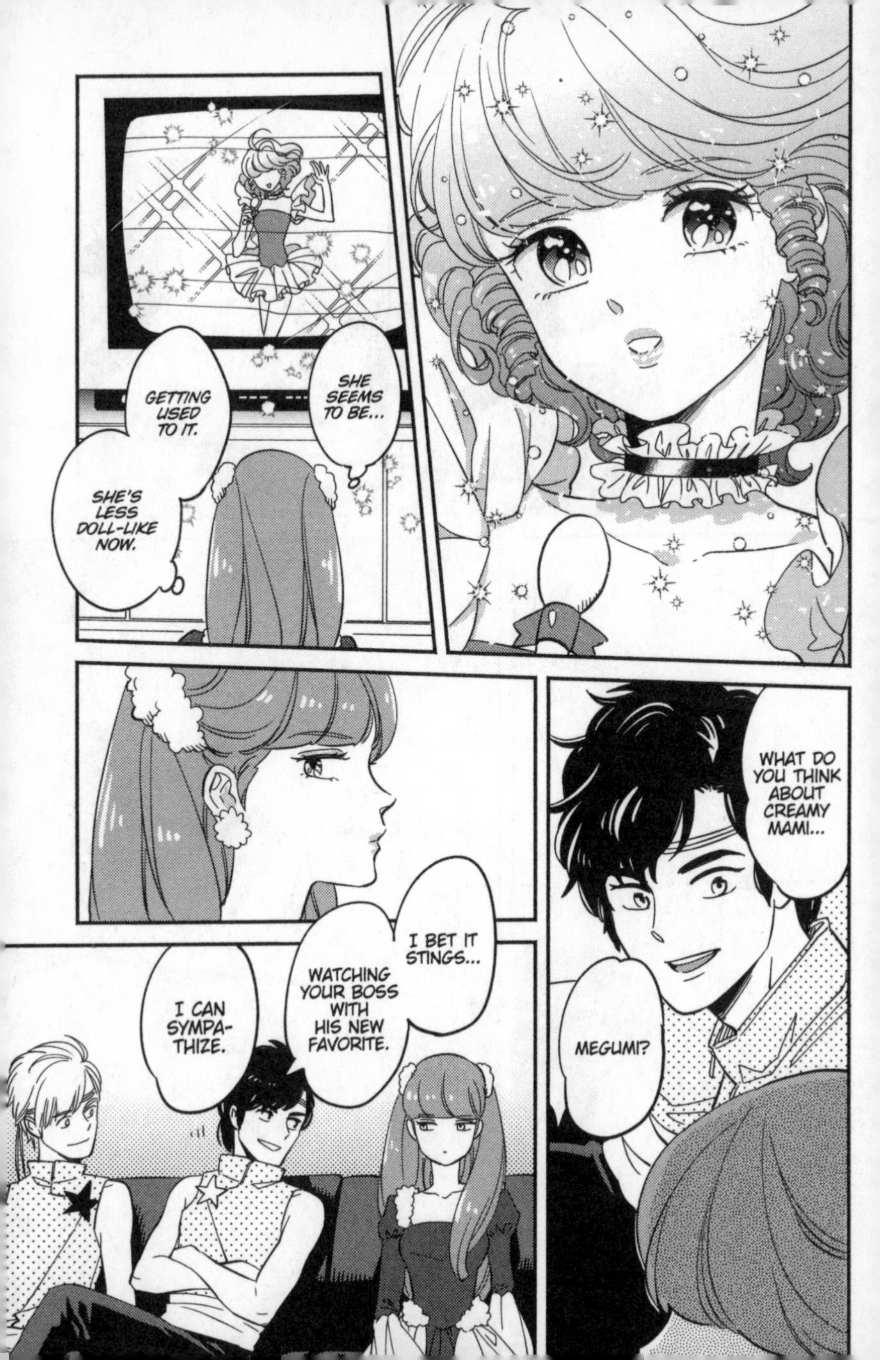
SHE SEEMS TO BE...
GETTING USED TO IT.
SHE'S LESS DOLL-LIKE NOW.
WHAT DO YOU THINK ABOUT CREAMY MAMI...
MEGUMI?
I BET IT STINGS...
WATCHING YOUR BOSS WITH HIS NEW FAVORITE.
I CAN SYMPA-THIZE.

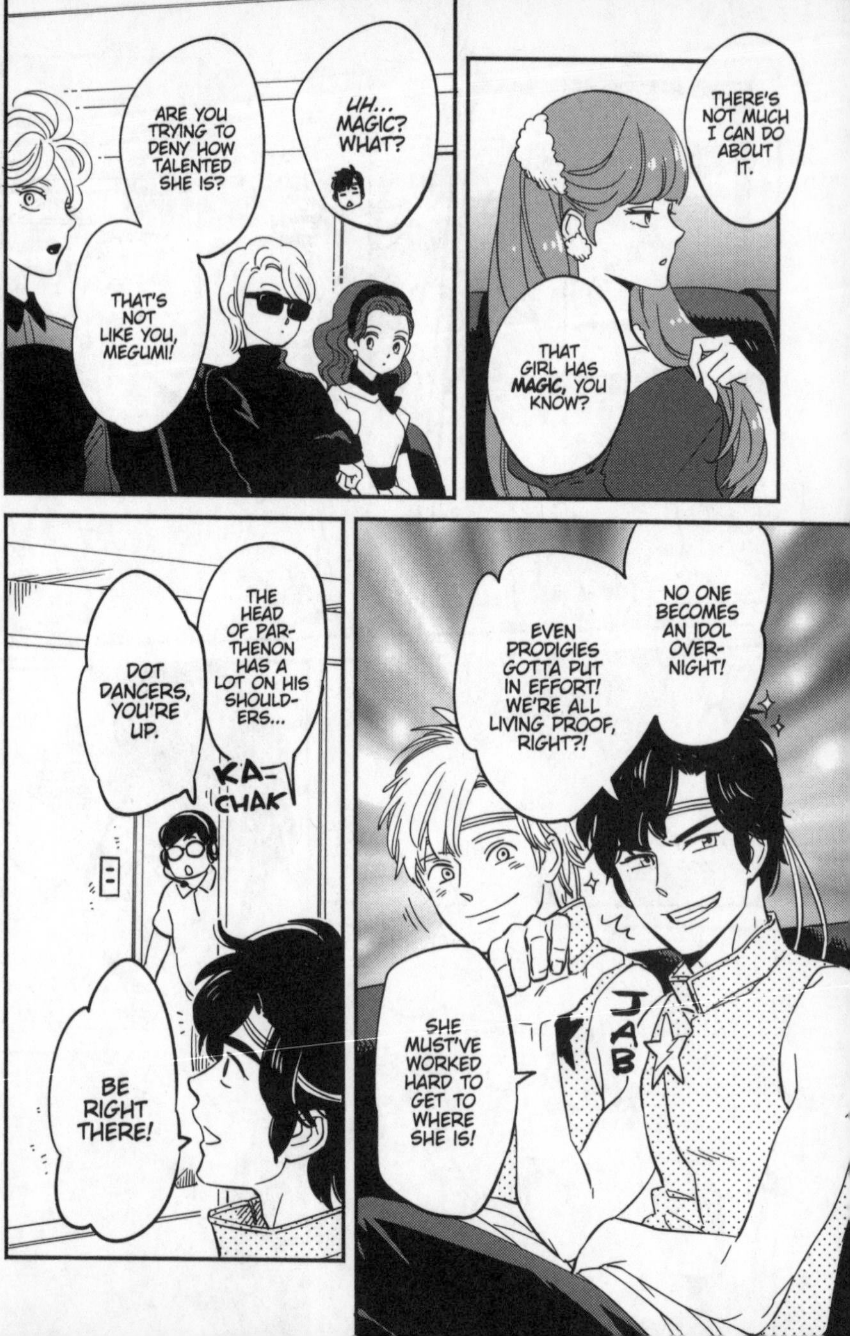
THERE'S NOT MUCH I CAN DO ABOUT IT.
THAT GIRL HAS MAGIC, YOU KNOW?
UH... MAGIC? WHAT?
ARE YOU TRYING TO DENY HOW TALENTED SHE IS?
THAT'S NOT LIKE YOU, MEGUMI!
NO ONE BECOMES AN IDOL OVERNIGHT!
EVEN PRODIGIES GOTTA PUT IN EFFORT! WE'RE ALL LIVING PROOF, RIGHT?!
JAB
SHE MUST'VE WORKED HARD TO GET TO WHERE SHE IS!
THE HEAD OF PARTHENON HAS A LOT ON HIS SHOULDERS...
DOT DANCERS, YOU'RE UP.
KA-CHAK
BE RIGHT THERE!

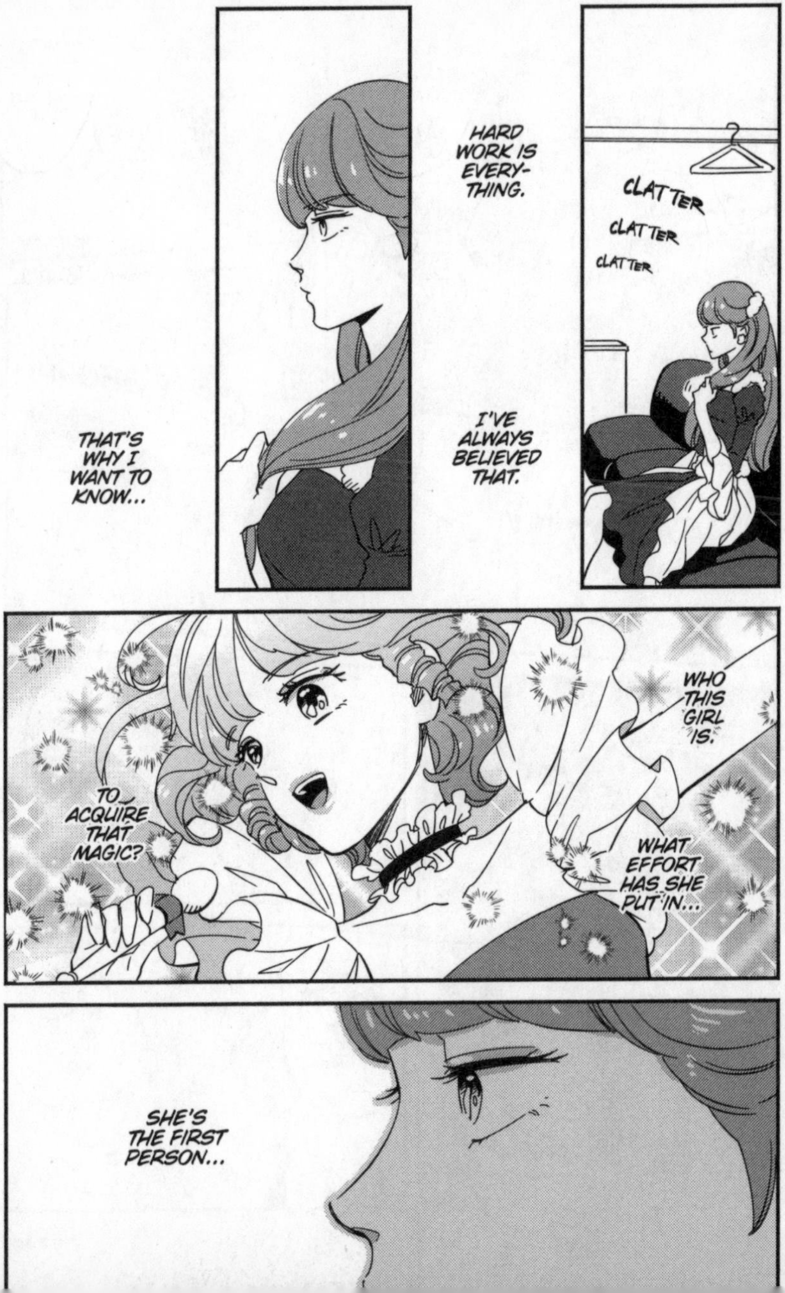
CLATTER
CLATTER
CLATTER
HARD WORK IS EVERYTHING.
I'VE ALWAYS BELIEVED THAT.
THAT'S WHY I WANT TO KNOW...
WHO THIS GIRL IS.
WHAT EFFORT HAS SHE PUT IN...
TO ACQUIRE THAT MAGIC?
SHE'S THE FIRST PERSON...

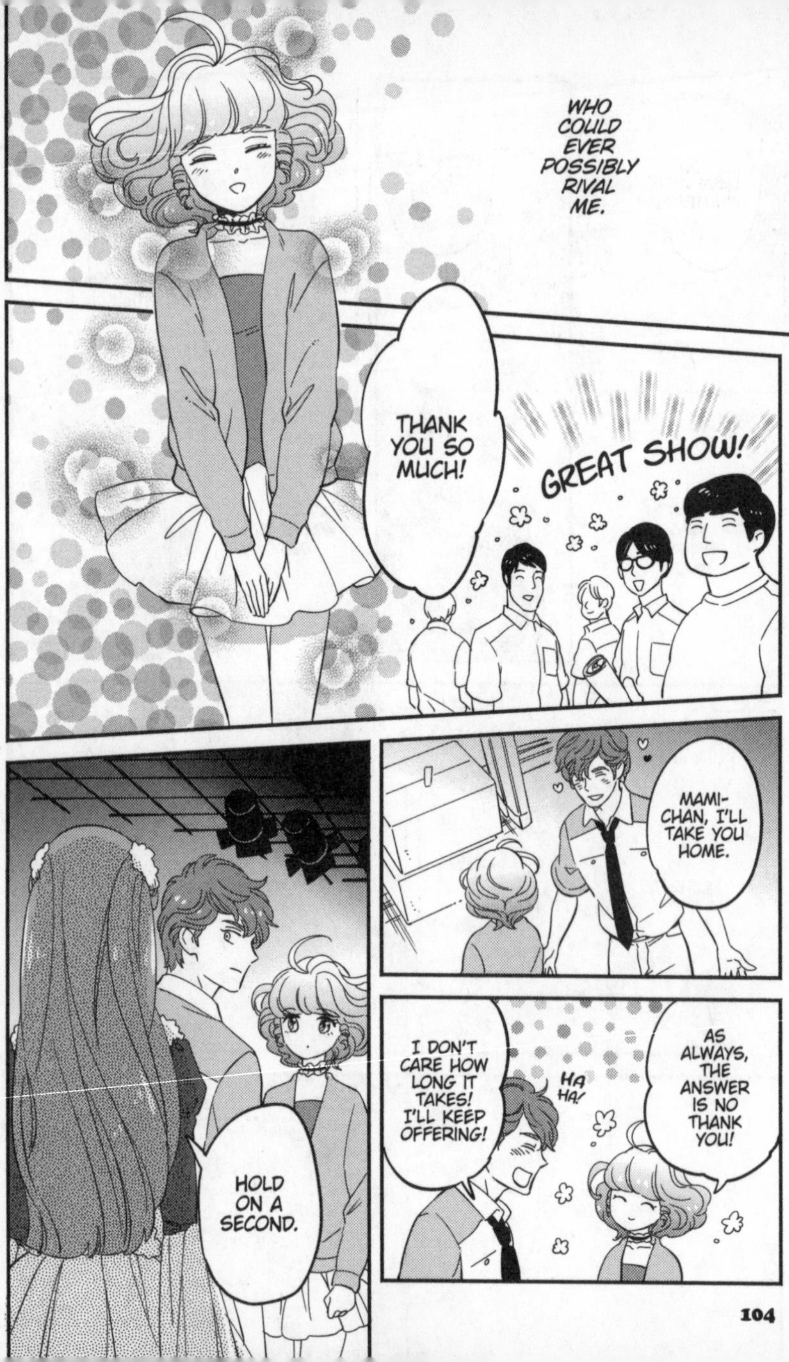
WHO COULD EVER POSSIBLY RIVAL ME.
GREAT SHOW!
THANK YOU SO MUCH!
MAMI-CHAN, I'LL TAKE YOU HOME.
AS ALWAYS, THE ANSWER IS NO THANK YOU!
HA HA!
I DON'T CARE HOW LONG IT TAKES! I'LL KEEP OFFERING!
HOLD ON A SECOND.

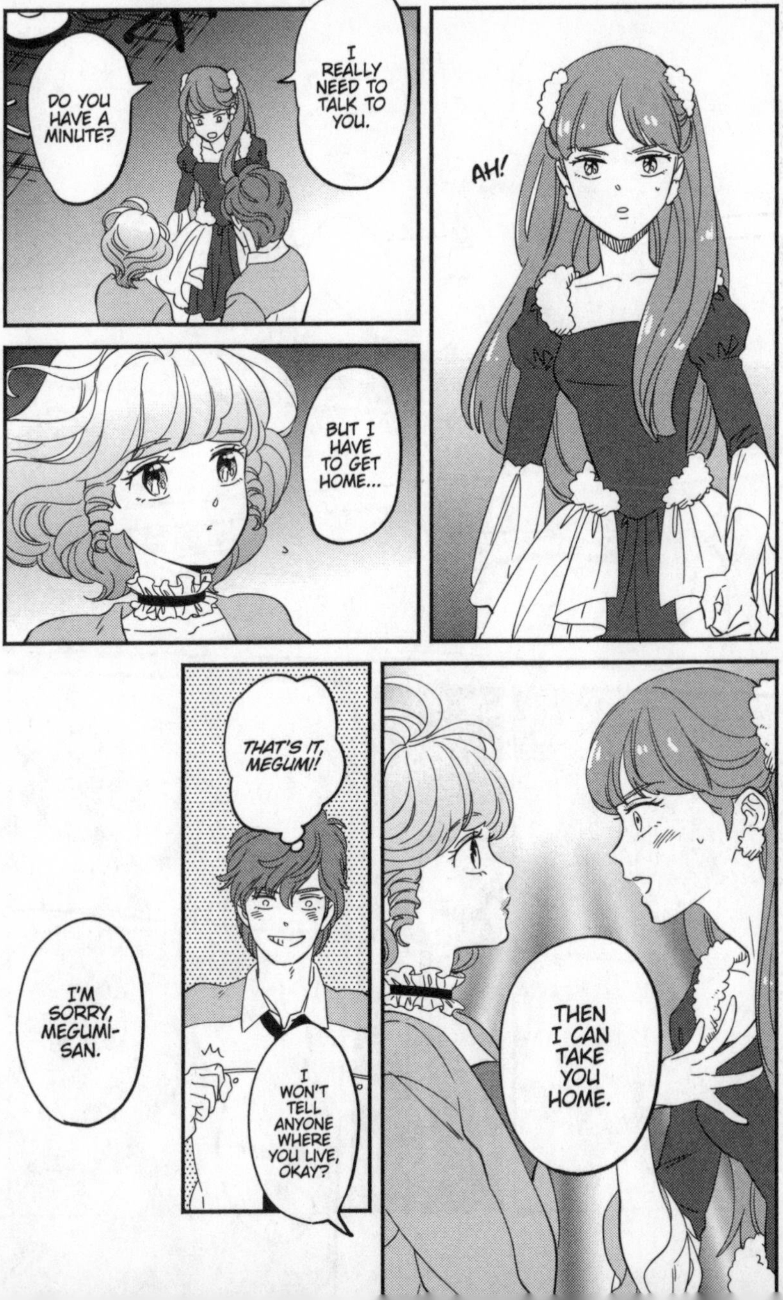
AH!
I REALLY NEED TO TALK TO YOU.
DO YOU HAVE A MINUTE?
BUT I HAVE TO GET HOME...
THEN I CAN TAKE YOU HOME.
THAT'S IT, MEGUMI!
I WON'T TELL ANYONE WHERE YOU LIVE, OKAY?
I'M SORRY, MEGUMI-SAN.

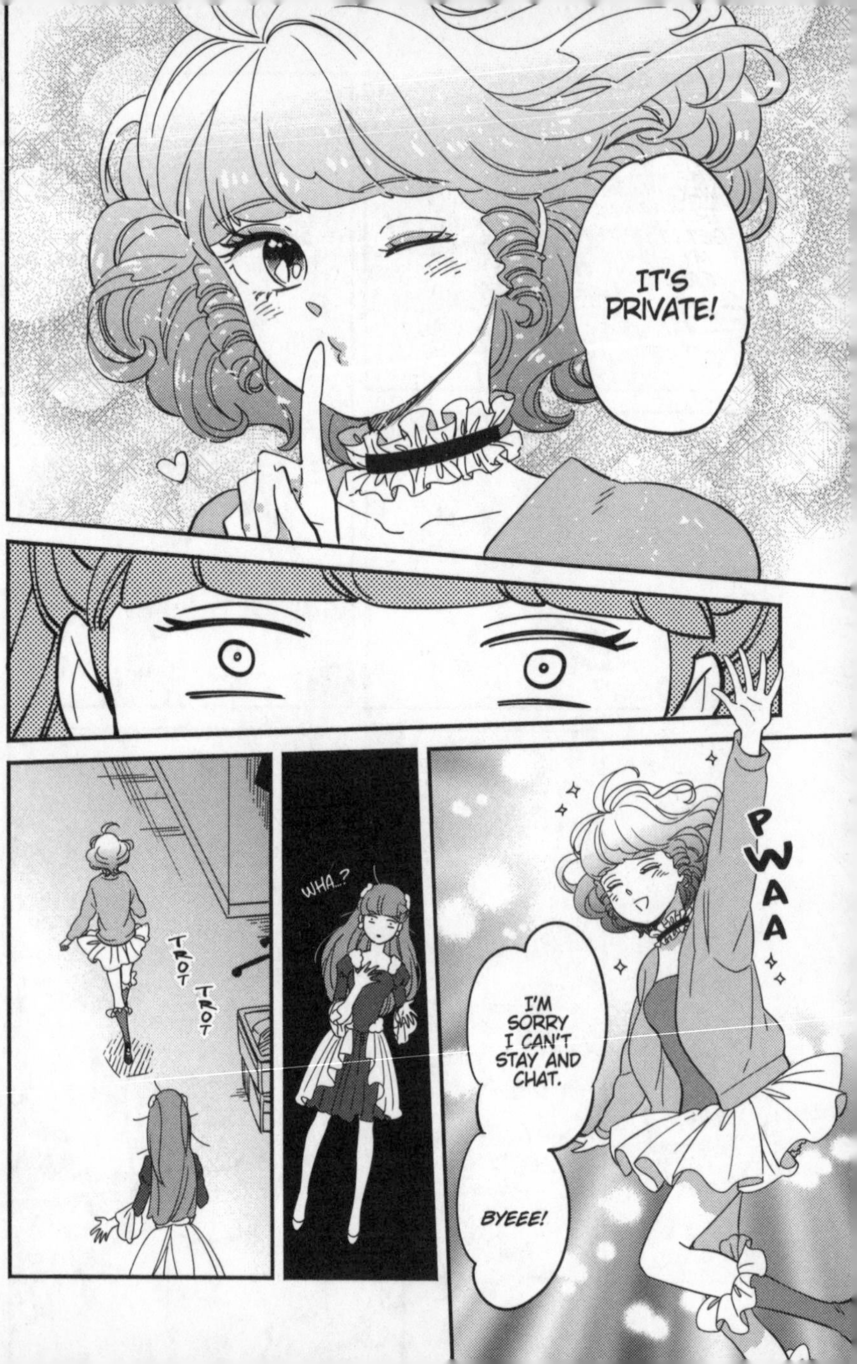
IT'S PRIVATE!
PWAA
I'M SORRY I CAN'T STAY AND CHAT.
BYEEE!
WHA...?
TROT TROT

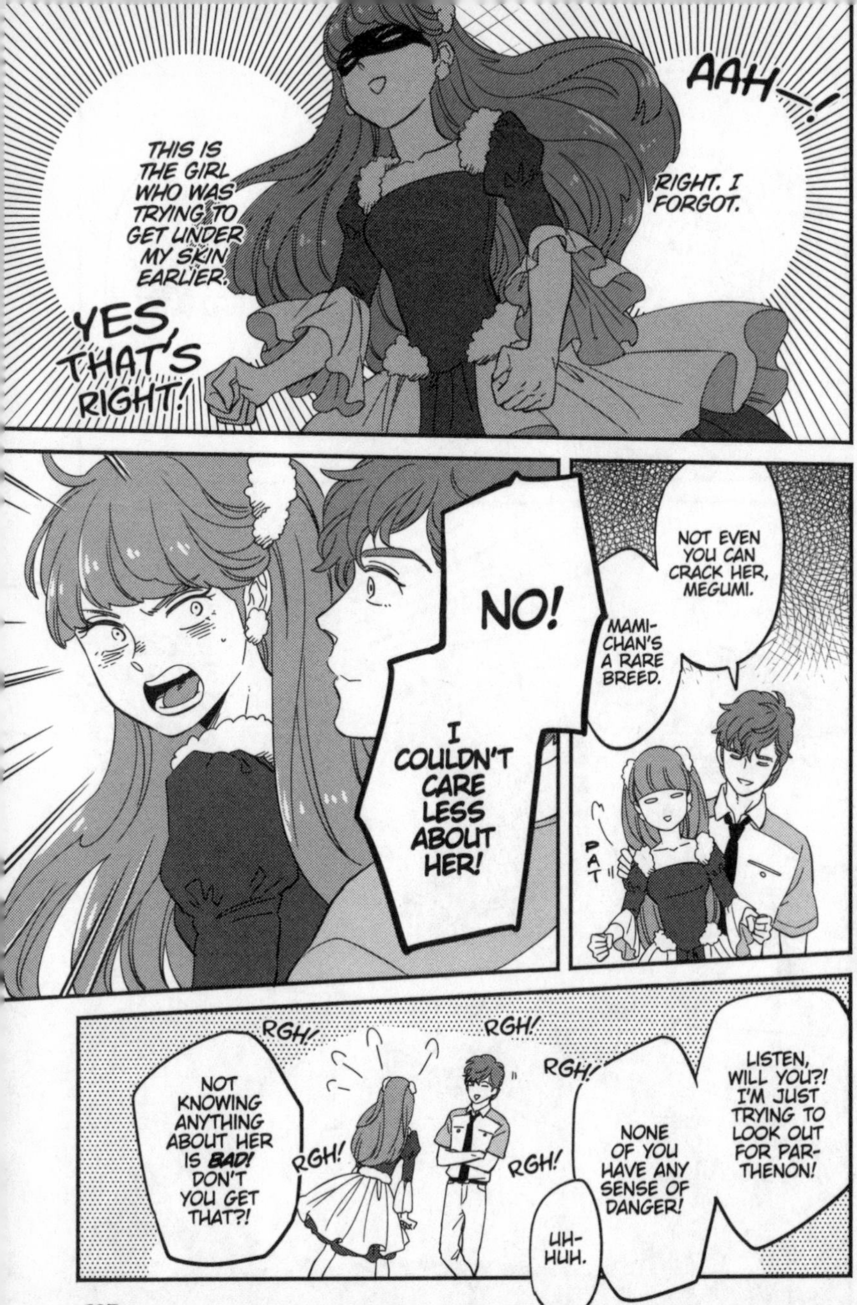
AAH—!
RIGHT. I FORGOT.
THIS IS THE GIRL WHO WAS TRYING TO GET UNDER MY SKIN EARLIER.
YES, THAT'S RIGHT!
NOT EVEN YOU CAN CRACK HER, MEGUMI.
MAMI-CHAN'S A RARE BREED.
PAT
NO!
I COULDN'T CARE LESS ABOUT HER!
LISTEN, WILL YOU?! I'M JUST TRYING TO LOOK OUT FOR PAR-THENON!
NONE OF YOU HAVE ANY SENSE OF DANGER!
RGH!
RGH!
RGH!
UH-HUH.
RGH!
RGH!
NOT KNOWING ANYTHING ABOUT HER IS *BAD!* DON'T YOU GET THAT?!

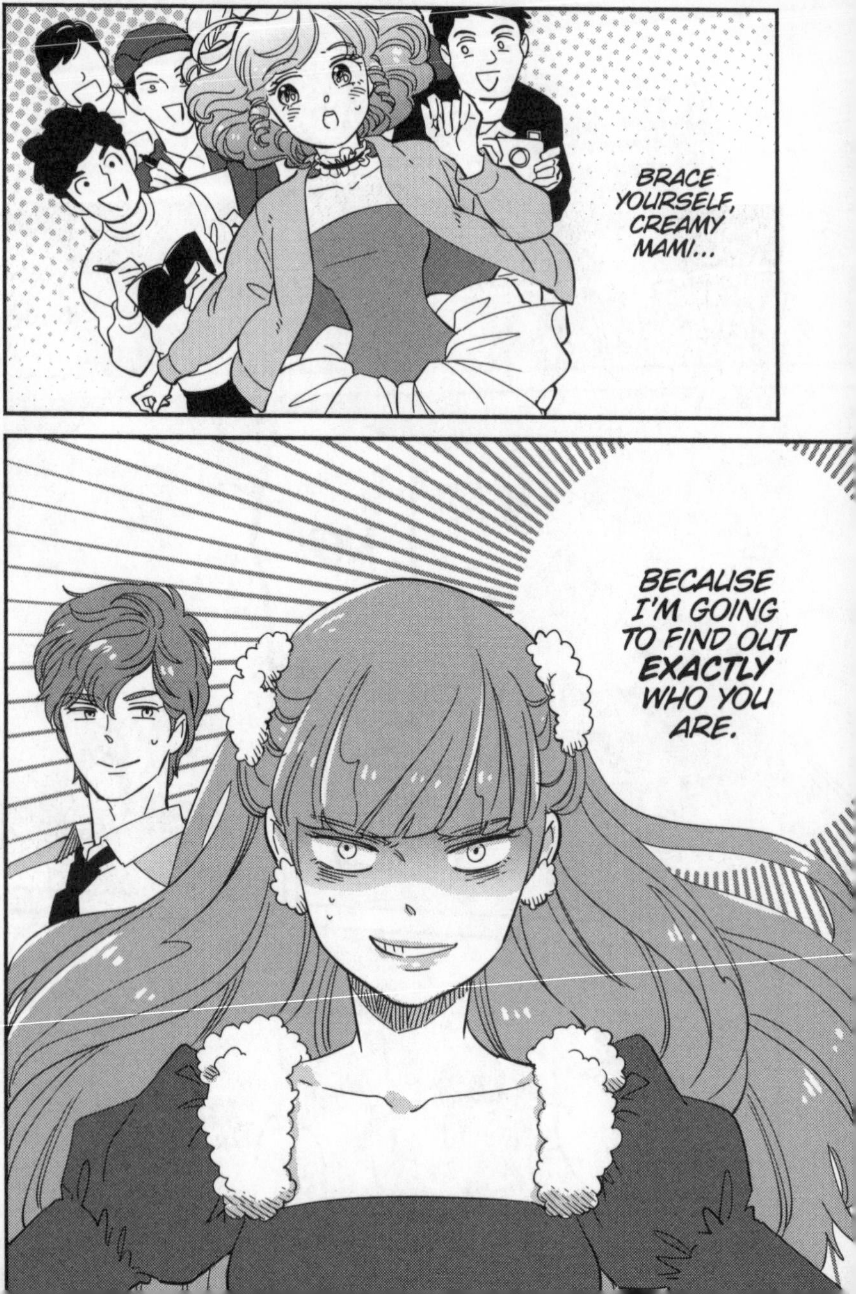
BRACE YOURSELF, CREAMY MAMI...
BECAUSE I'M GOING TO FIND OUT **EXACTLY** WHO YOU ARE.

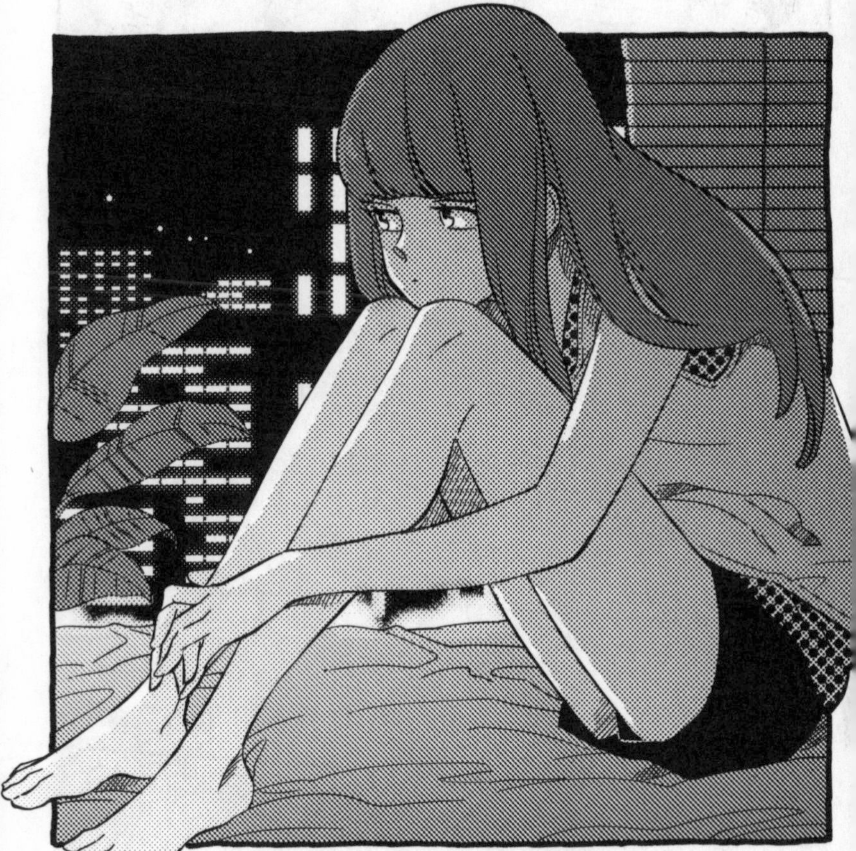

6 The Illusory Performance

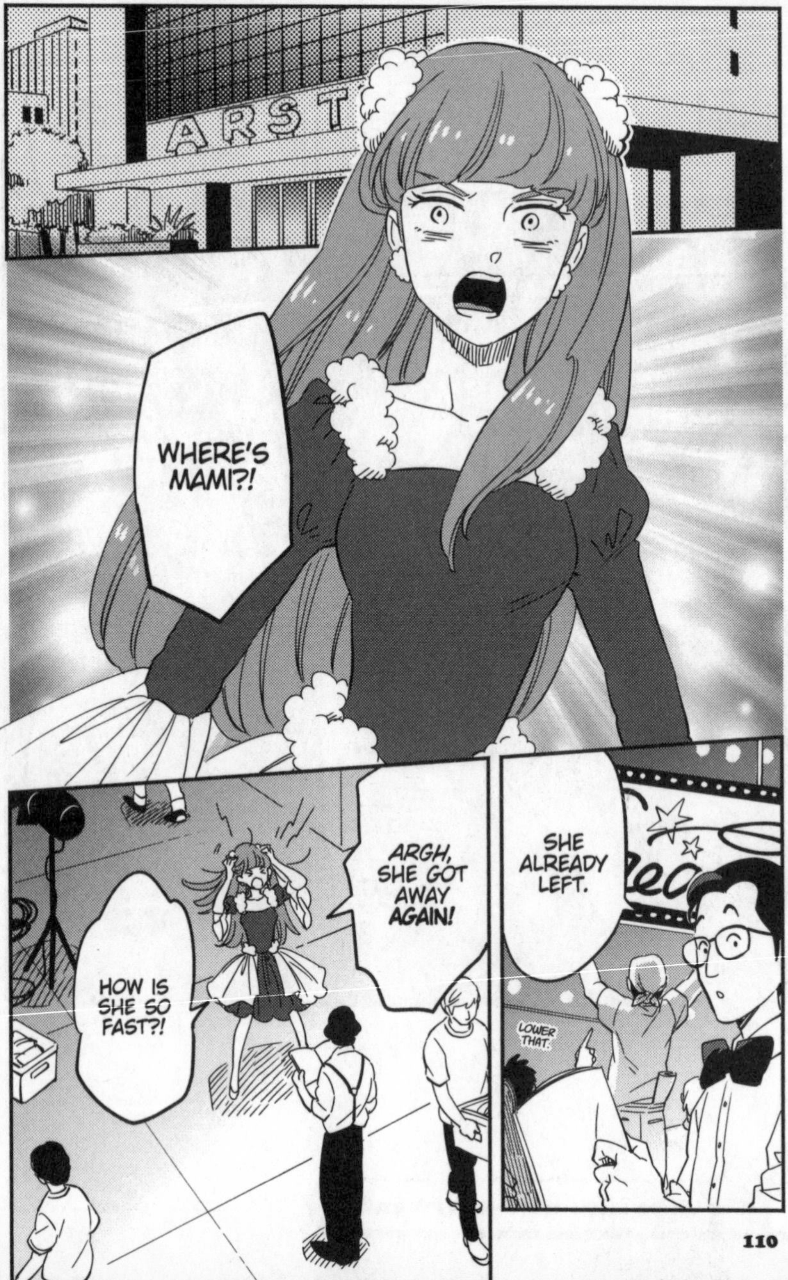
WHERE'S MAMI?!
SHE ALREADY LEFT.
LOWER THAT.
ARGH, SHE GOT AWAY AGAIN!
HOW IS SHE SO FAST?!

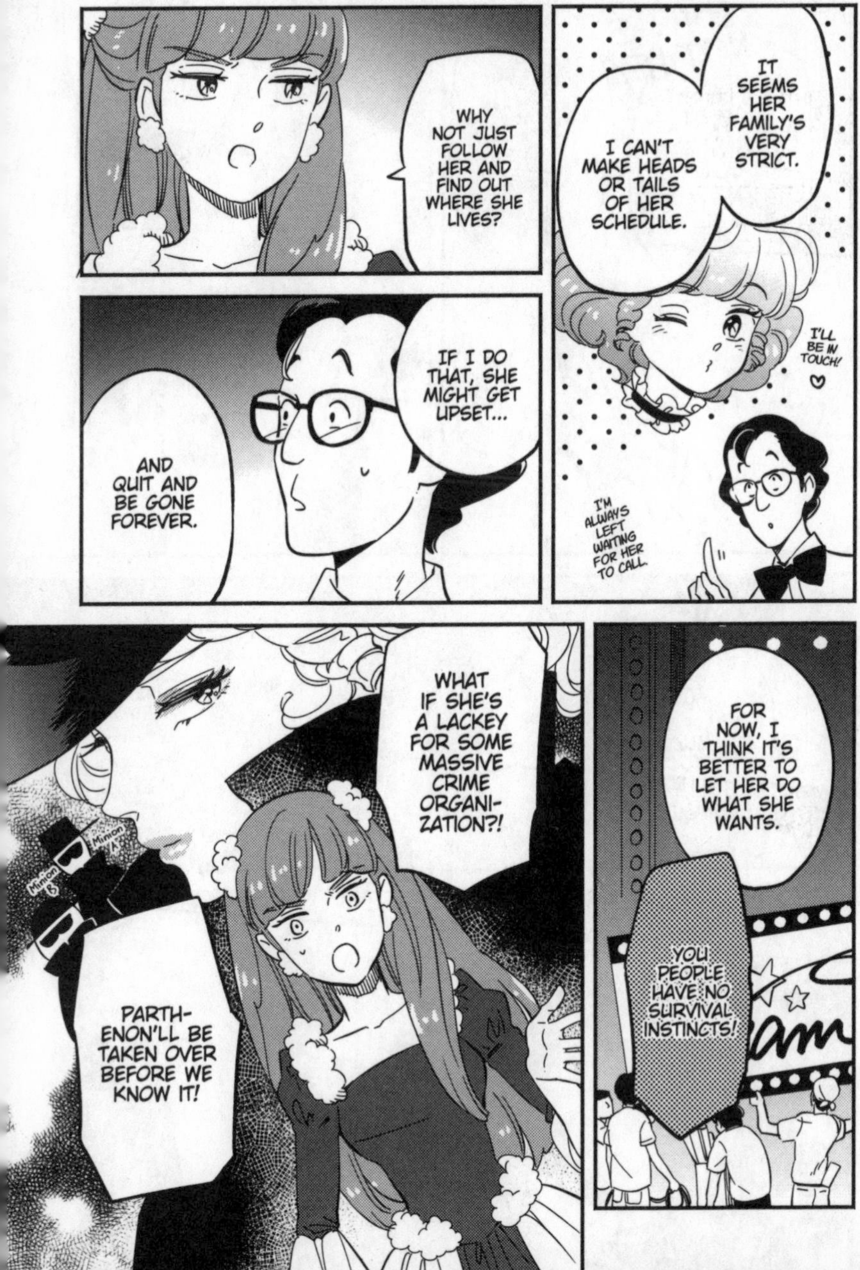
IT SEEMS HER FAMILY'S VERY STRICT.
I CAN'T MAKE HEADS OR TAILS OF HER SCHEDULE.
I'LL BE IN TOUCH! ♥
I'M ALWAYS LEFT WAITING FOR HER TO CALL.
WHY NOT JUST FOLLOW HER AND FIND OUT WHERE SHE LIVES?
IF I DO THAT, SHE MIGHT GET UPSET...
AND QUIT AND BE GONE FOREVER.
FOR NOW, I THINK IT'S BETTER TO LET HER DO WHAT SHE WANTS.
YOU PEOPLE HAVE NO SURVIVAL INSTINCTS!
WHAT IF SHE'S A LACKEY FOR SOME MASSIVE CRIME ORGANIZATION?!
Minion A
Minion B
PARTH-ENON'LL BE TAKEN OVER BEFORE WE KNOW IT!

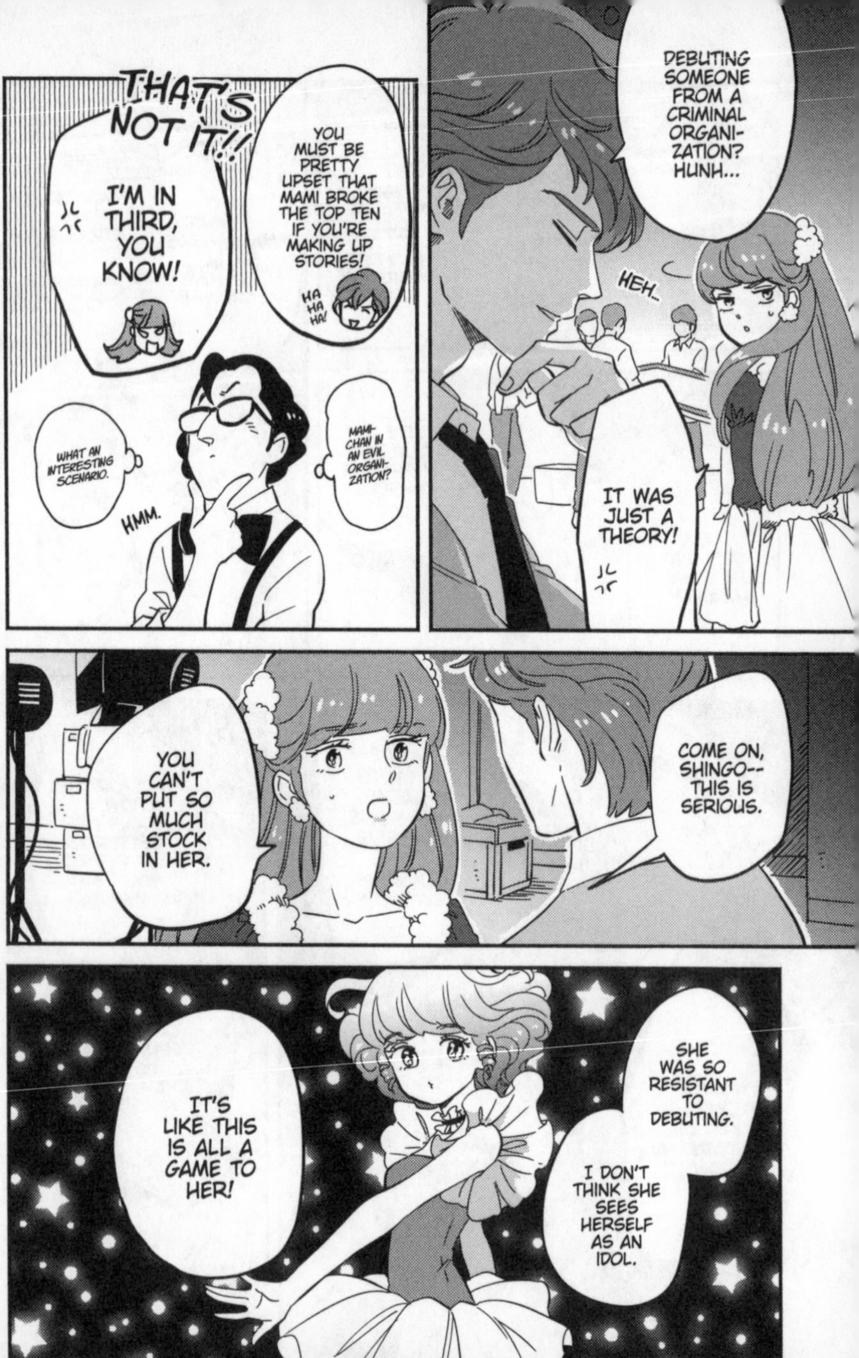
DEBUTING SOMEONE FROM A CRIMINAL ORGANIZATION? HUNH...
HEH...
IT WAS JUST A THEORY!
YOU MUST BE PRETTY UPSET THAT MAMI BROKE THE TOP TEN IF YOU'RE MAKING UP STORIES!
HA HA HA!
THAT'S NOT IT!!
I'M IN THIRD, YOU KNOW!
MAMI-CHAN IN AN EVIL ORGANIZATION?
WHAT AN INTERESTING SCENARIO.
HMM.
COME ON, SHINGO-- THIS IS SERIOUS.
YOU CAN'T PUT SO MUCH STOCK IN HER.
SHE WAS SO RESISTANT TO DEBUTING.
I DON'T THINK SHE SEES HERSELF AS AN IDOL.
IT'S LIKE THIS IS ALL A GAME TO HER!

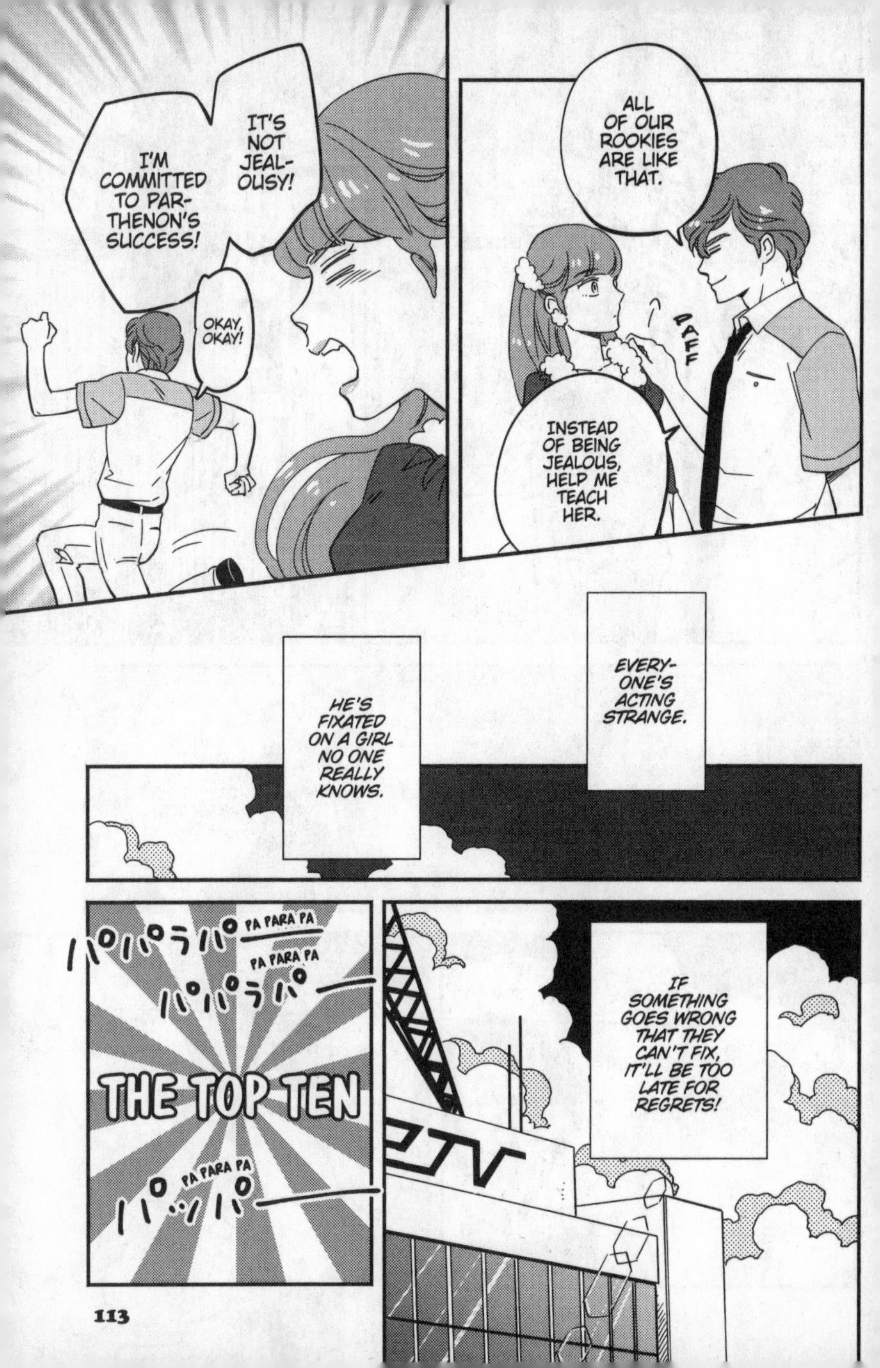
ALL OF OUR ROOKIES ARE LIKE THAT.
PAFF
INSTEAD OF BEING JEALOUS, HELP ME TEACH HER.
IT'S NOT JEAL-OUSY!
I'M COMMITTED TO PAR-THENON'S SUCCESS!
OKAY, OKAY!
EVERY-ONE'S ACTING STRANGE.
HE'S FIXATED ON A GIRL NO ONE REALLY KNOWS.
IF SOMETHING GOES WRONG THAT THEY CAN'T FIX, IT'LL BE TOO LATE FOR REGRETS!
パパラパ PA PARA PA
パパラパー PA PARA PA
THE TOP TEN
パッパー PA PARA PA

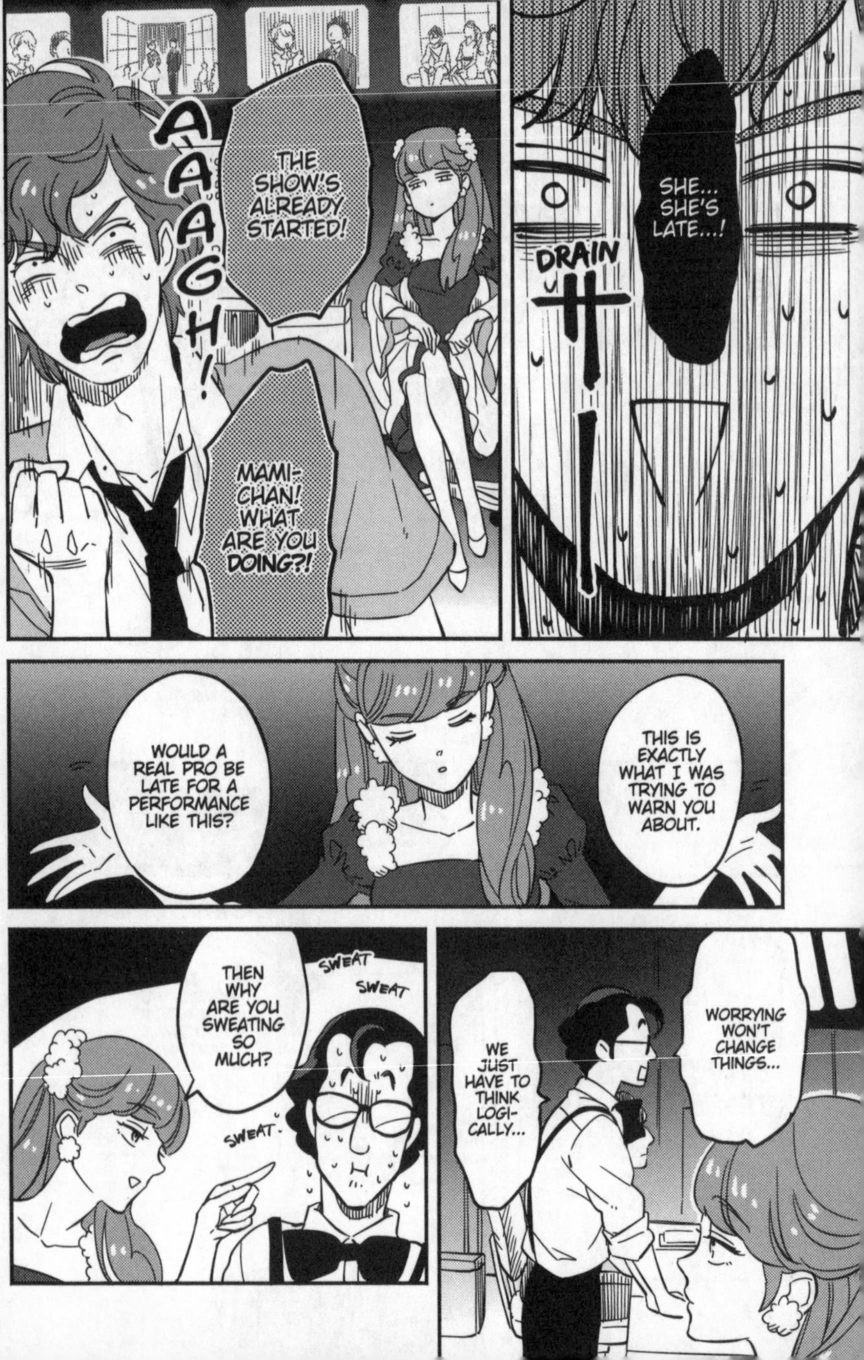
SHE... SHE'S LATE...!
DRAIN
AAAGH!
THE SHOW'S ALREADY STARTED!
MAMI-CHAN! WHAT ARE YOU DOING?!
THIS IS EXACTLY WHAT I WAS TRYING TO WARN YOU ABOUT.
WOULD A REAL PRO BE LATE FOR A PERFORMANCE LIKE THIS?
WORRYING WON'T CHANGE THINGS...
WE JUST HAVE TO THINK LOGI-CALLY...
THEN WHY ARE YOU SWEATING SO MUCH?
SWEAT
SWEAT
SWEAT

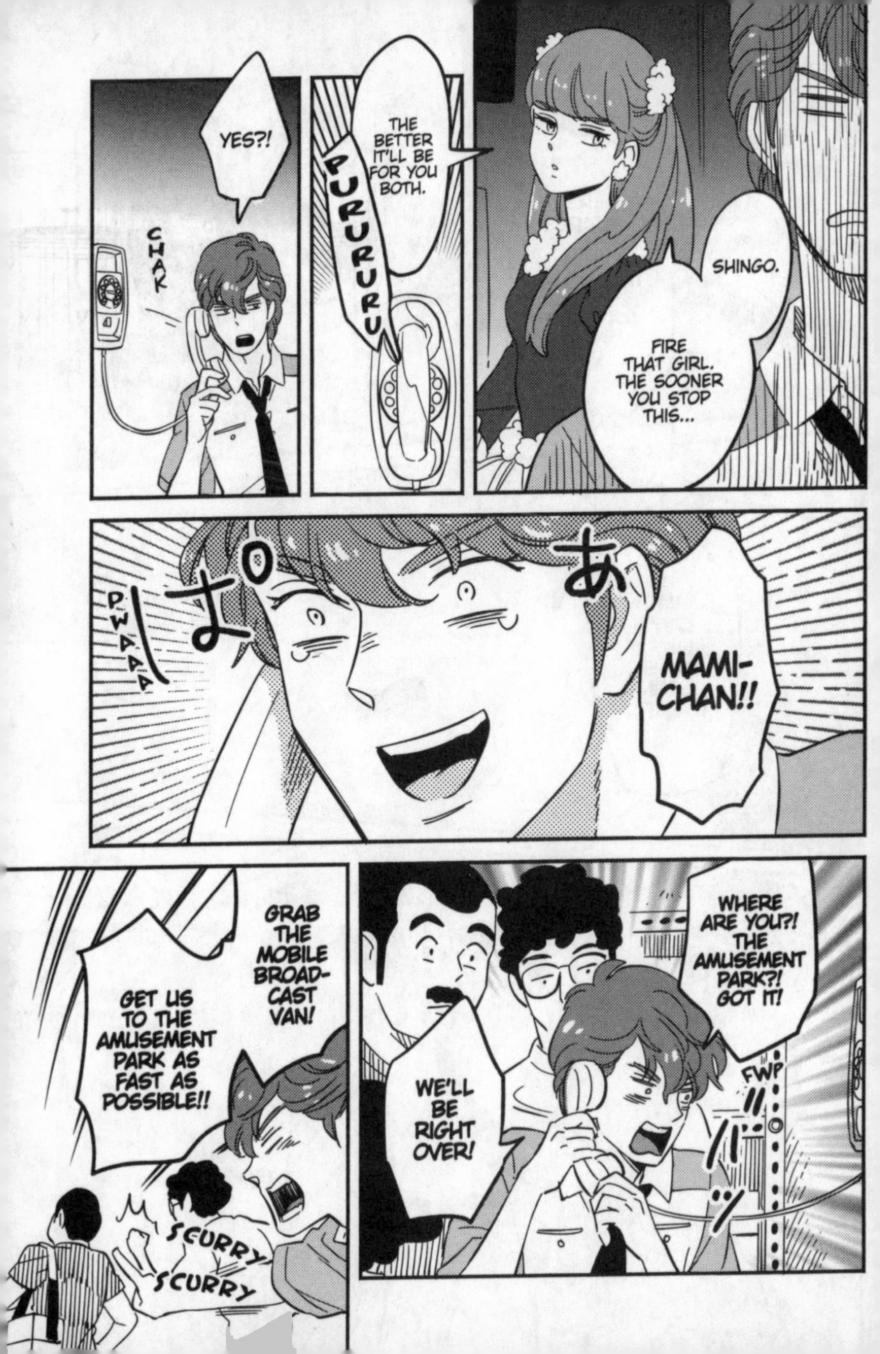
SHINGO.
FIRE THAT GIRL. THE SOONER YOU STOP THIS...
THE BETTER IT'LL BE FOR YOU BOTH.
PURURURURU
YES?!
CHAK
MAMI-CHAN!!
あ
よ
PWAAA
WHERE ARE YOU?! THE AMUSEMENT PARK?! GOT IT!
FWP
WE'LL BE RIGHT OVER!
GRAB THE MOBILE BROADCAST VAN!
GET US TO THE AMUSEMENT PARK AS FAST AS POSSIBLE!!
SCURRY
SCURRY

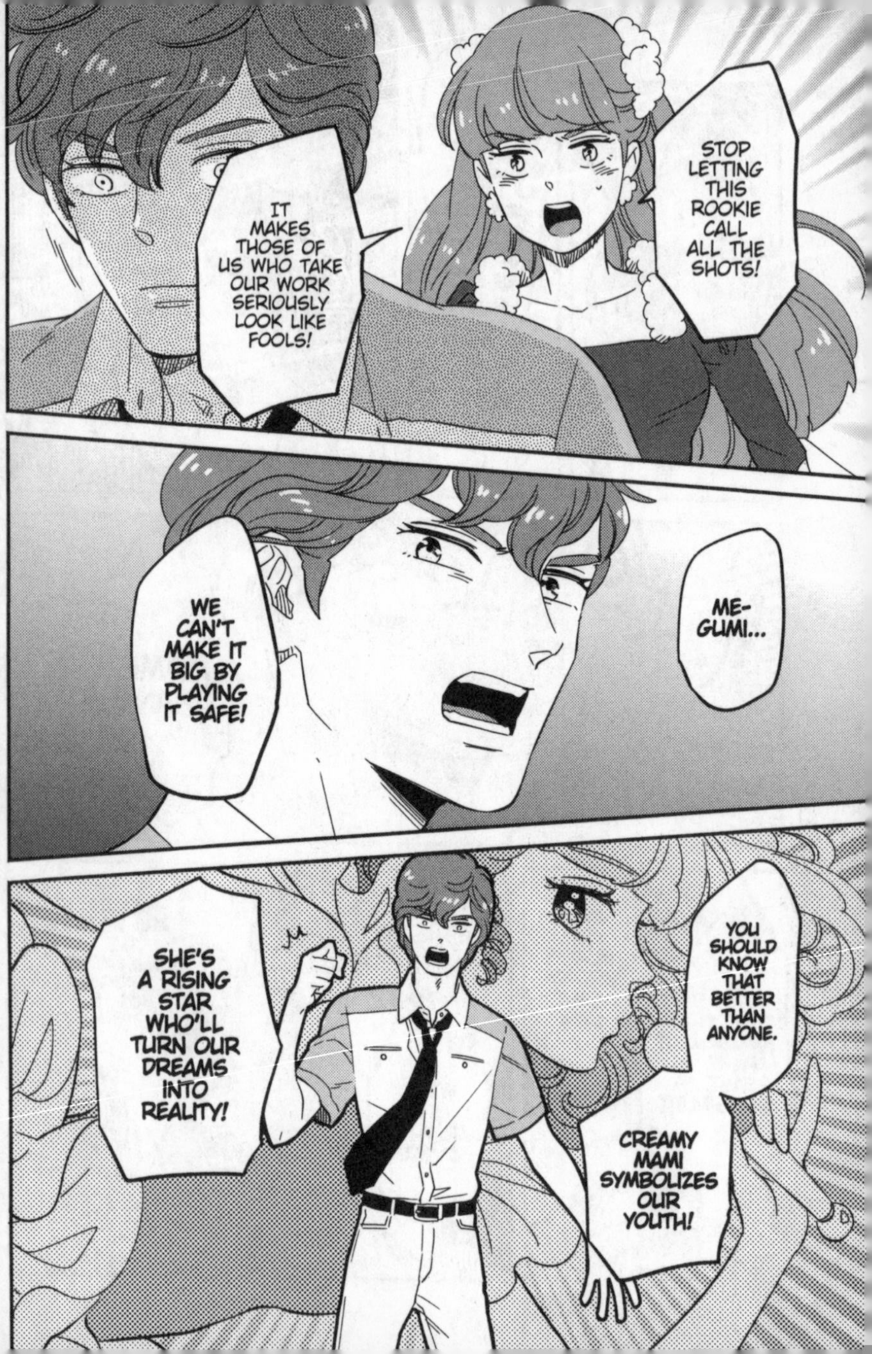
STOP LETTING THIS ROOKIE CALL ALL THE SHOTS!
IT MAKES THOSE OF US WHO TAKE OUR WORK SERIOUSLY LOOK LIKE FOOLS!
ME-GUMI...
WE CAN'T MAKE IT BIG BY PLAYING IT SAFE!
YOU SHOULD KNOW THAT BETTER THAN ANYONE.
SHE'S A RISING STAR WHO'LL TURN OUR DREAMS INTO REALITY!
CREAMY MAMI SYMBOLIZES OUR YOUTH!

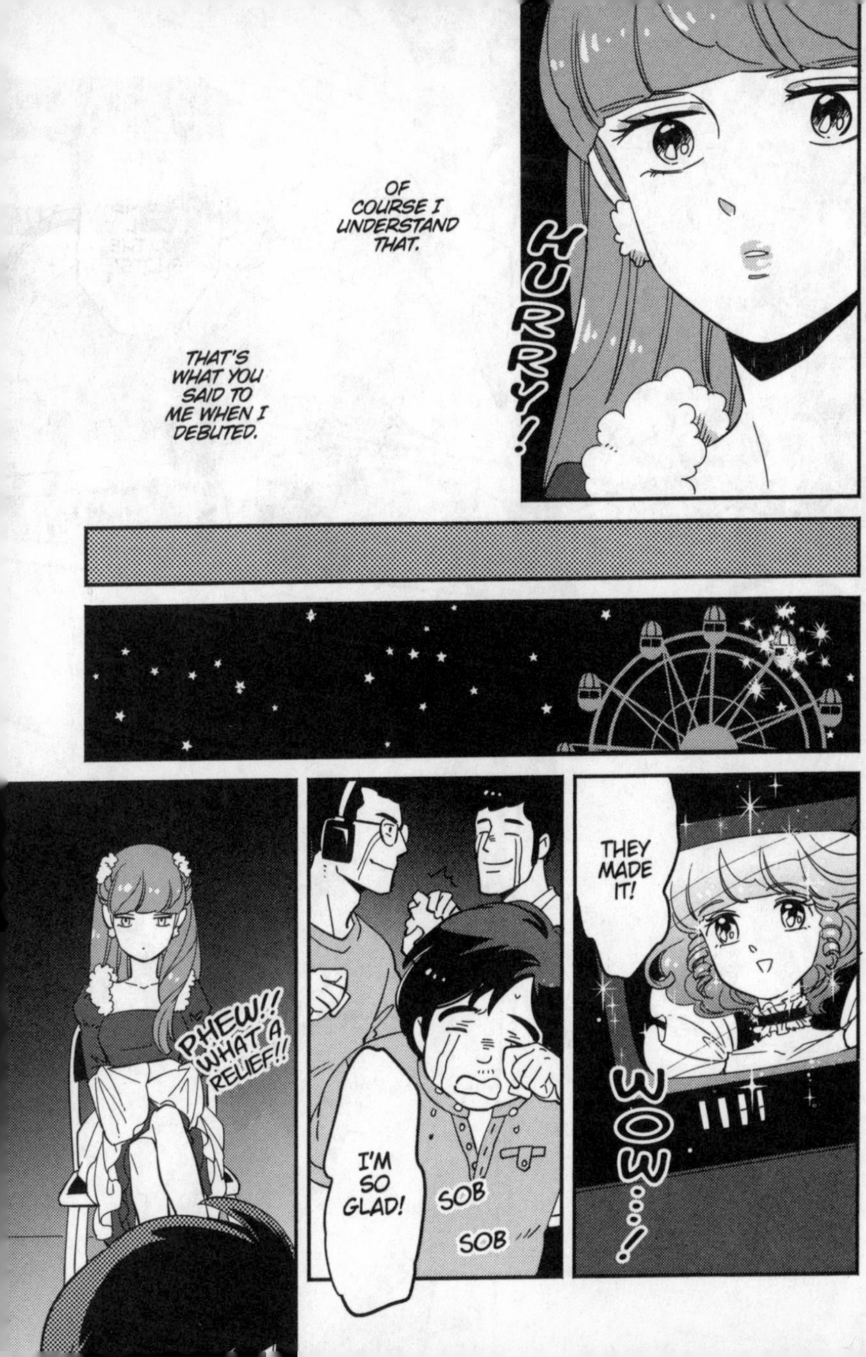
HURRY!
OF COURSE I UNDERSTAND THAT.
THAT'S WHAT YOU SAID TO ME WHEN I DEBUTED.
THEY MADE IT!
WOW...!
I'M SO GLAD!
SOB
SOB
PHEW!! WHAT A RELIEF!!

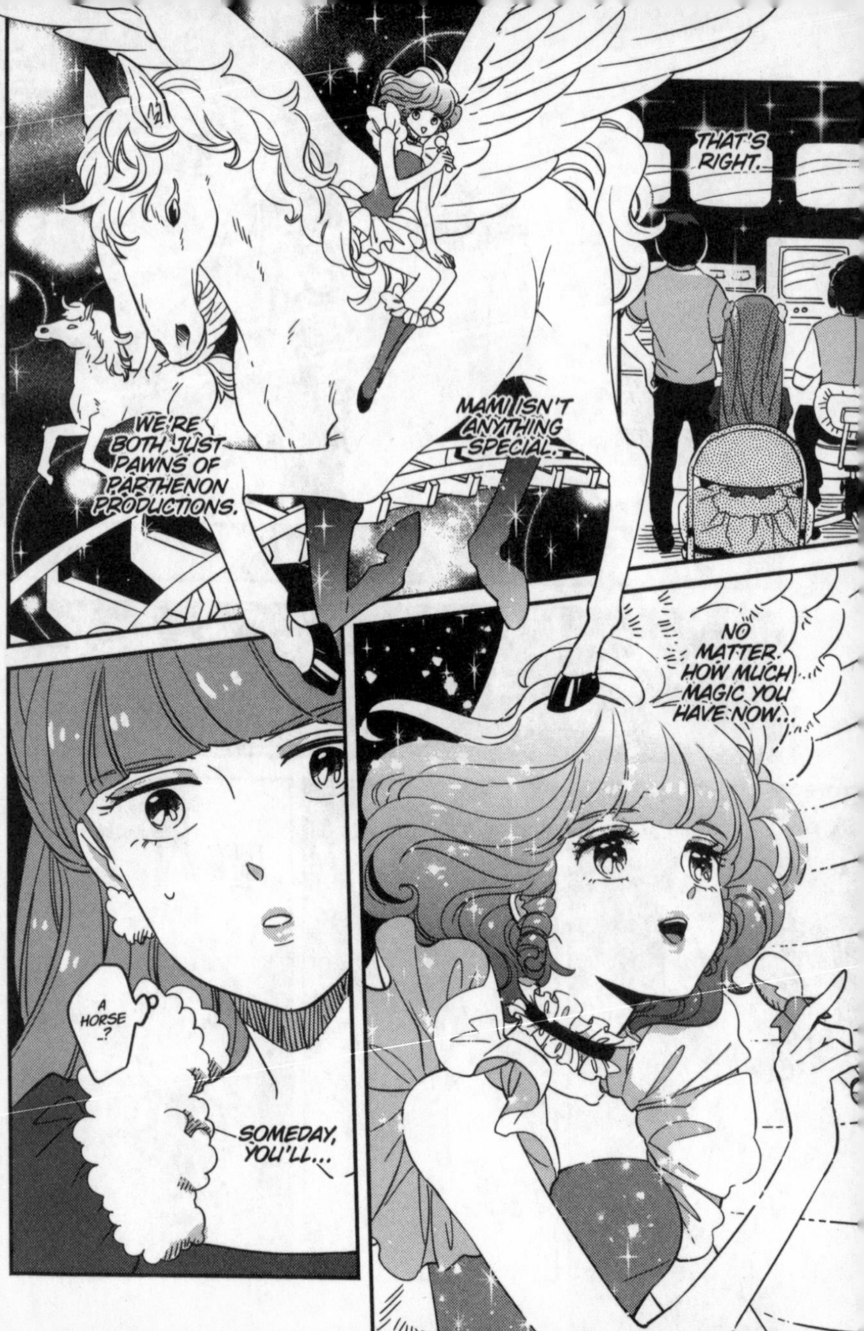
THAT'S RIGHT.
MAMI ISN'T ANYTHING SPECIAL.
WE'RE BOTH JUST PAWNS OF PARTHENON PRODUCTIONS.
NO MATTER HOW MUCH MAGIC YOU HAVE NOW...
A HORSE...?
SOMEDAY, YOU'LL...

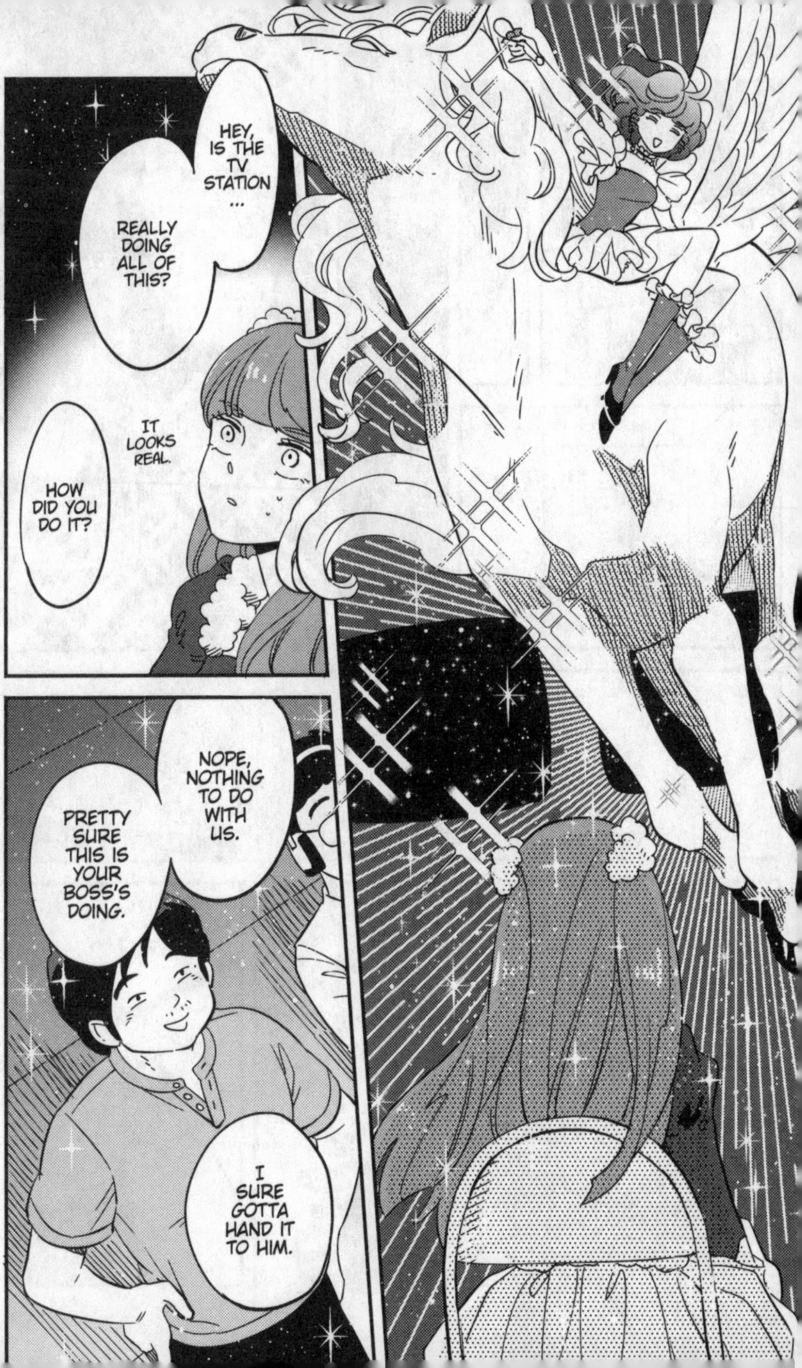
HEY, IS THE TV STATION ...
REALLY DOING ALL OF THIS?
IT LOOKS REAL.
HOW DID YOU DO IT?
NOPE, NOTHING TO DO WITH US.
PRETTY SURE THIS IS YOUR BOSS'S DOING.
I SURE GOTTA HAND IT TO HIM.

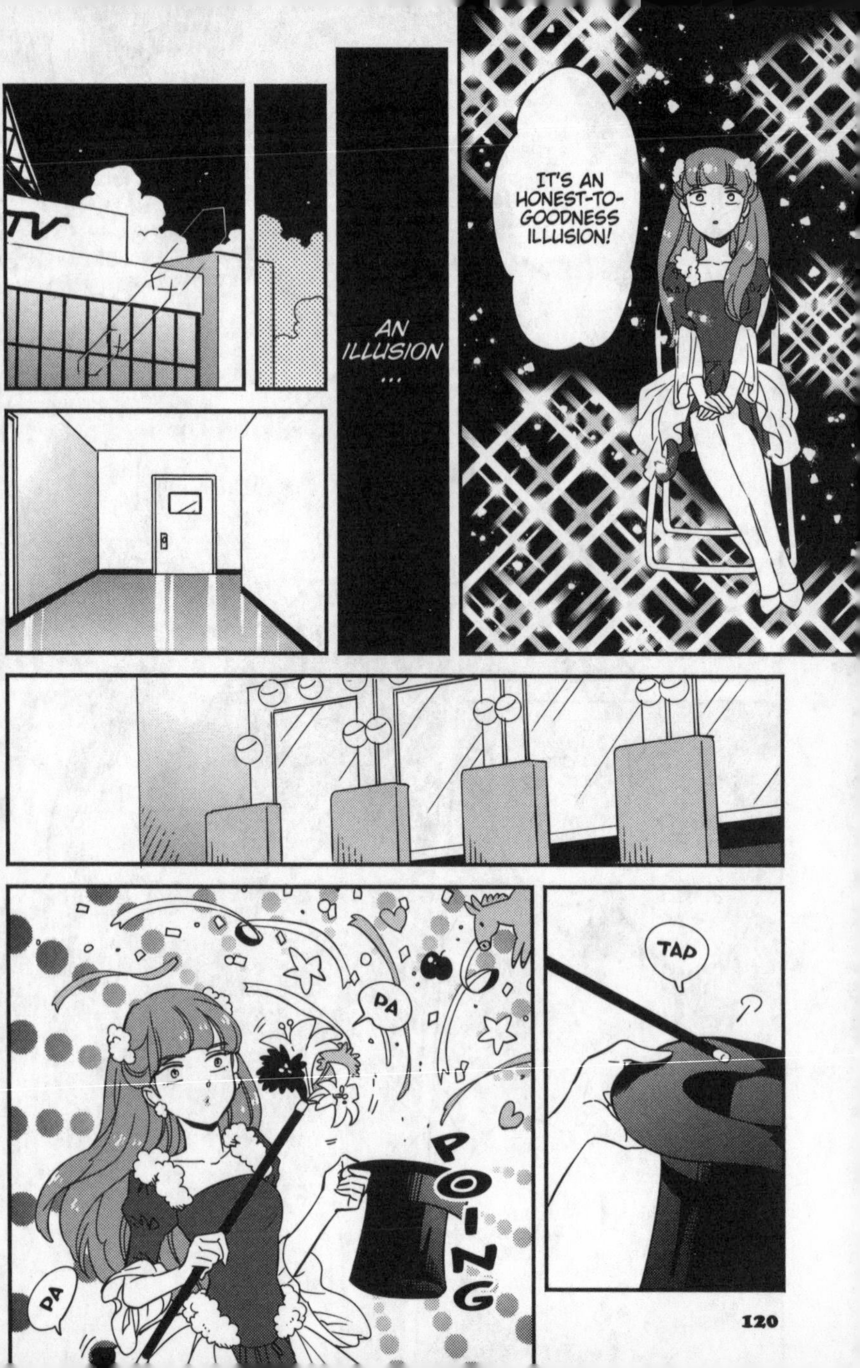
IT'S AN HONEST-TO-GOODNESS ILLUSION!
AN ILLUSION ...
TV
TAP
PA
POING
PA

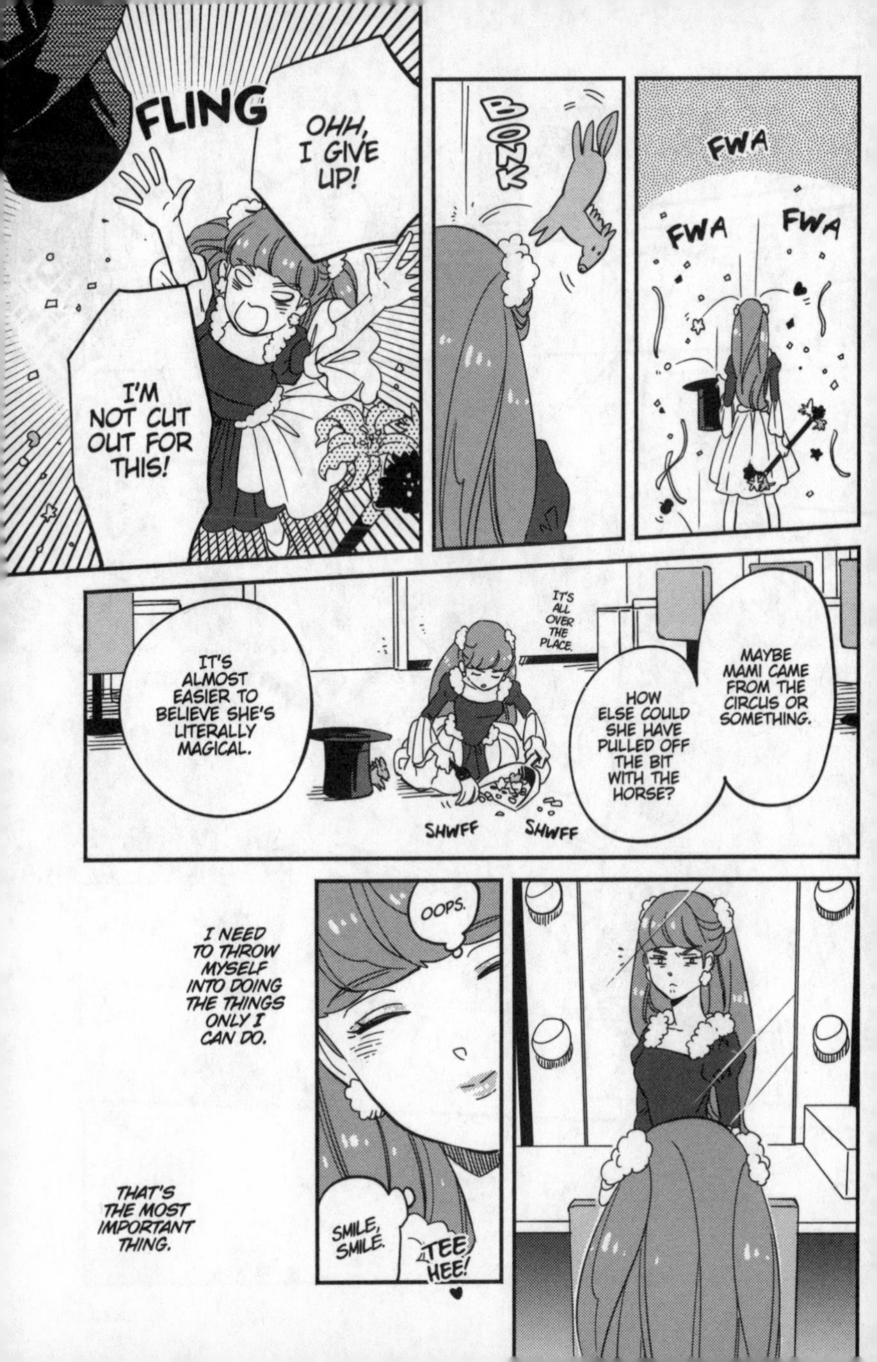
FWA
FWA
FWA
BONK
FLING
OHH, I GIVE UP!
I'M NOT CUT OUT FOR THIS!
MAYBE MAMI CAME FROM THE CIRCUS OR SOMETHING.
HOW ELSE COULD SHE HAVE PULLED OFF THE BIT WITH THE HORSE?
IT'S ALL OVER THE PLACE.
IT'S ALMOST EASIER TO BELIEVE SHE'S LITERALLY MAGICAL.
SHWFF
SHWFF
OOPS.
SMILE, SMILE.
TEE HEE!
I NEED TO THROW MYSELF INTO DOING THE THINGS ONLY I CAN DO.
THAT'S THE MOST IMPORTANT THING.

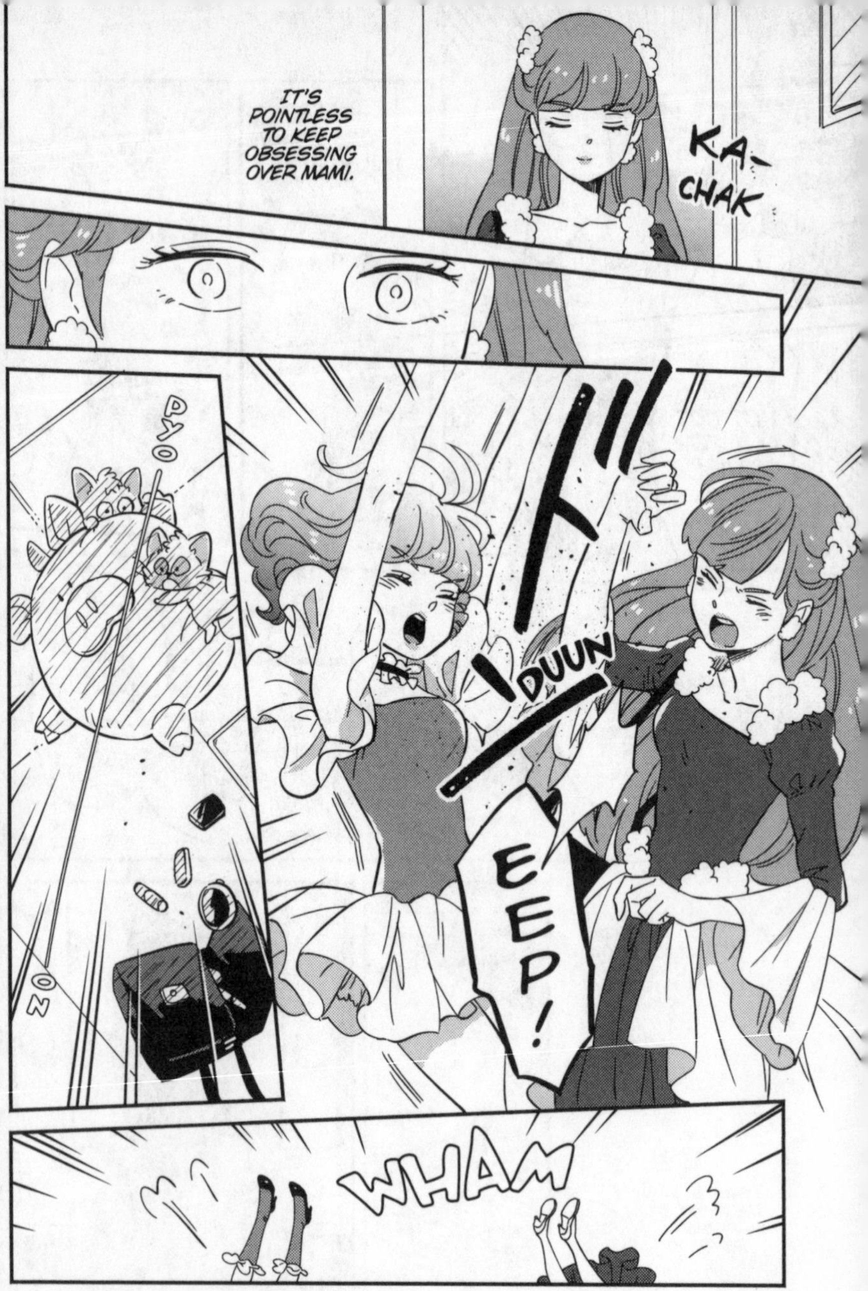
IT'S POINTLESS TO KEEP OBSESSING OVER MAMI.
KA-CHAK
ド
DUUN
EEP!
PYO
ON
WHAM

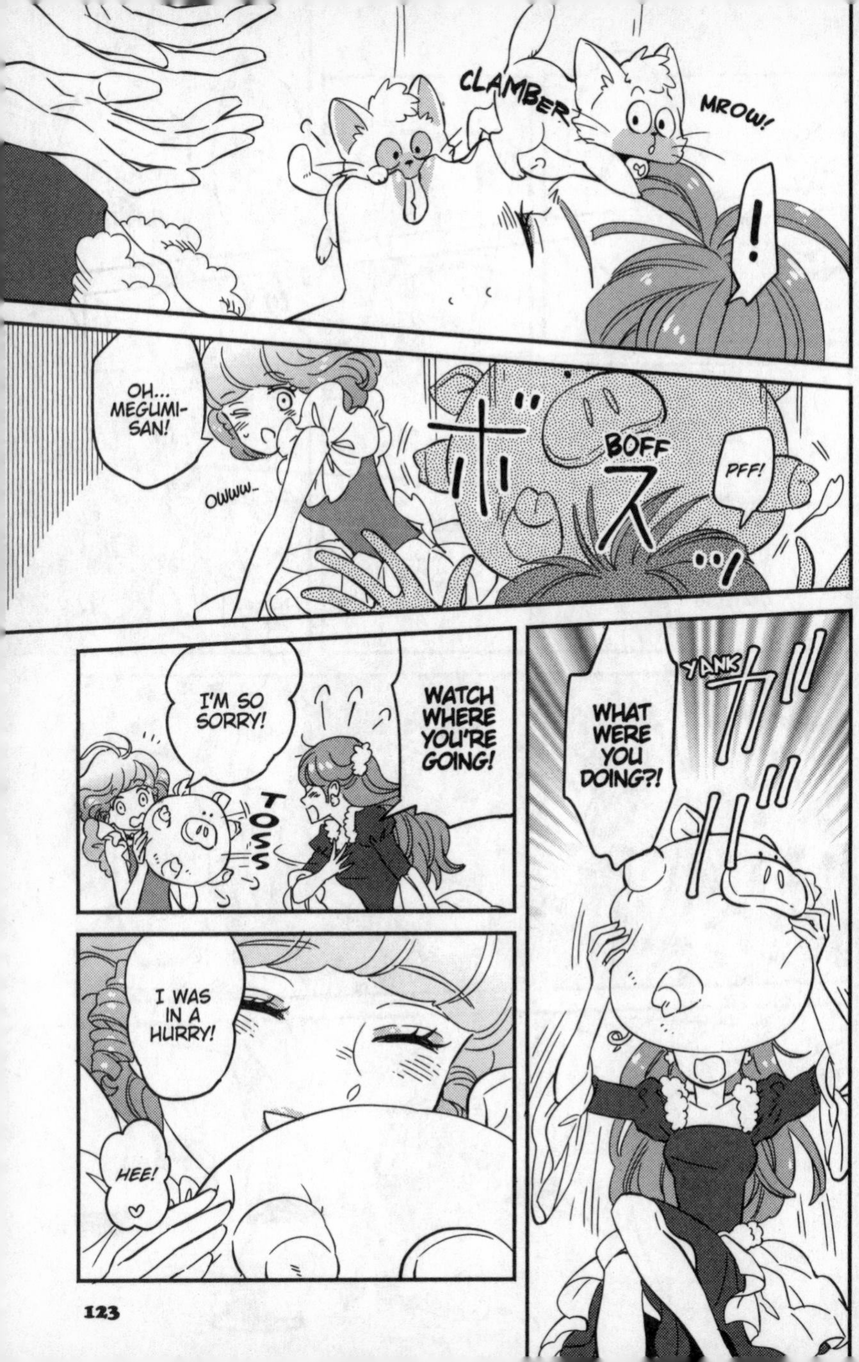
MROW!
CLAMBER
!
PFF!
BOFF
ボス
OH... MEGUMI-SAN!
OWWW...
YANK
WHAT WERE YOU DOING?!
WATCH WHERE YOU'RE GOING!
I'M SO SORRY!
TOSS
I WAS IN A HURRY!
HEE!

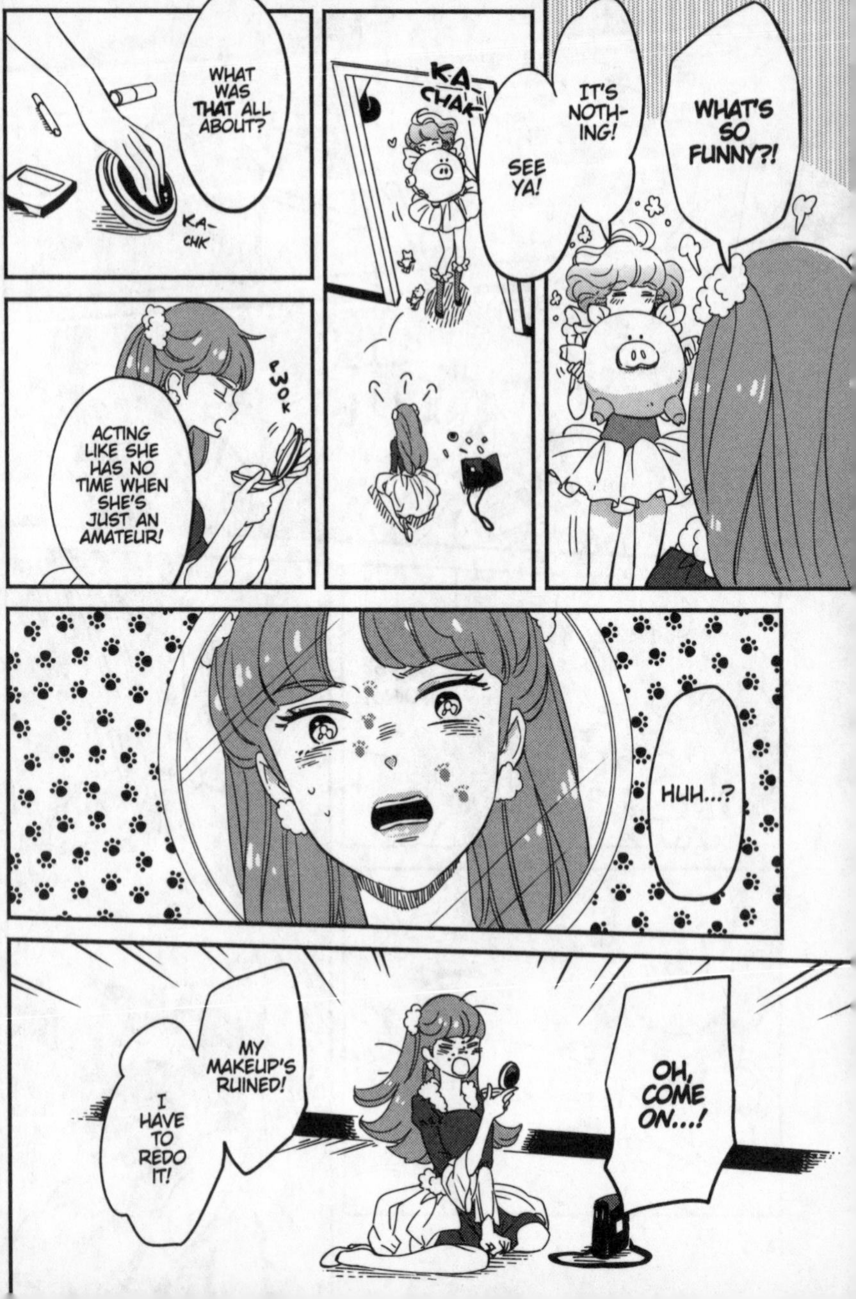
WHAT'S SO FUNNY?!
IT'S NOTH-ING!
SEE YA!
KA-CHAK
WHAT WAS THAT ALL ABOUT?
KA-CHK
PWOK
ACTING LIKE SHE HAS NO TIME WHEN SHE'S JUST AN AMATEUR!
HUH...?
OH, COME ON...!
MY MAKEUP'S RUINED!
I HAVE TO REDO IT!

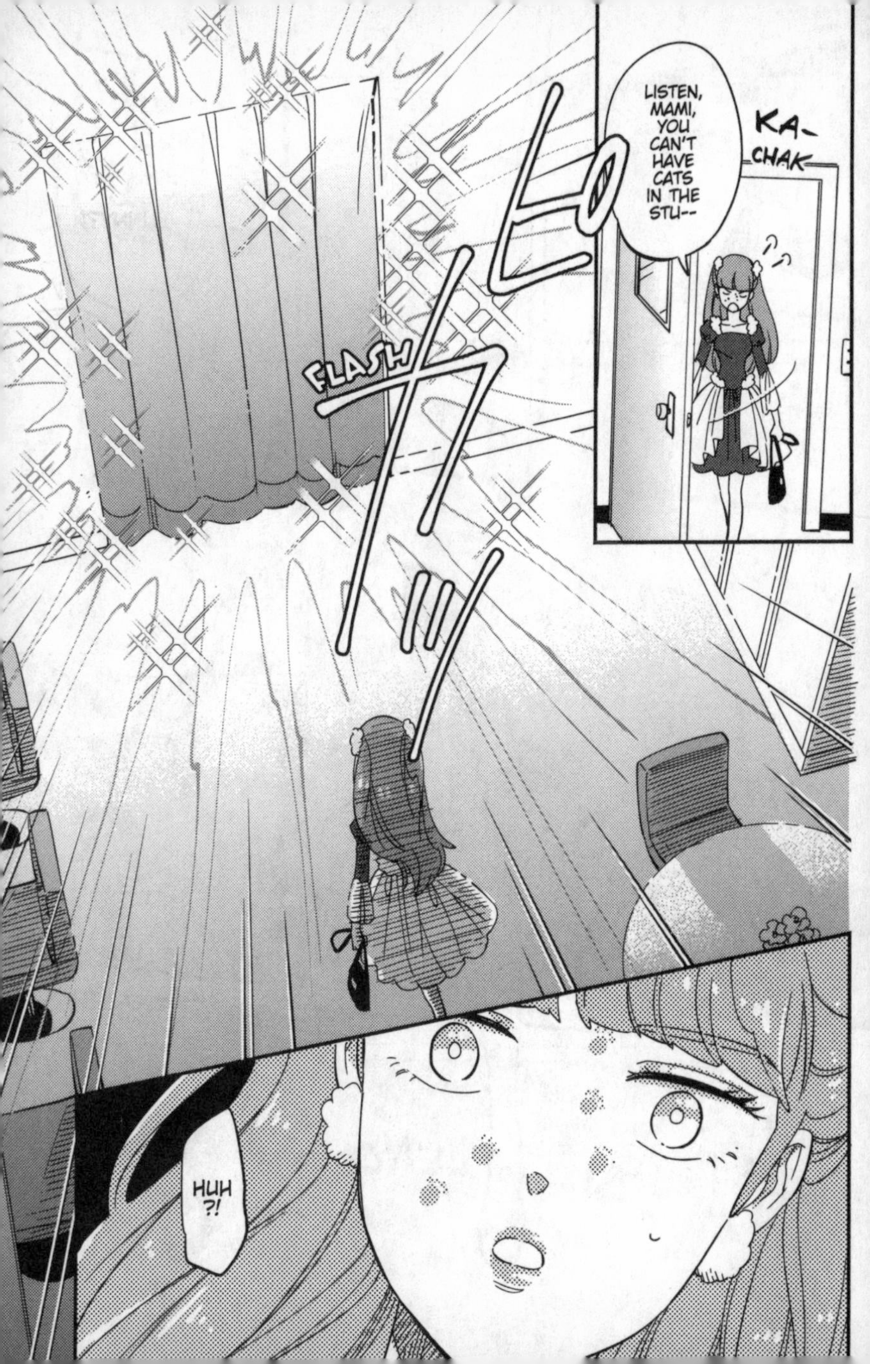
LISTEN, MAMI, YOU CAN'T HAVE CATS IN THE STU--
KA-CHAK
FLASH
HUH?!

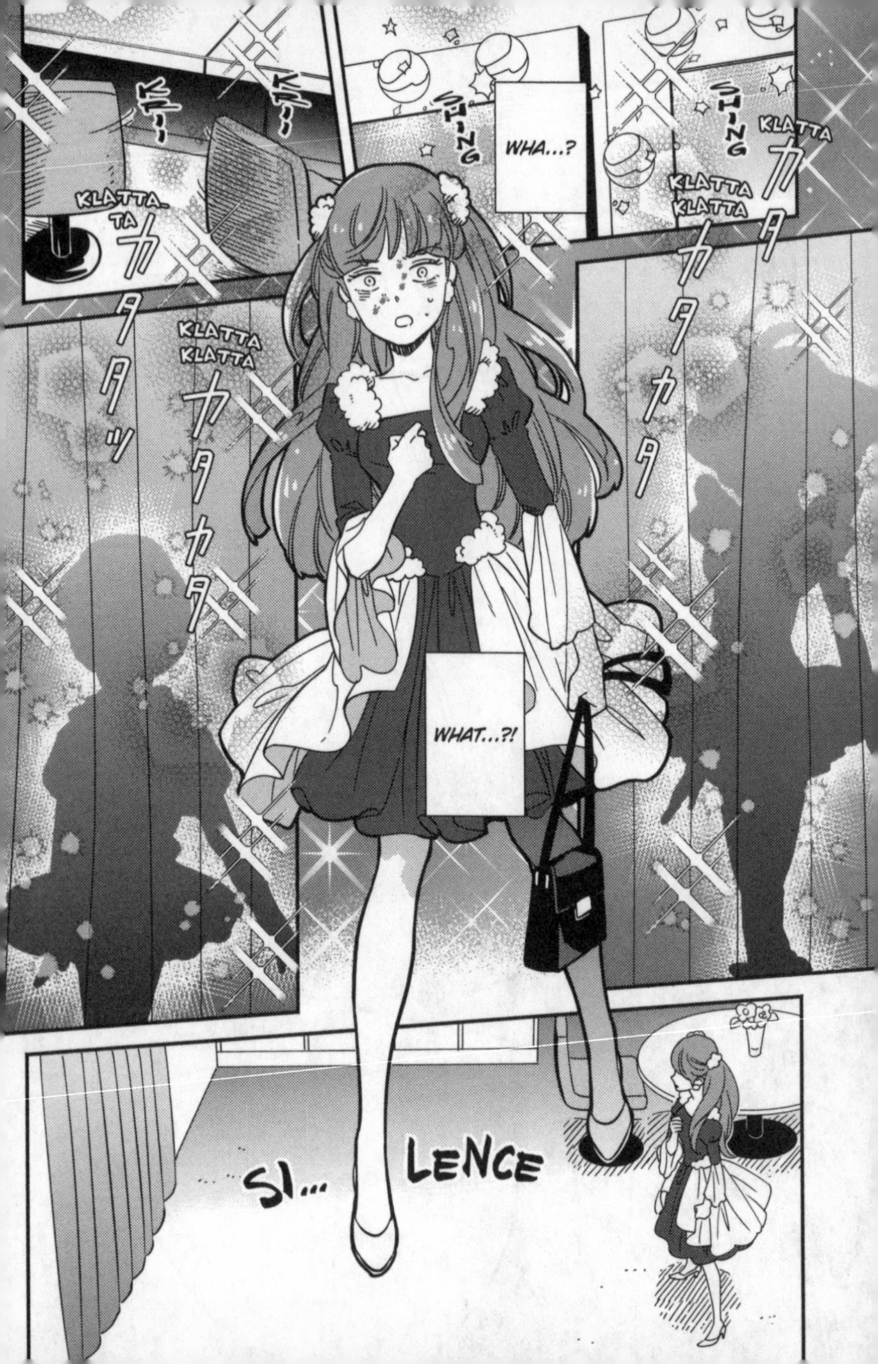
SHING
KLATTA
KLATTA KLATTA
WHA...?
SHING
KRI—
KRI—
KLATTA-TA
KLATTA KLATTA
WHAT...?!
SI... LENCE

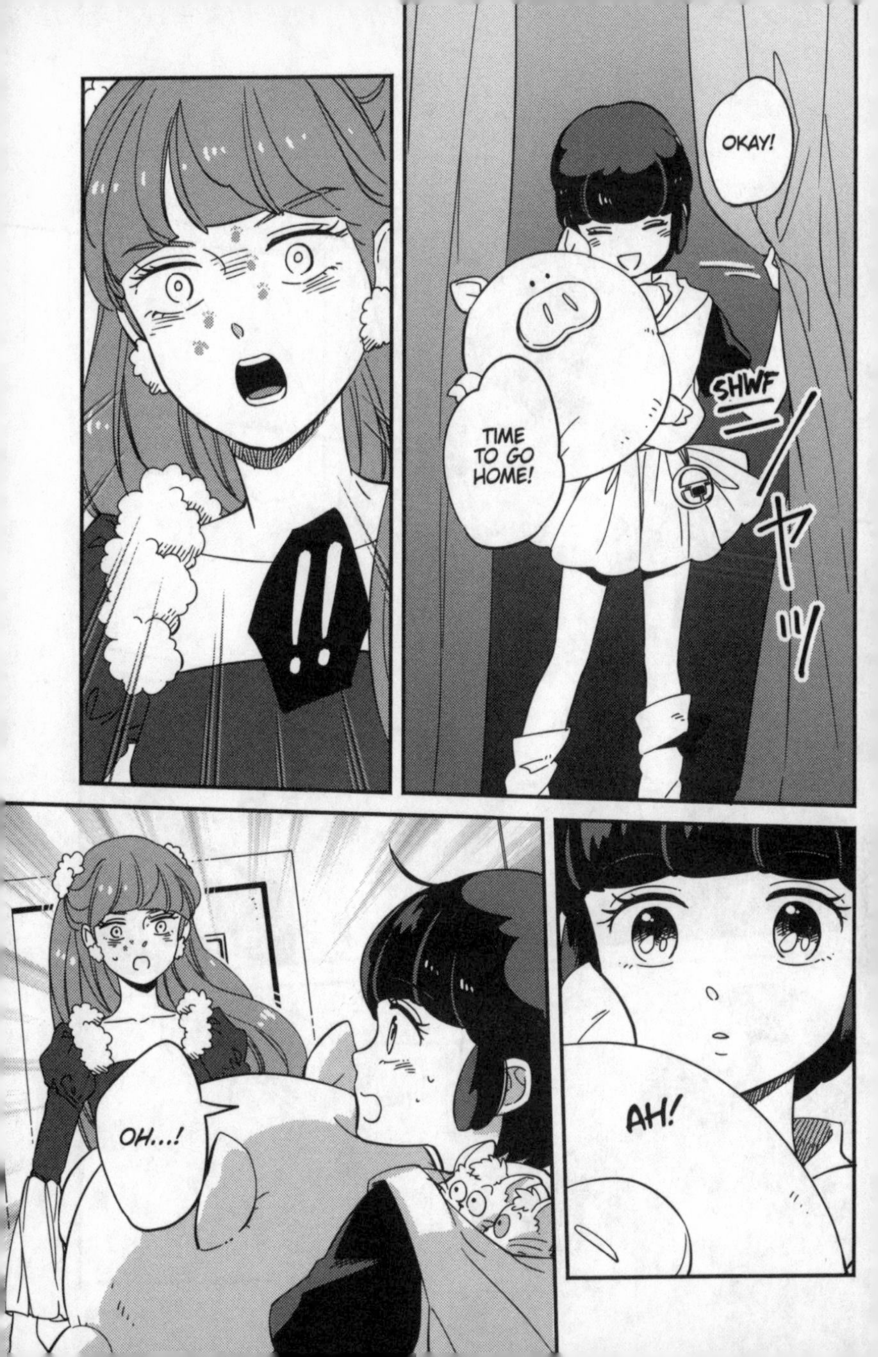
OKAY!
TIME TO GO HOME!
SHWF
!!
AH!
OH...!

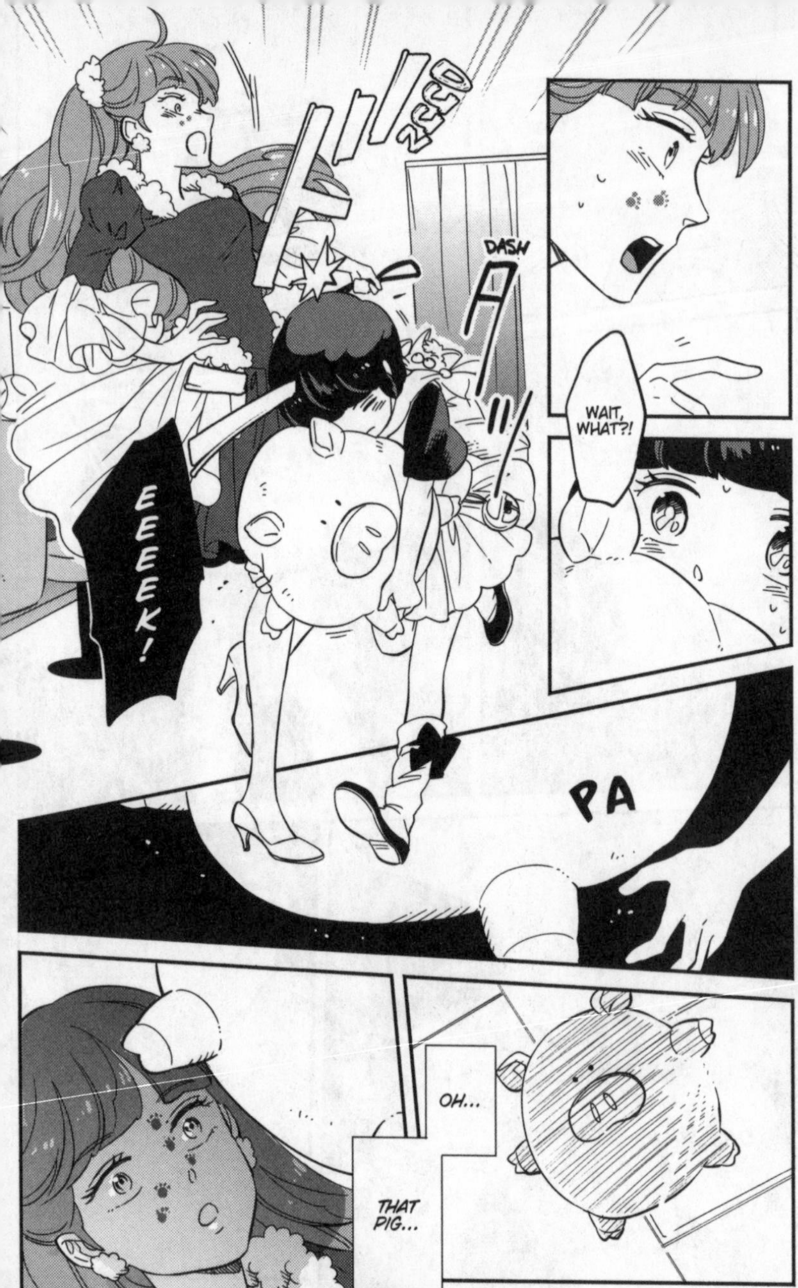
WAIT, WHAT?!
DASH
EEEEK!
PA
OH...
THAT PIG...

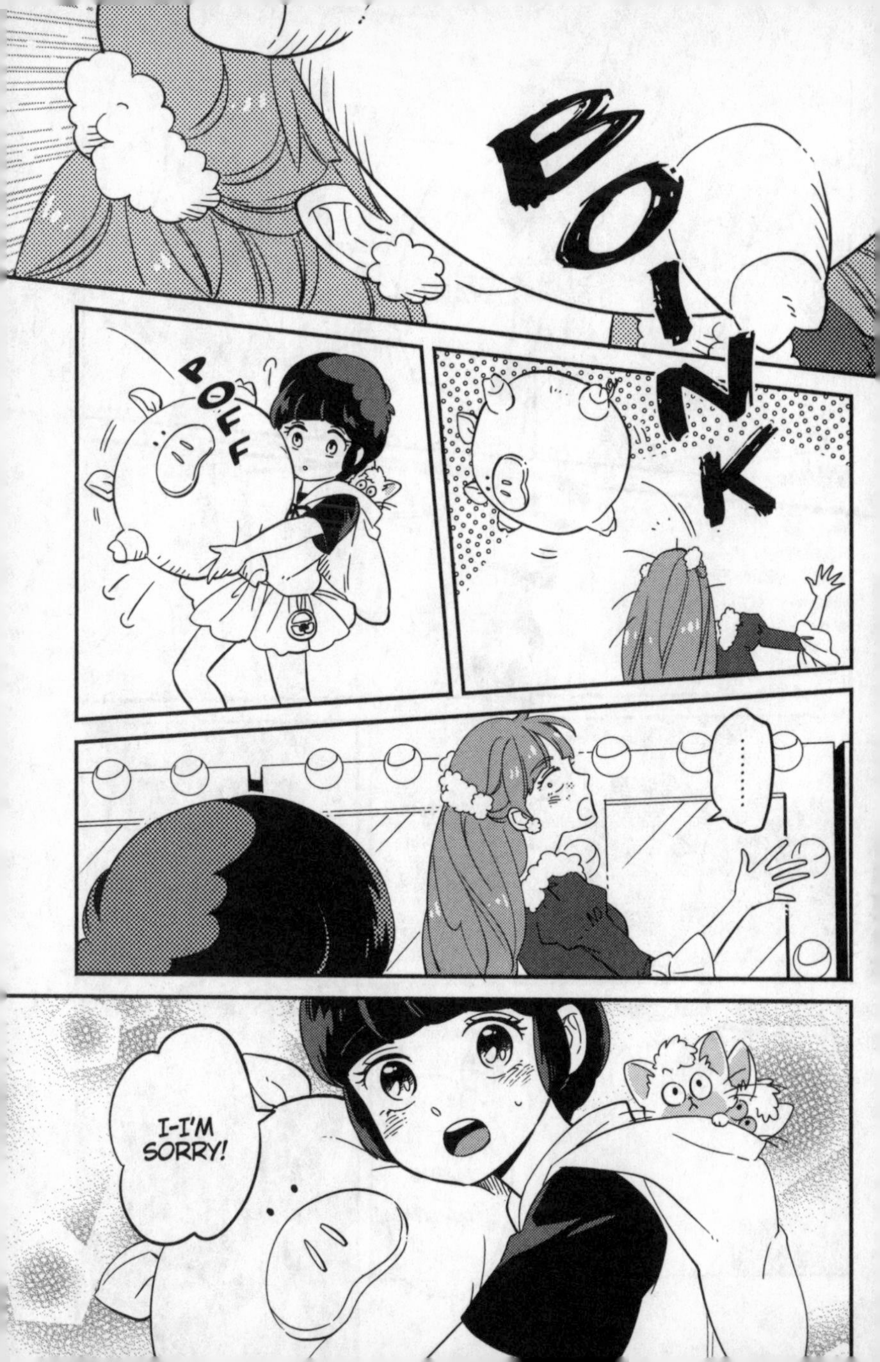
BOINK
POFF
......
I-I'M SORRY!

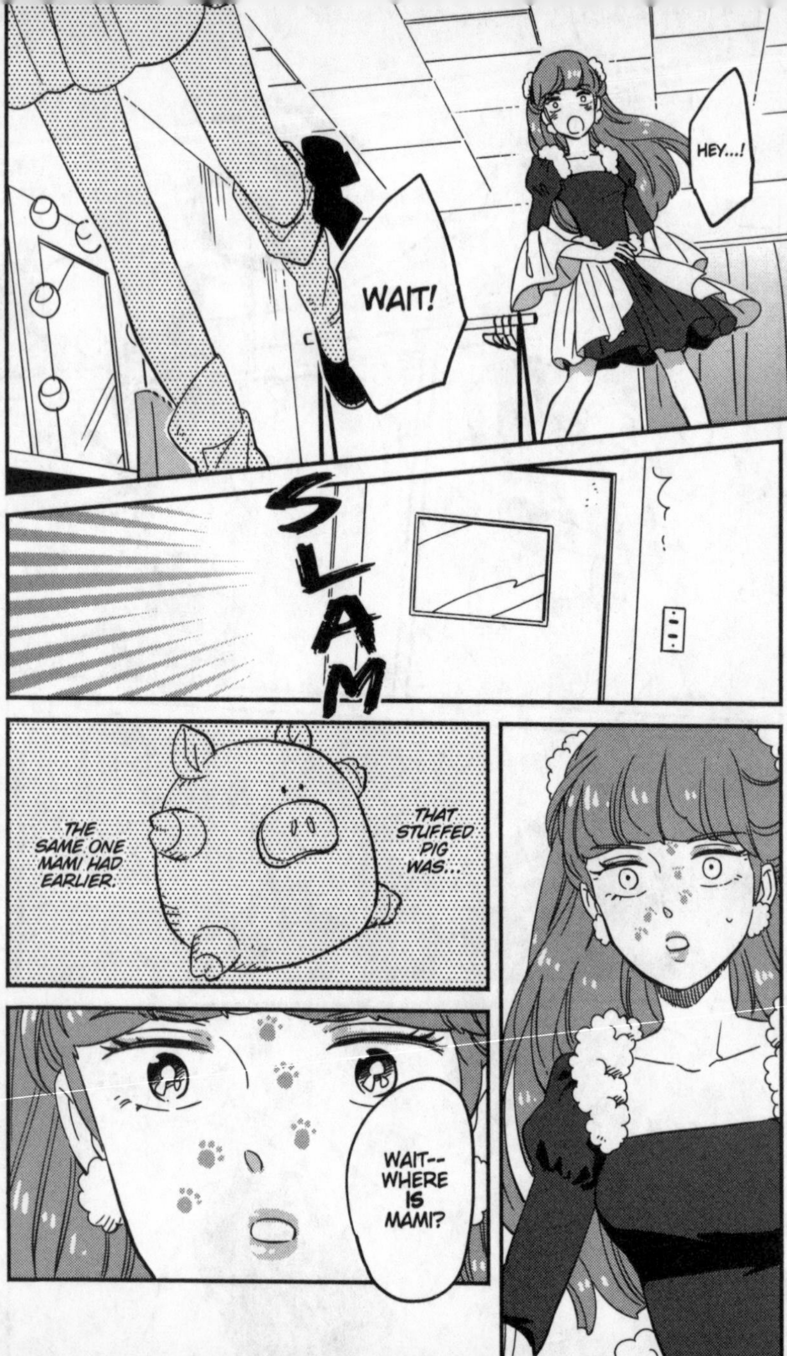
HEY...!
WAIT!
SLAM
THAT STUFFED PIG WAS...
THE SAME ONE MAMI HAD EARLIER.
WAIT-- WHERE IS MAMI?

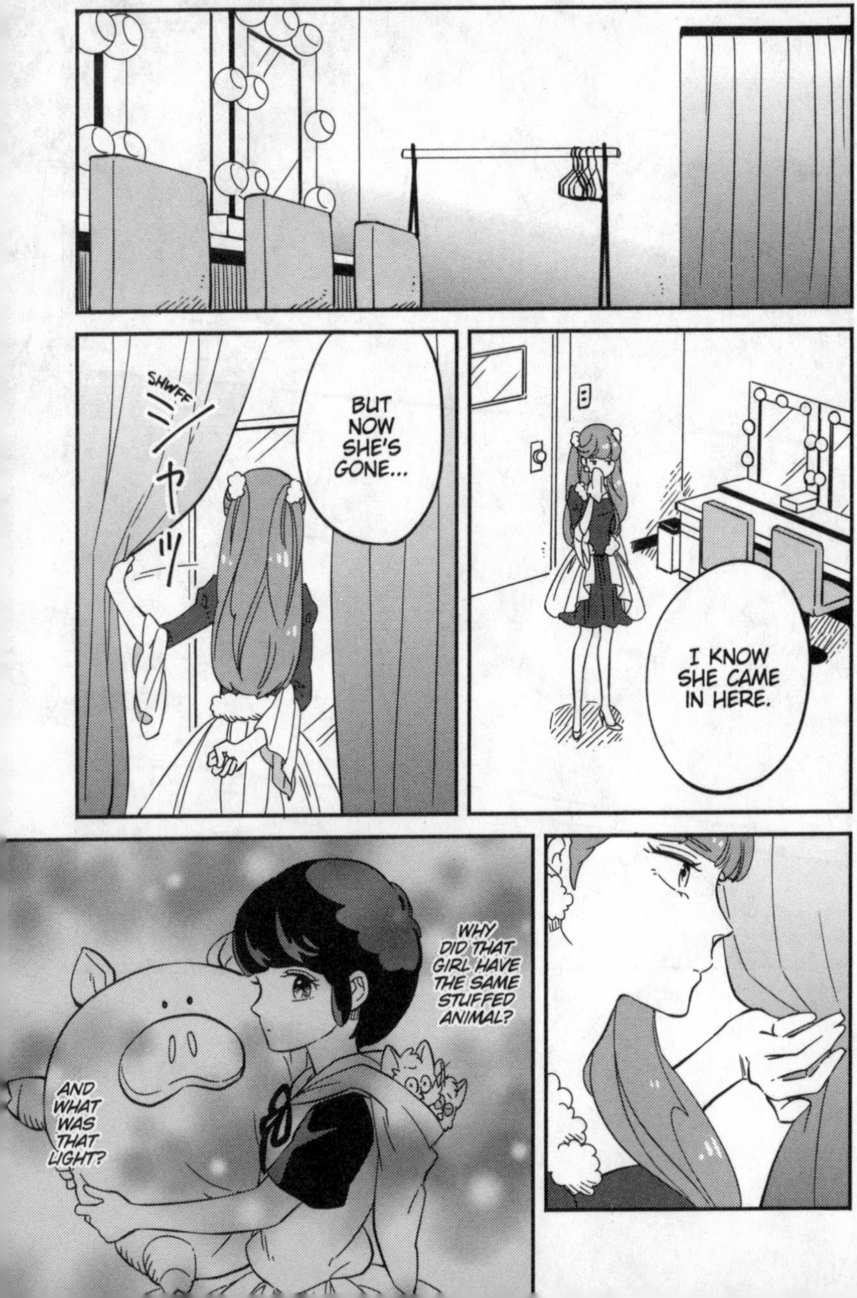
I KNOW SHE CAME IN HERE.
BUT NOW SHE'S GONE...
SHWFF
シャッ
WHY DID THAT GIRL HAVE THE SAME STUFFED ANIMAL?
AND WHAT WAS THAT LIGHT?

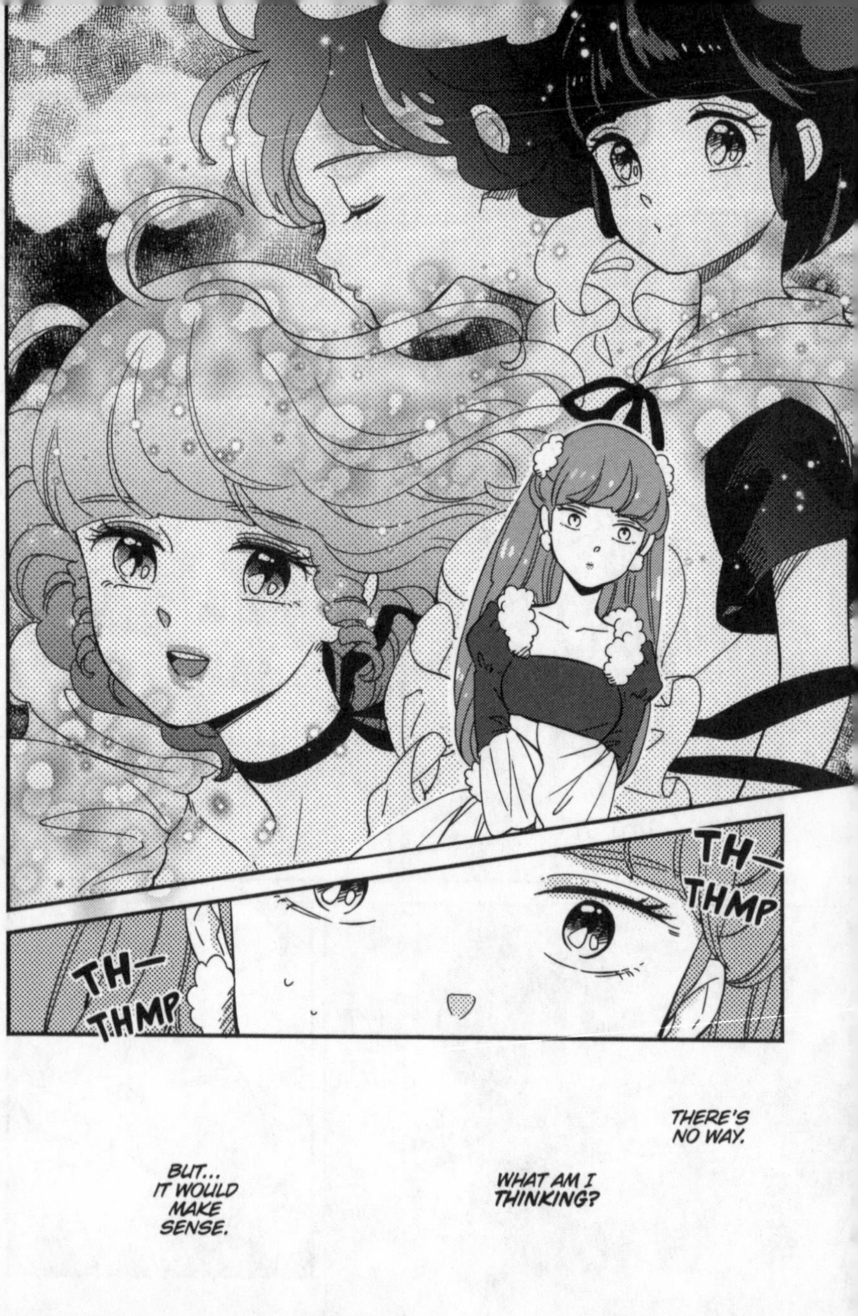
TH—THMP
TH—THMP
THERE'S NO WAY.
WHAT AM I THINKING?
BUT... IT WOULD MAKE SENSE.

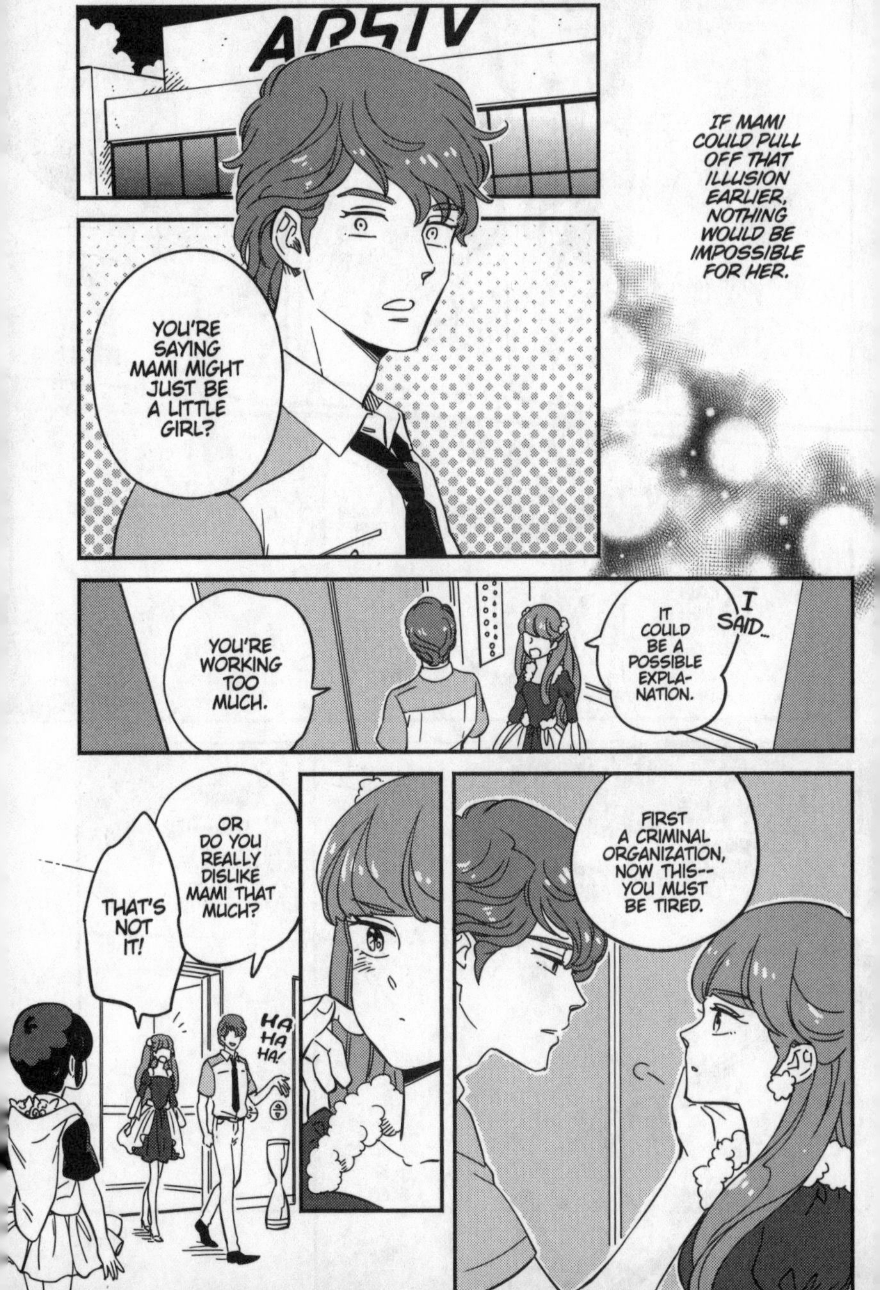
IF MAMI COULD PULL OFF THAT ILLUSION EARLIER, NOTHING WOULD BE IMPOSSIBLE FOR HER.
YOU'RE SAYING MAMI MIGHT JUST BE A LITTLE GIRL?
I SAID..
IT COULD BE A POSSIBLE EXPLANATION.
YOU'RE WORKING TOO MUCH.
FIRST A CRIMINAL ORGANIZATION, NOW THIS-- YOU MUST BE TIRED.
OR DO YOU REALLY DISLIKE MAMI THAT MUCH?
THAT'S NOT IT!
HA HA HA!

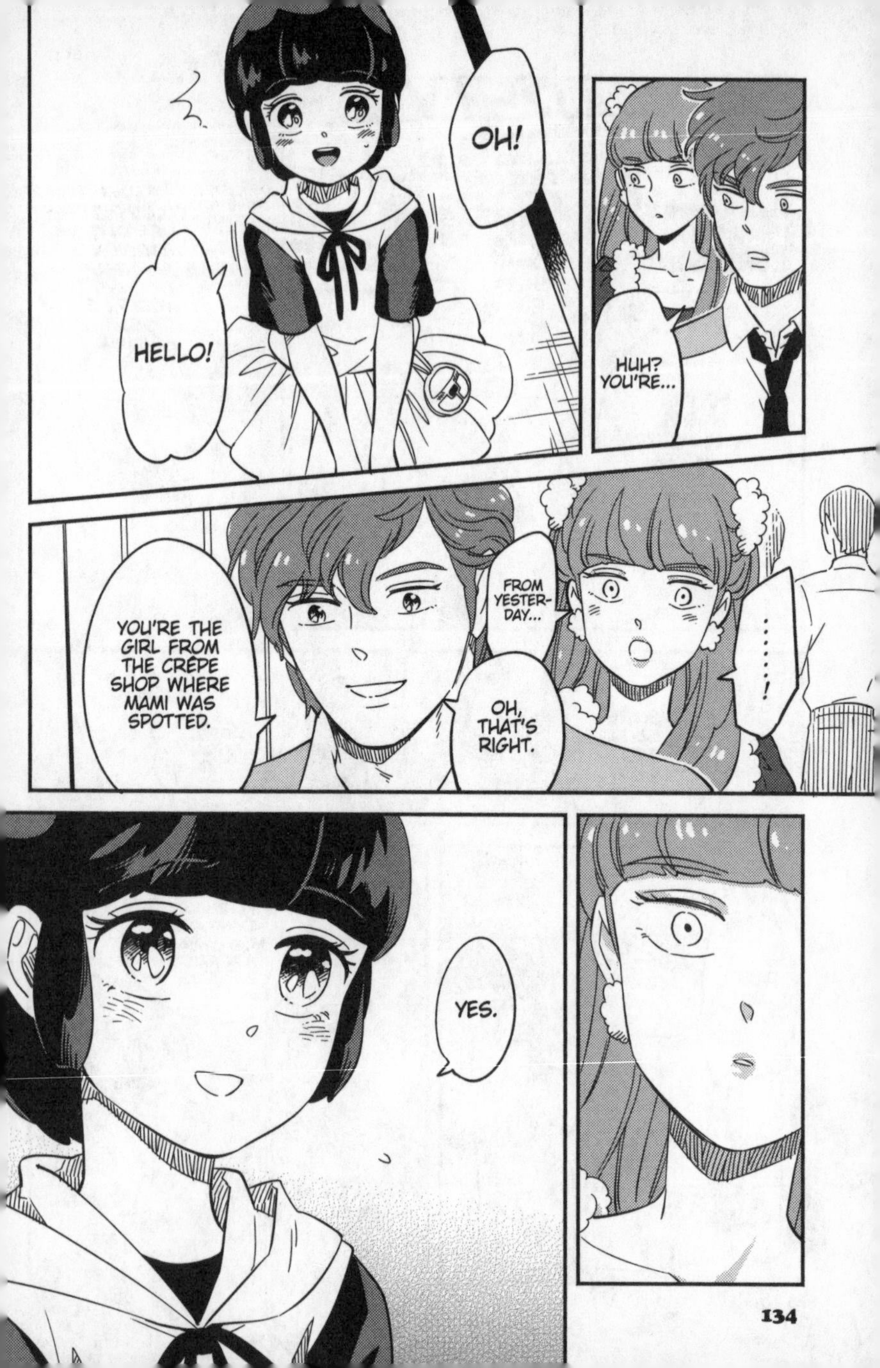
HUH? YOU'RE...
OH!
HELLO!
......!
FROM YESTER-DAY...
OH, THAT'S RIGHT.
YOU'RE THE GIRL FROM THE CRÊPE SHOP WHERE MAMI WAS SPOTTED.
YES.

Back When Creamy Mami Was Airing

1983 Tokyo Disneyland Opens

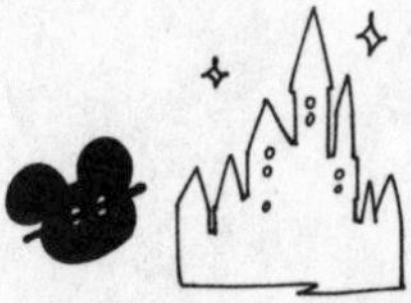

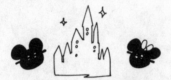

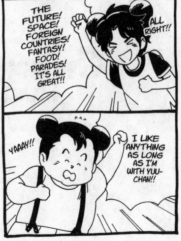

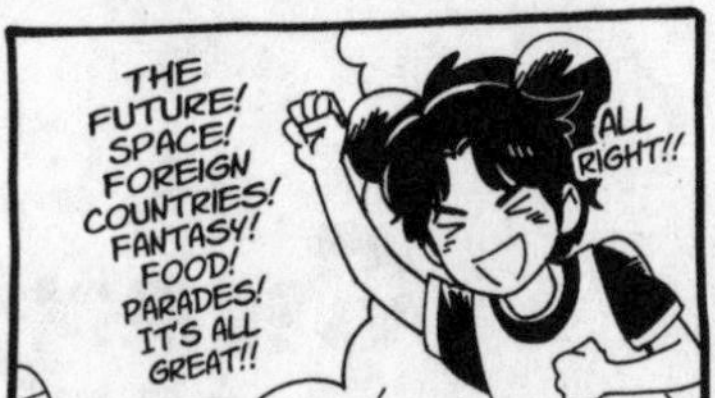
THE FUTURE! SPACE! FOREIGN COUNTRIES! FANTASY! FOOD! PARADES! IT'S ALL GREAT!!
ALL RIGHT!!

People Who Preferred Toshimaen's Shuttle Loop

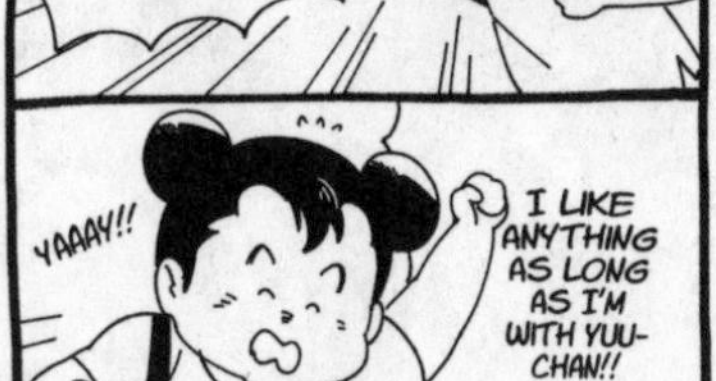
I LIKE ANYTHING AS LONG AS I'M WITH YUU-CHAN!!
YAAAY!!

People Who Preferred Mukogaoka Amusement Park's Big Ferris Wheel

Magical Angel Creamy Mami and the Spoiled Princess

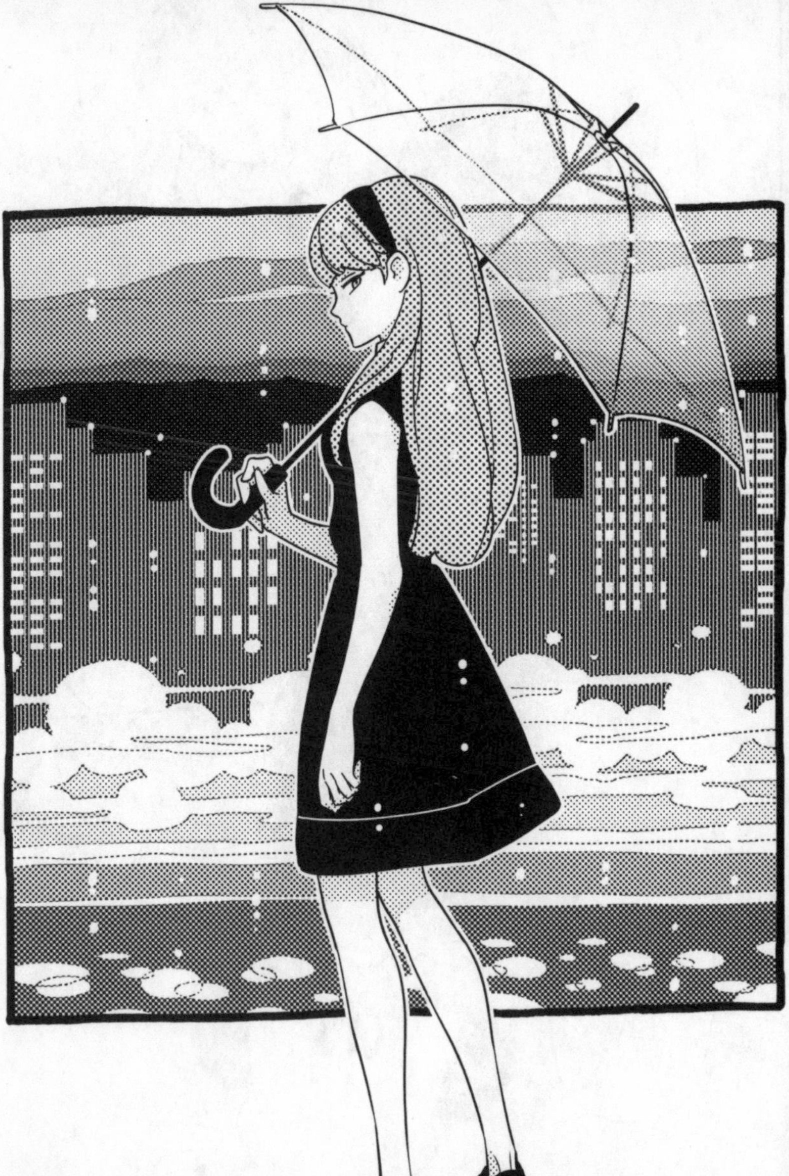

7 Revealing Mami's Secret!

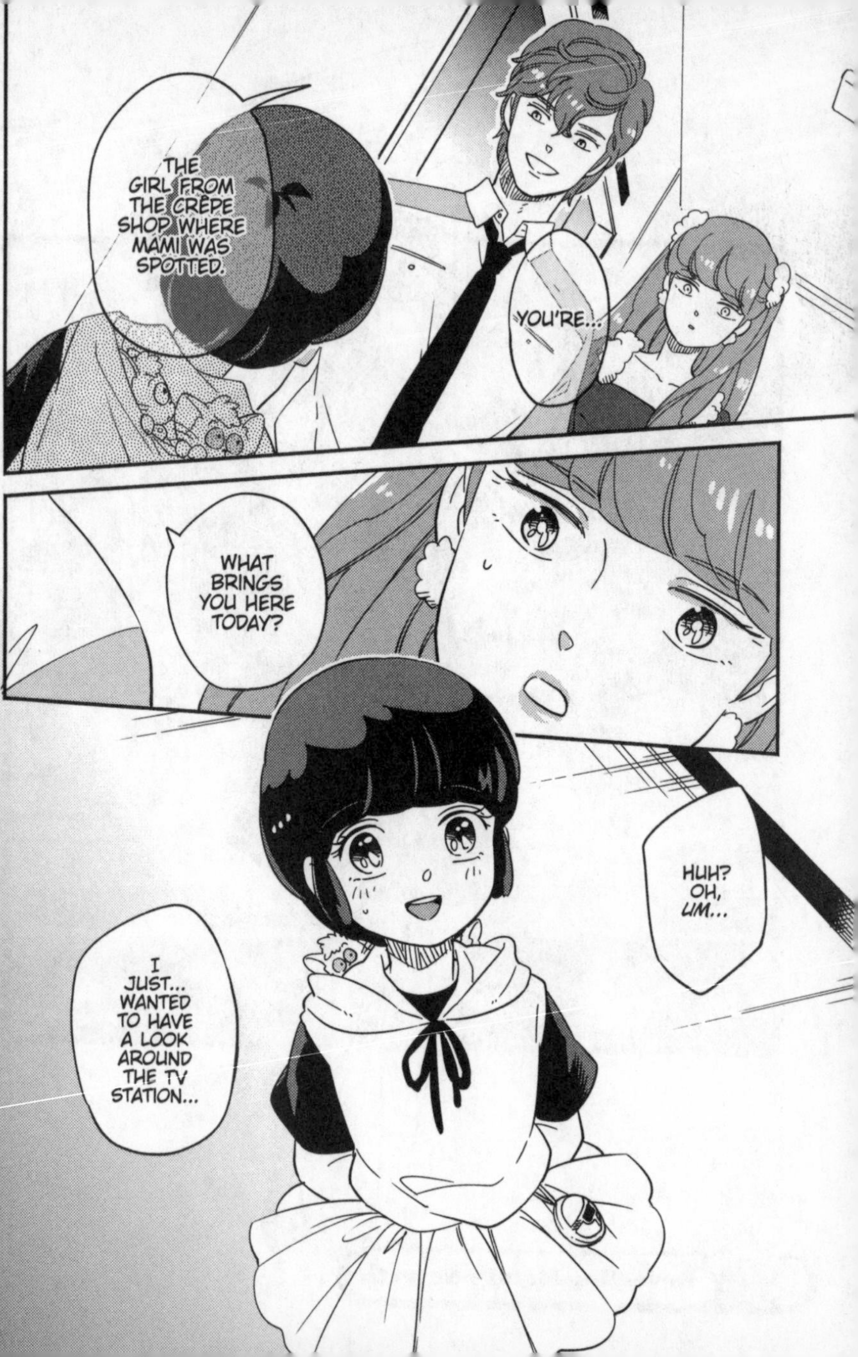
YOU'RE...
THE GIRL FROM THE CRÊPE SHOP WHERE MAMI WAS SPOTTED.
WHAT BRINGS YOU HERE TODAY?
HUH? OH, UM...
I JUST... WANTED TO HAVE A LOOK AROUND THE TV STATION...

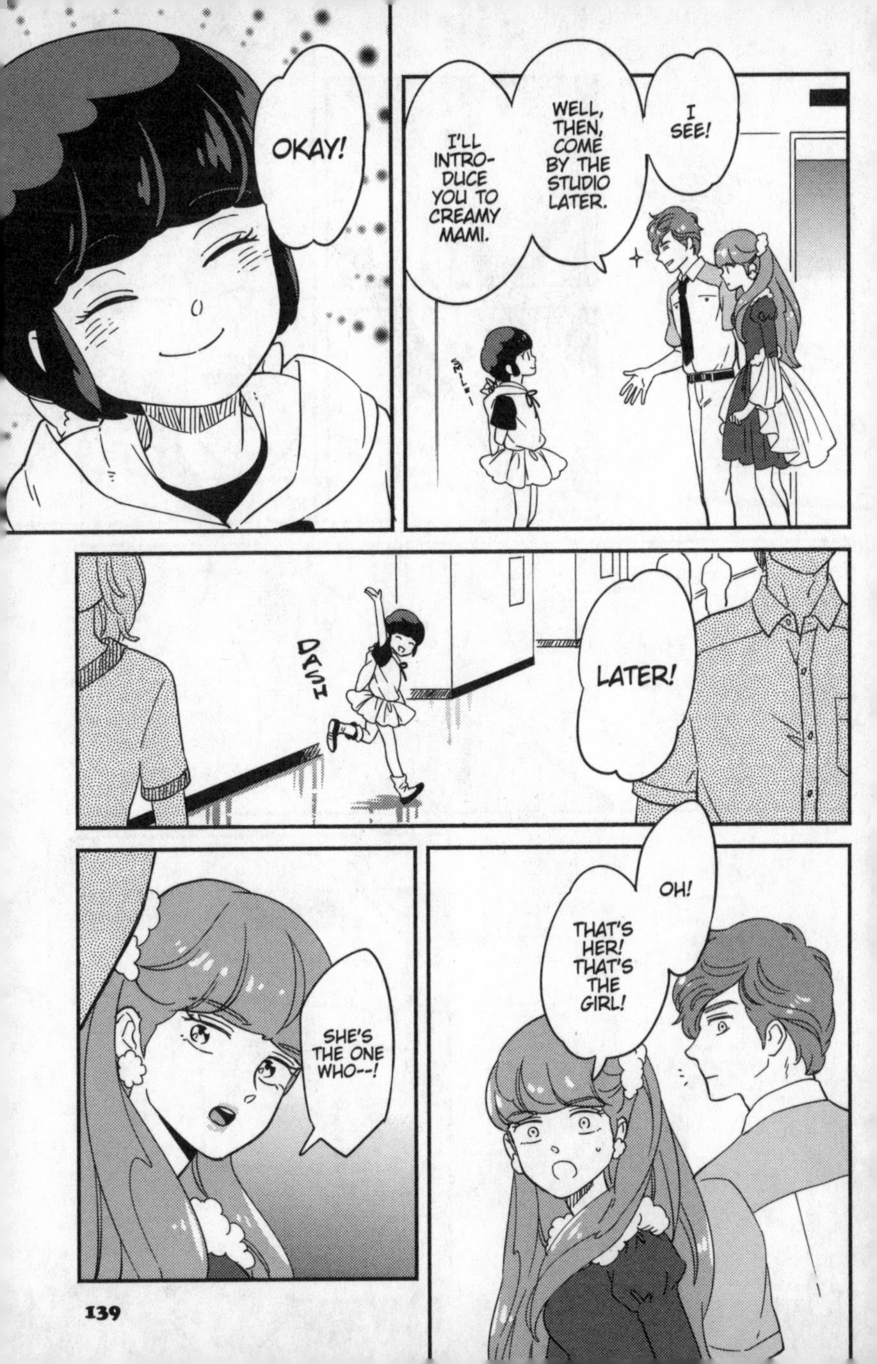
I SEE!
WELL, THEN, COME BY THE STUDIO LATER.
I'LL INTRODUCE YOU TO CREAMY MAMI.
OKAY!
LATER!
DASH
OH!
THAT'S HER! THAT'S THE GIRL!
SHE'S THE ONE WHO--!

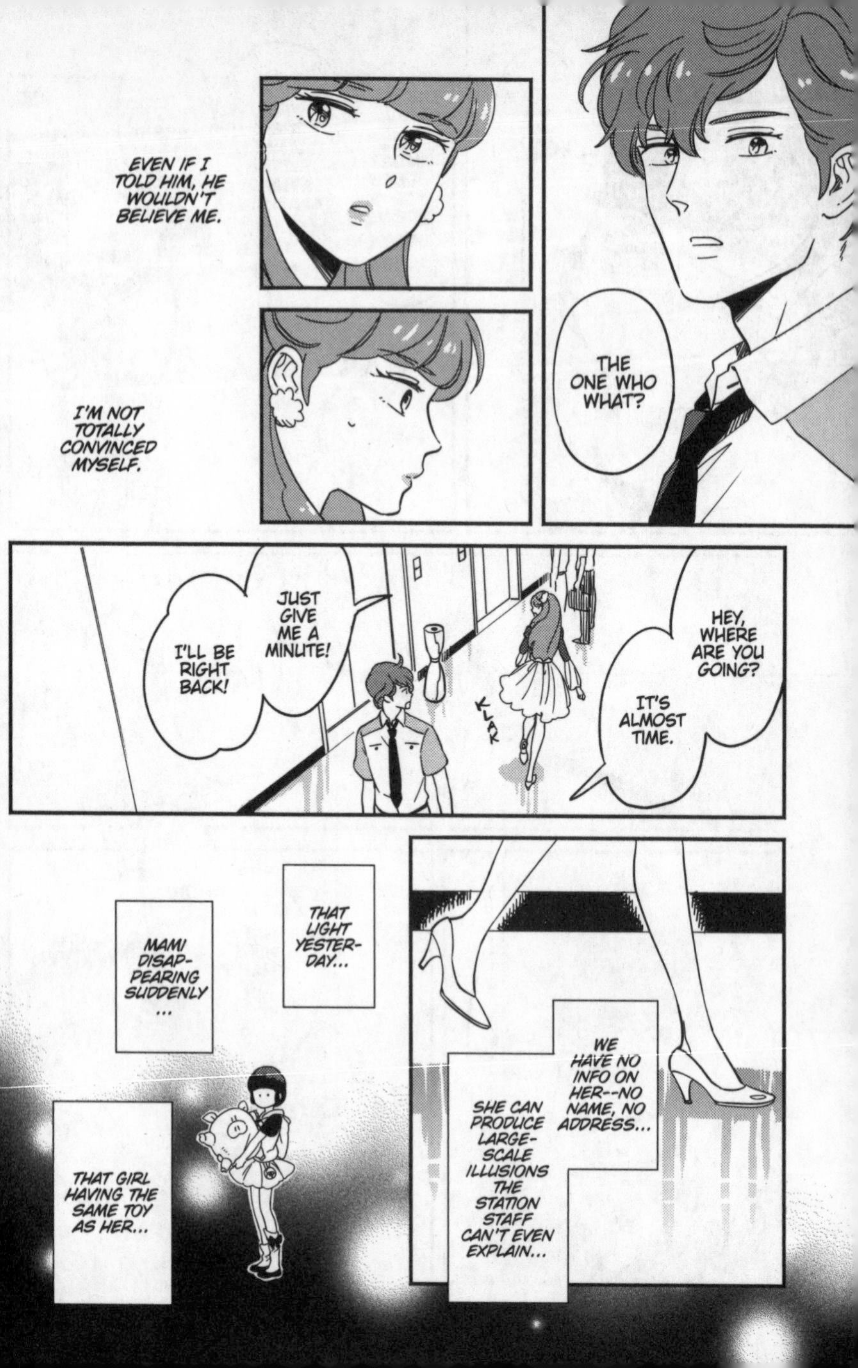
THE ONE WHO WHAT?
EVEN IF I TOLD HIM, HE WOULDN'T BELIEVE ME.
I'M NOT TOTALLY CONVINCED MYSELF.
HEY, WHERE ARE YOU GOING?
IT'S ALMOST TIME.
KLAK
JUST GIVE ME A MINUTE!
I'LL BE RIGHT BACK!
WE HAVE NO INFO ON HER--NO NAME, NO ADDRESS...
SHE CAN PRODUCE LARGE-SCALE ILLUSIONS THE STATION STAFF CAN'T EVEN EXPLAIN...
THAT LIGHT YESTERDAY...
MAMI DISAPPEARING SUDDENLY...
THAT GIRL HAVING THE SAME TOY AS HER...

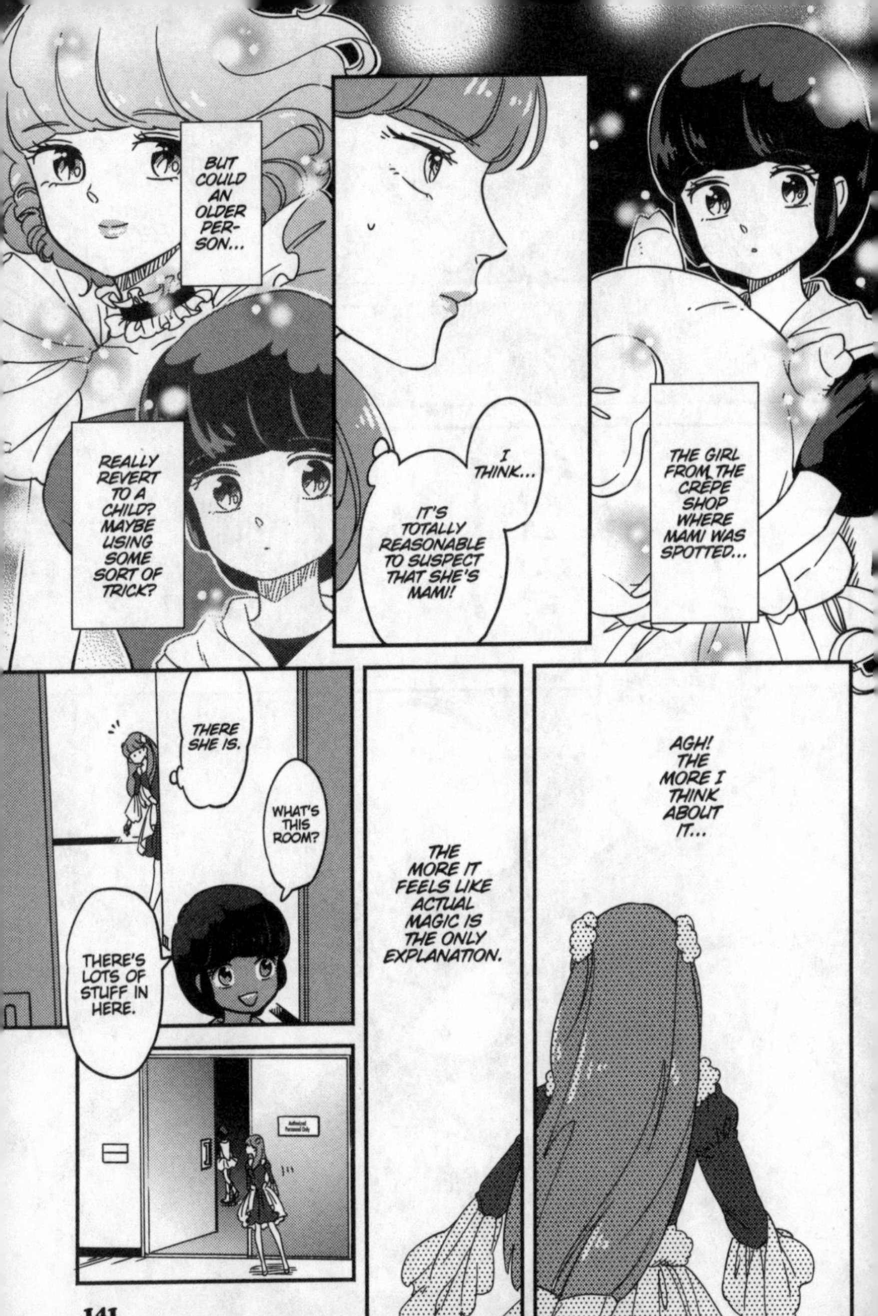
THE GIRL FROM THE CRÊPE SHOP WHERE MAMI WAS SPOTTED...
I THINK...
IT'S TOTALLY REASONABLE TO SUSPECT THAT SHE'S MAMI!
BUT COULD AN OLDER PER-SON...
REALLY REVERT TO A CHILD? MAYBE USING SOME SORT OF TRICK?
AGH! THE MORE I THINK ABOUT IT...
THE MORE IT FEELS LIKE ACTUAL MAGIC IS THE ONLY EXPLANATION.
THERE SHE IS.
WHAT'S THIS ROOM?
THERE'S LOTS OF STUFF IN HERE.

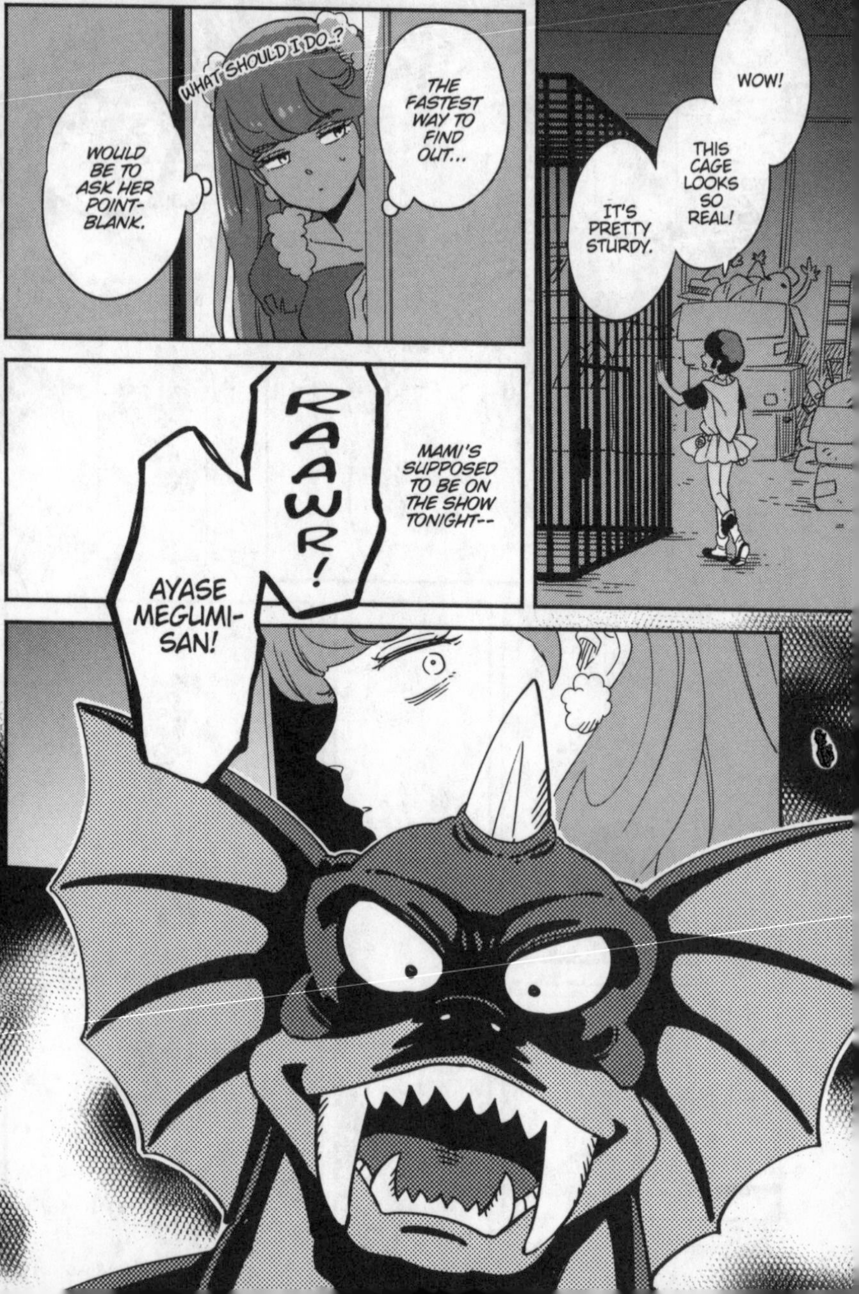
WOW!
THIS CAGE LOOKS SO REAL!
IT'S PRETTY STURDY.
WHAT SHOULD I DO..?
THE FASTEST WAY TO FIND OUT...
WOULD BE TO ASK HER POINT-BLANK.
MAMI'S SUPPOSED TO BE ON THE SHOW TONIGHT--
RAAWR!
AYASE MEGUMI-SAN!

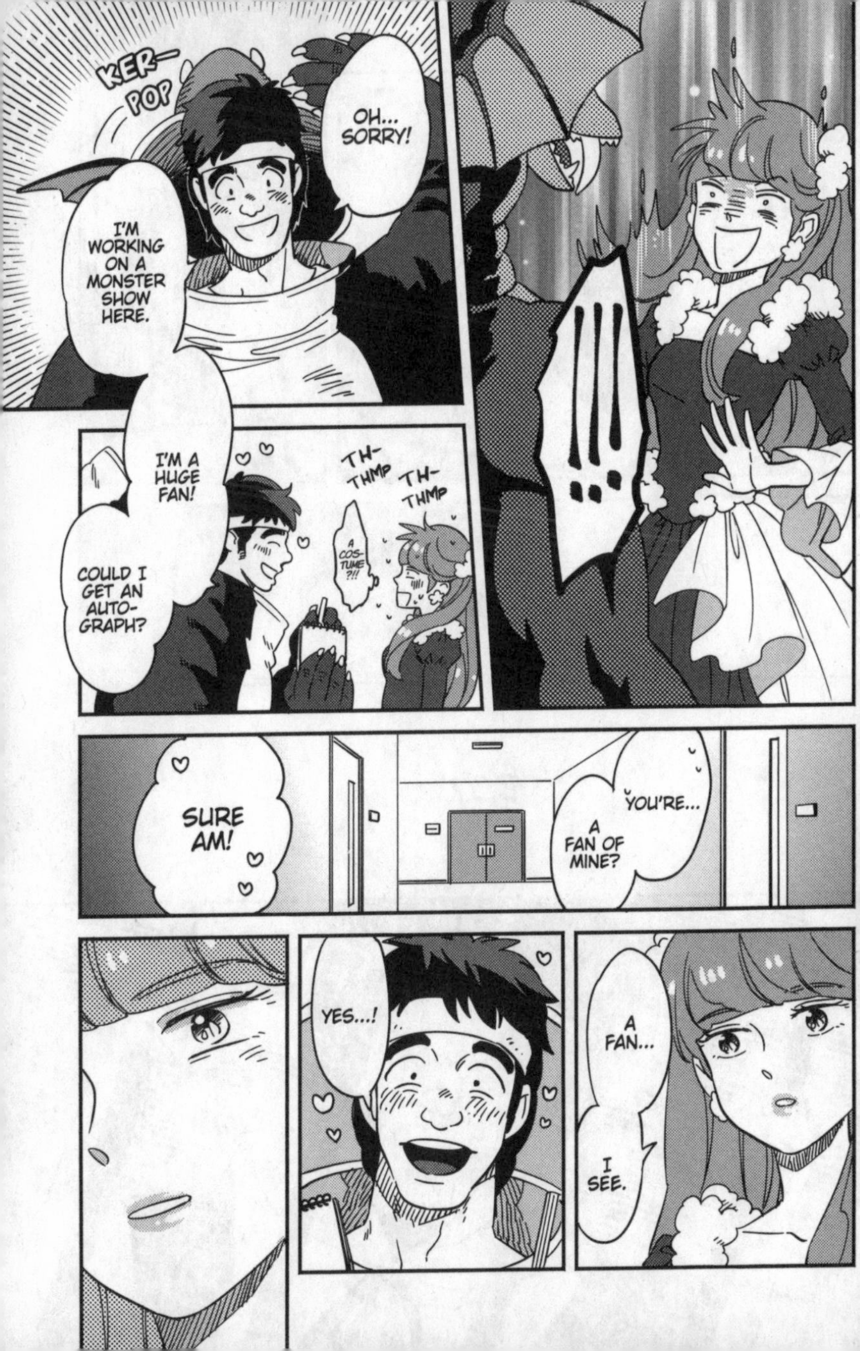
!!
KER-POP
OH... SORRY!
I'M WORKING ON A MONSTER SHOW HERE.
I'M A HUGE FAN!
TH-THMP
TH-THMP
A COSTUME?!!
COULD I GET AN AUTOGRAPH?
YOU'RE... A FAN OF MINE?
SURE AM!
A FAN...
I SEE.
YES...!

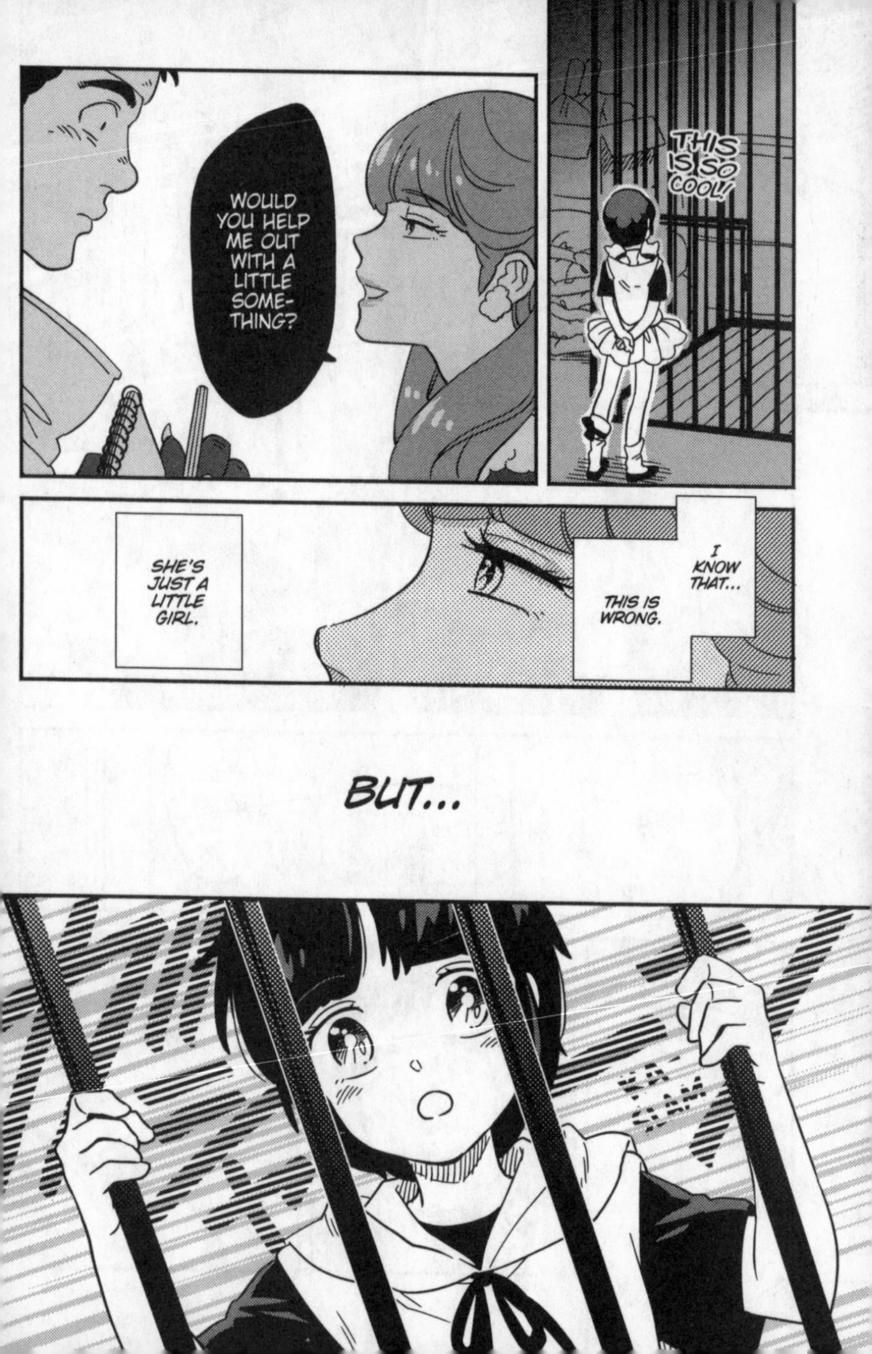
THIS IS SO COOL!
WOULD YOU HELP ME OUT WITH A LITTLE SOME-THING?
I KNOW THAT...
THIS IS WRONG.
SHE'S JUST A LITTLE GIRL.
BUT...
KA-SLAM

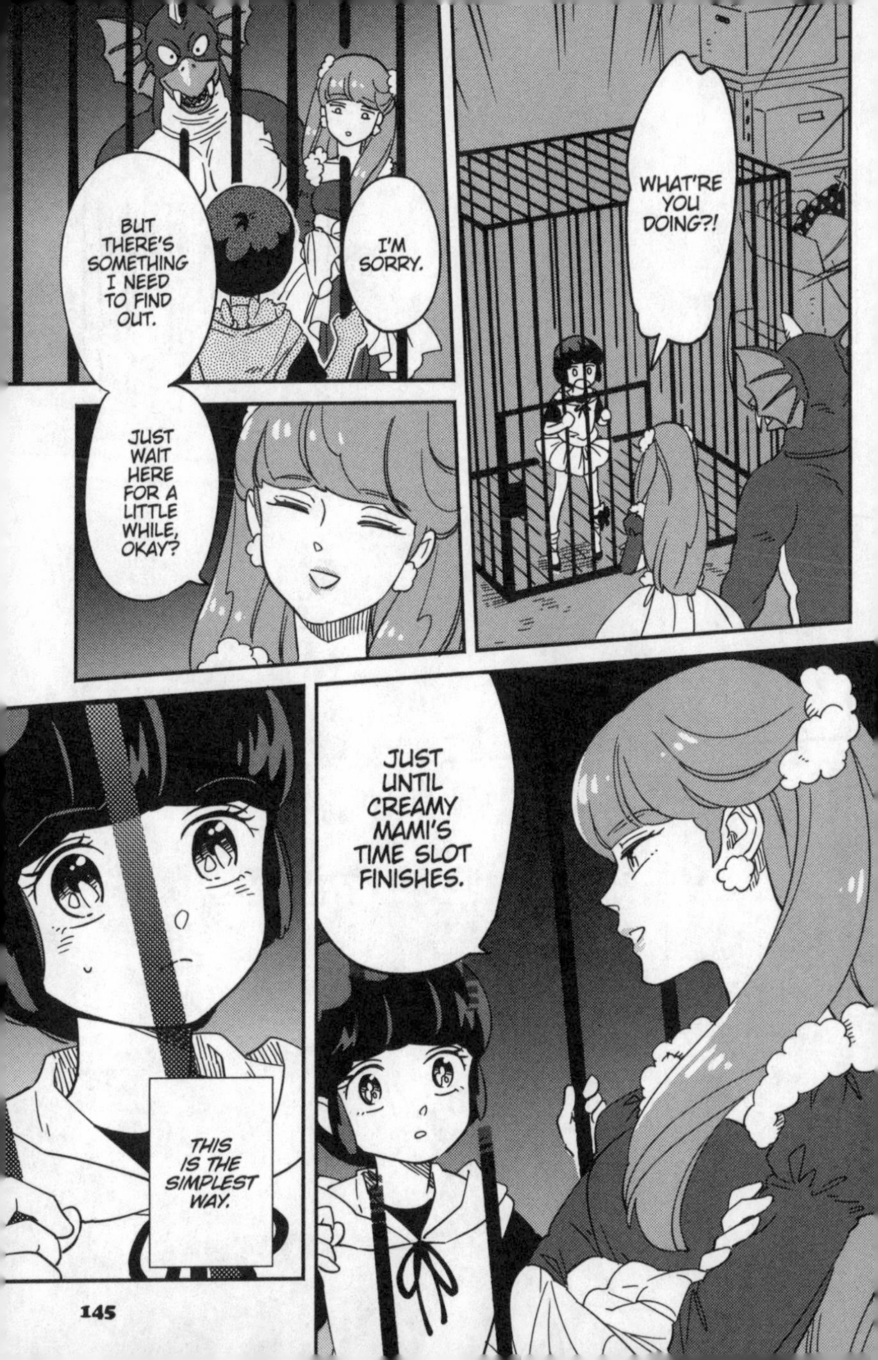
WHAT'RE YOU DOING?!
I'M SORRY.
BUT THERE'S SOMETHING I NEED TO FIND OUT.
JUST WAIT HERE FOR A LITTLE WHILE, OKAY?
JUST UNTIL CREAMY MAMI'S TIME SLOT FINISHES.
THIS IS THE SIMPLEST WAY.

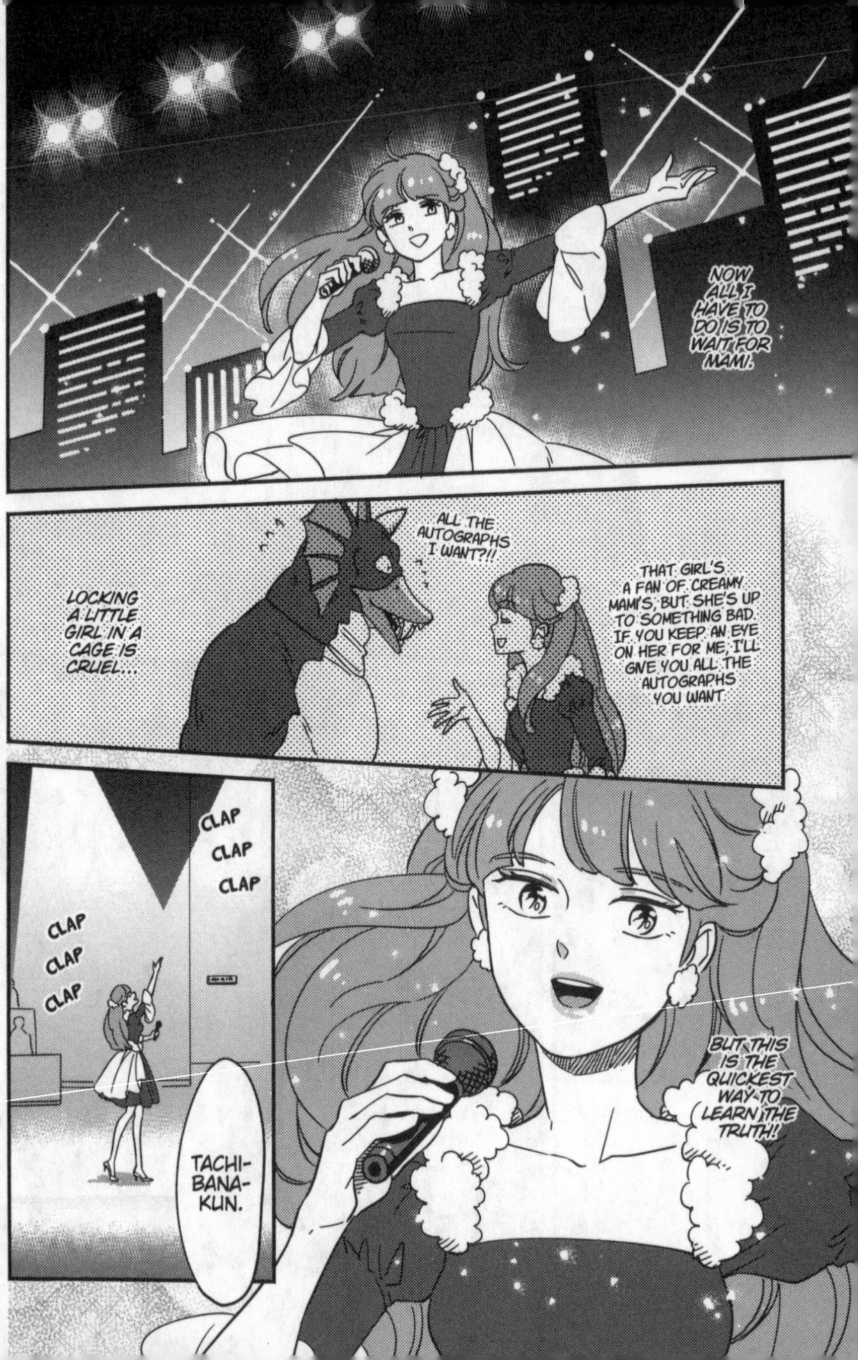
NOW ALL I HAVE TO DO IS TO WAIT FOR MAMI.
THAT GIRL'S A FAN OF CREAMY MAMI'S, BUT SHE'S UP TO SOMETHING BAD. IF YOU KEEP AN EYE ON HER FOR ME, I'LL GIVE YOU ALL THE AUTOGRAPHS YOU WANT.
ALL THE AUTOGRAPHS I WANT?!!
LOCKING A LITTLE GIRL IN A CAGE IS CRUEL...
BUT THIS IS THE QUICKEST WAY TO LEARN THE TRUTH!
CLAP CLAP CLAP
CLAP CLAP CLAP
TACHI-BANA-KUN.

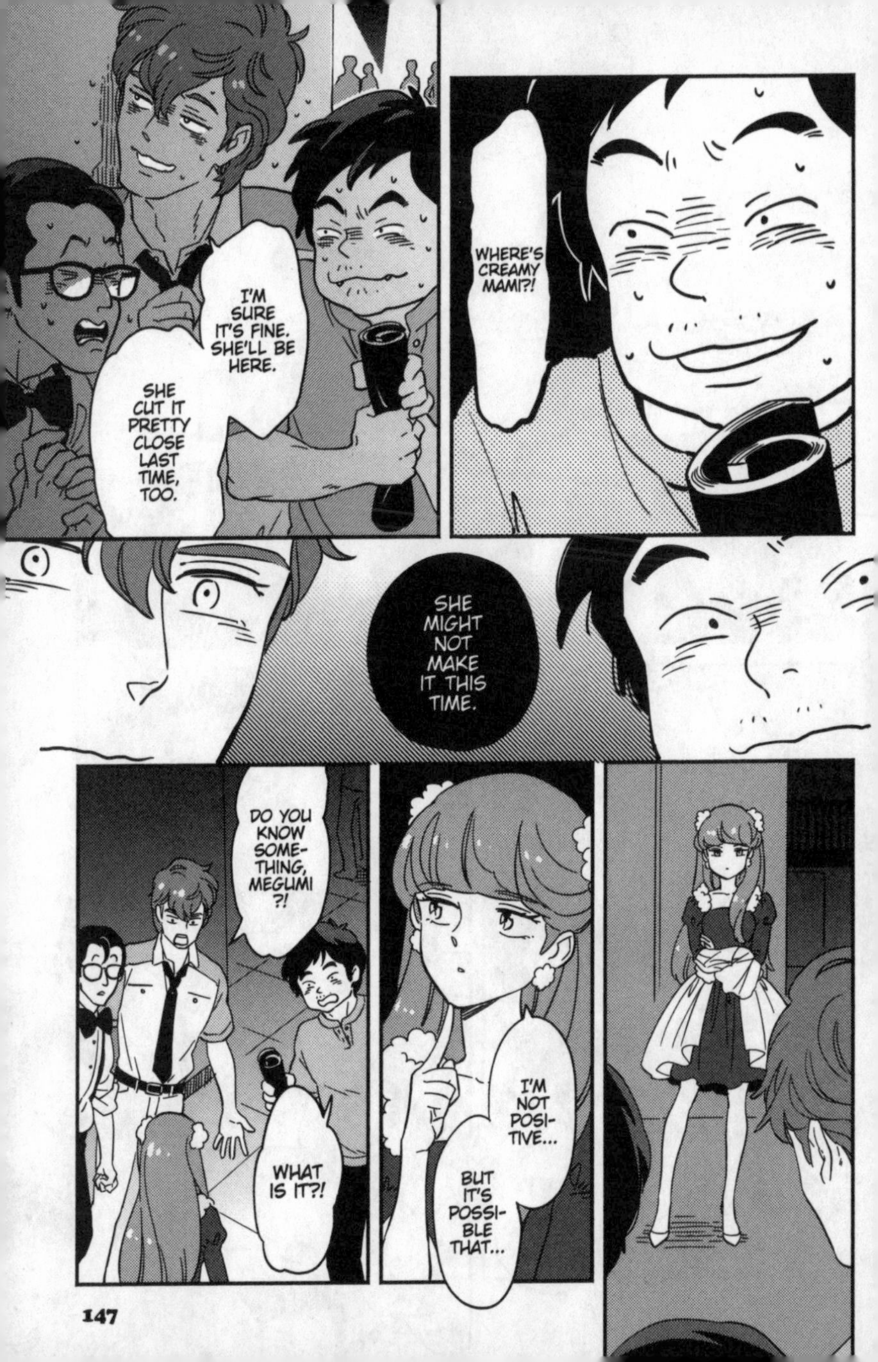
WHERE'S CREAMY MAMI?!
I'M SURE IT'S FINE. SHE'LL BE HERE.
SHE CUT IT PRETTY CLOSE LAST TIME, TOO.
SHE MIGHT NOT MAKE IT THIS TIME.
I'M NOT POSITIVE...
BUT IT'S POSSIBLE THAT...
DO YOU KNOW SOMETHING, MEGUMI?!
WHAT IS IT?!

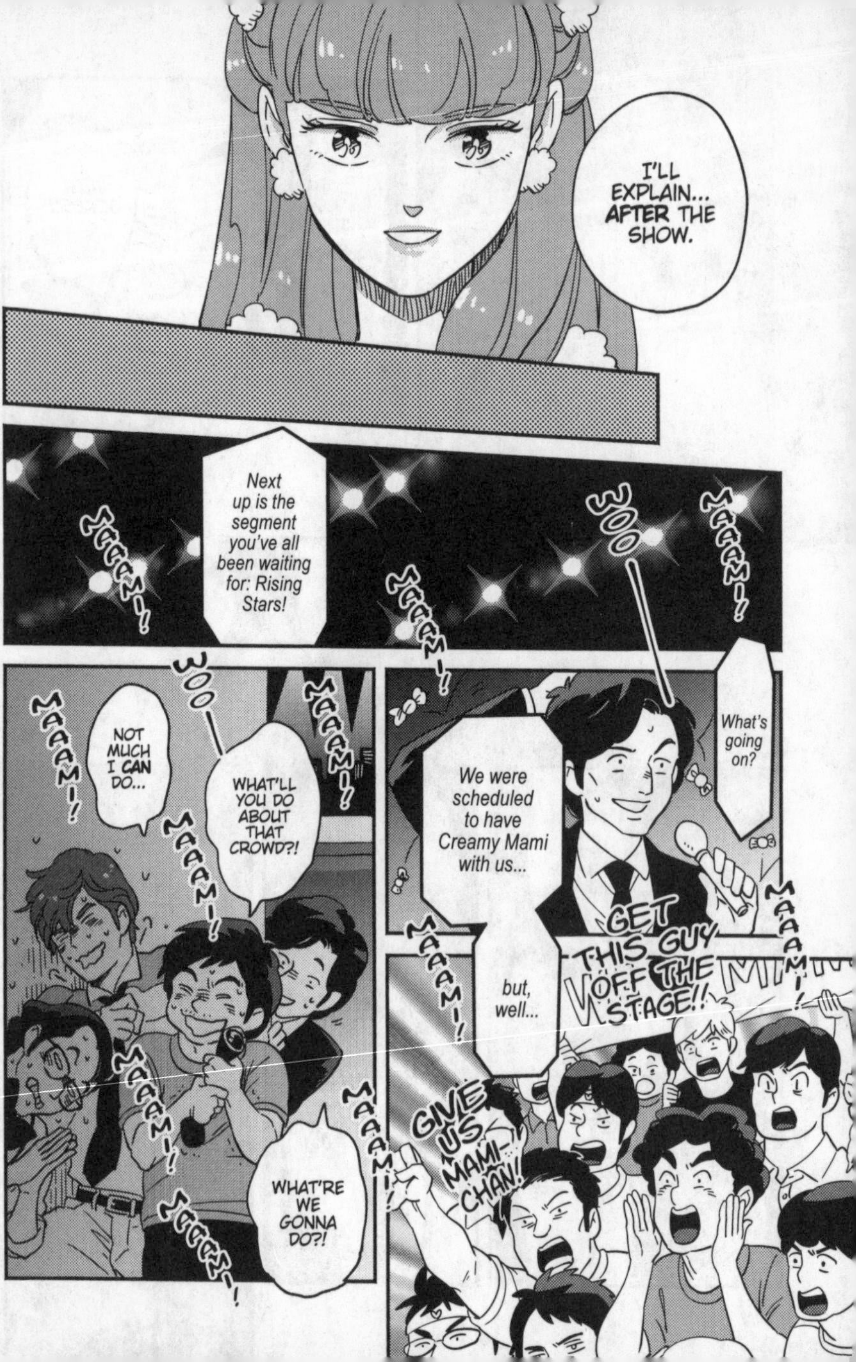
I'LL EXPLAIN... AFTER THE SHOW.
MAAAMI!
WOO—
MAAAMI!
Next up is the segment you've all been waiting for: Rising Stars!
MAAAMI!
What's going on?
We were scheduled to have Creamy Mami with us...
MAAAMI!
but, well...
GET THIS GUY OFF THE STAGE!!
MAAAMI!
GIVE US MAMI-CHAN!
MAAAMI!
WOO—
WHAT'LL YOU DO ABOUT THAT CROWD?!
NOT MUCH I CAN DO...
MAAAMI!
MAAAMI!
MAAAMI!
WHAT'RE WE GONNA DO?!
MAAAMI!

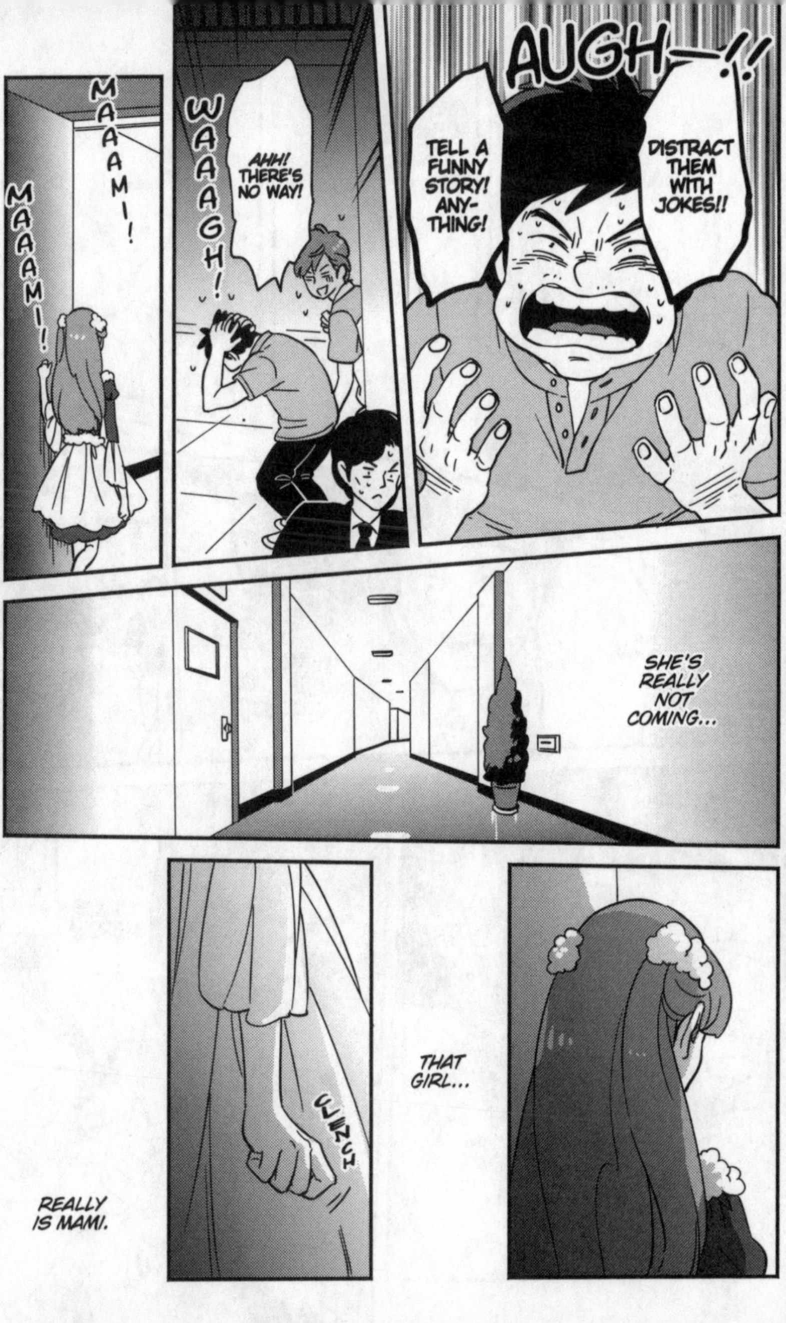
AUGH—!!
DISTRACT THEM WITH JOKES!!
TELL A FUNNY STORY! ANY-THING!
WAAAAGH!
AHH! THERE'S NO WAY!
MAAAAMI!
MAAAAMI!
SHE'S REALLY NOT COMING...
THAT GIRL...
CLENCH
REALLY IS MAMI.

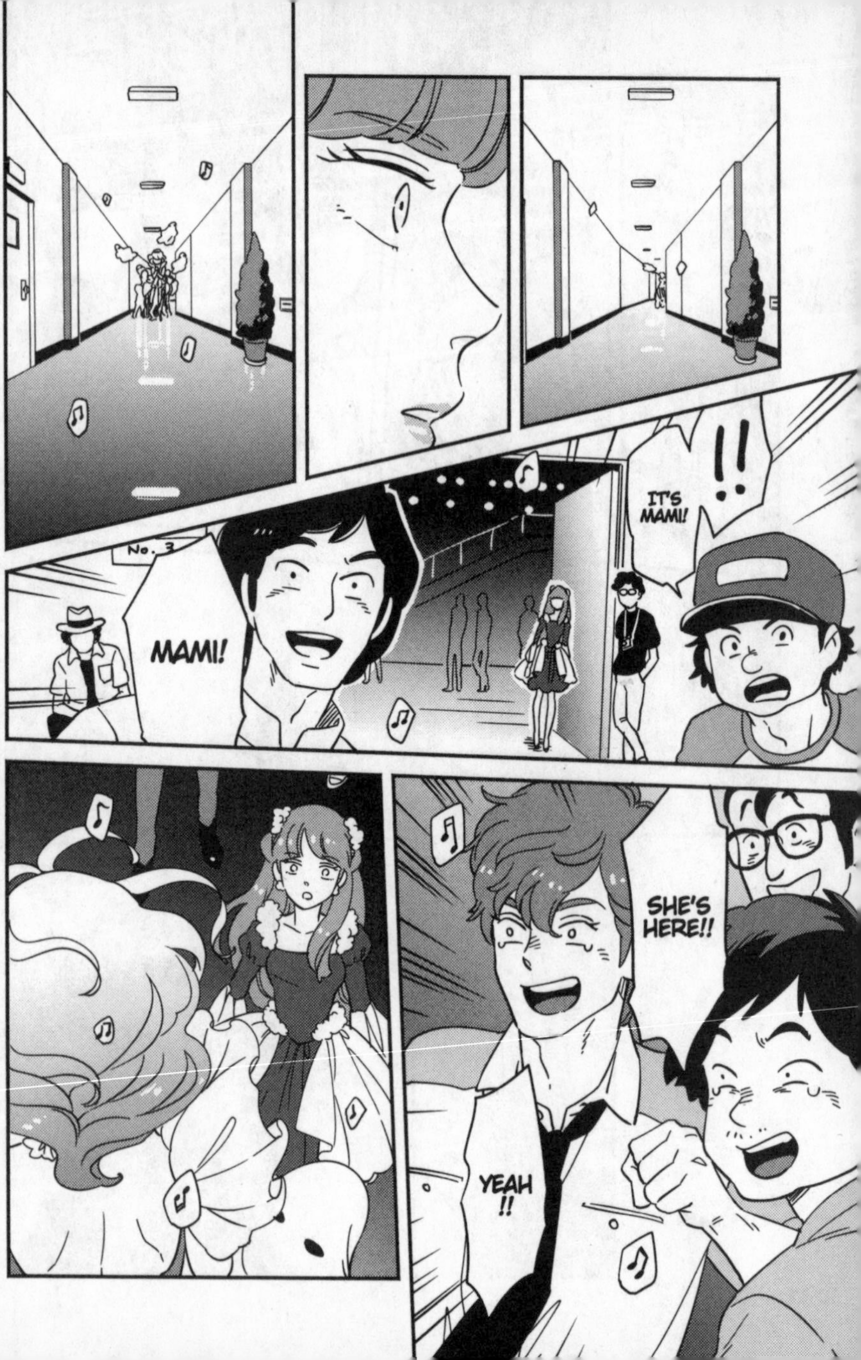
!!
IT'S MAMI!
No. 3
MAMI!
SHE'S HERE!!
YEAH !!

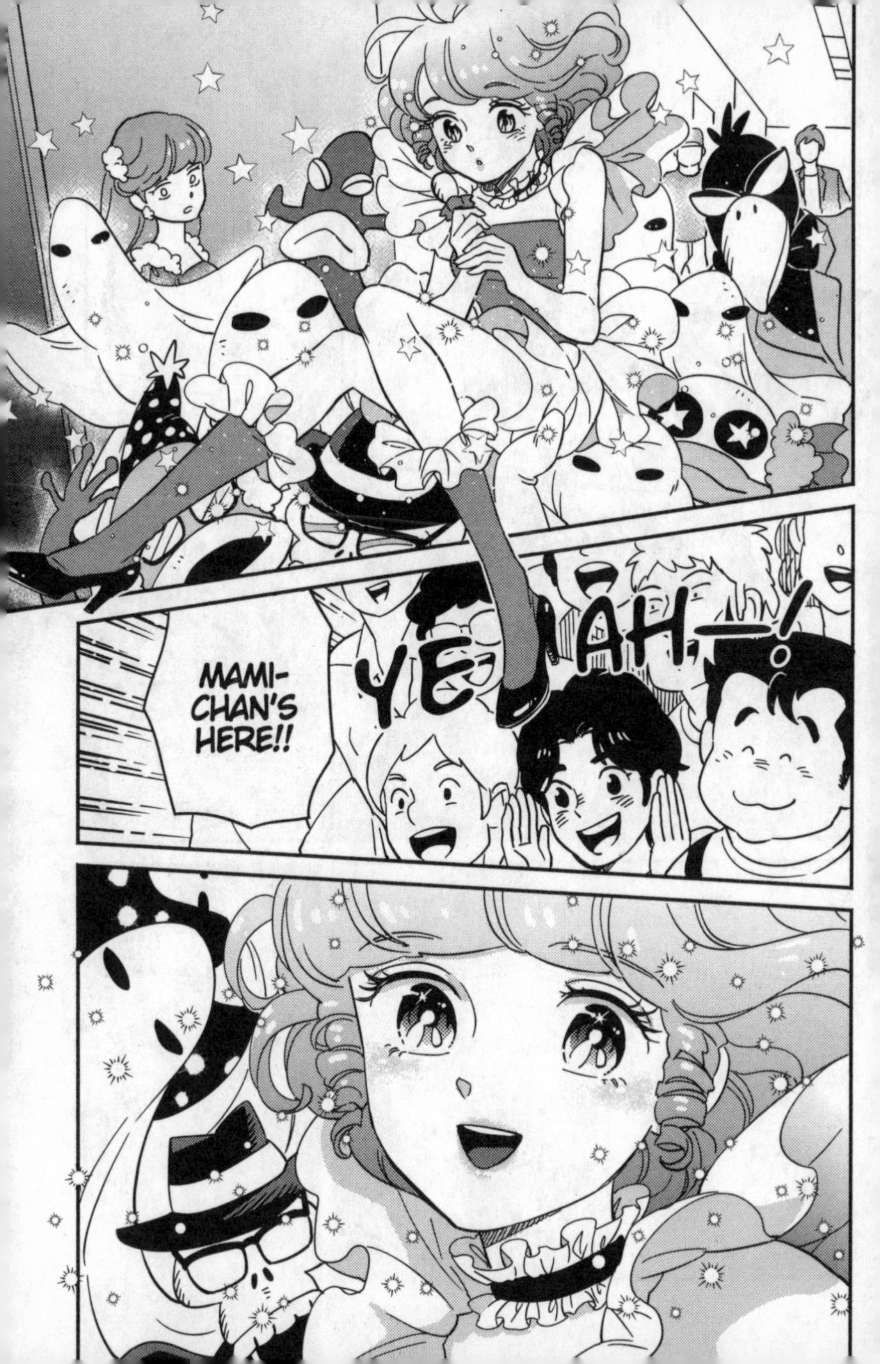
YEAAAH—!
MAMI-CHAN'S HERE!!

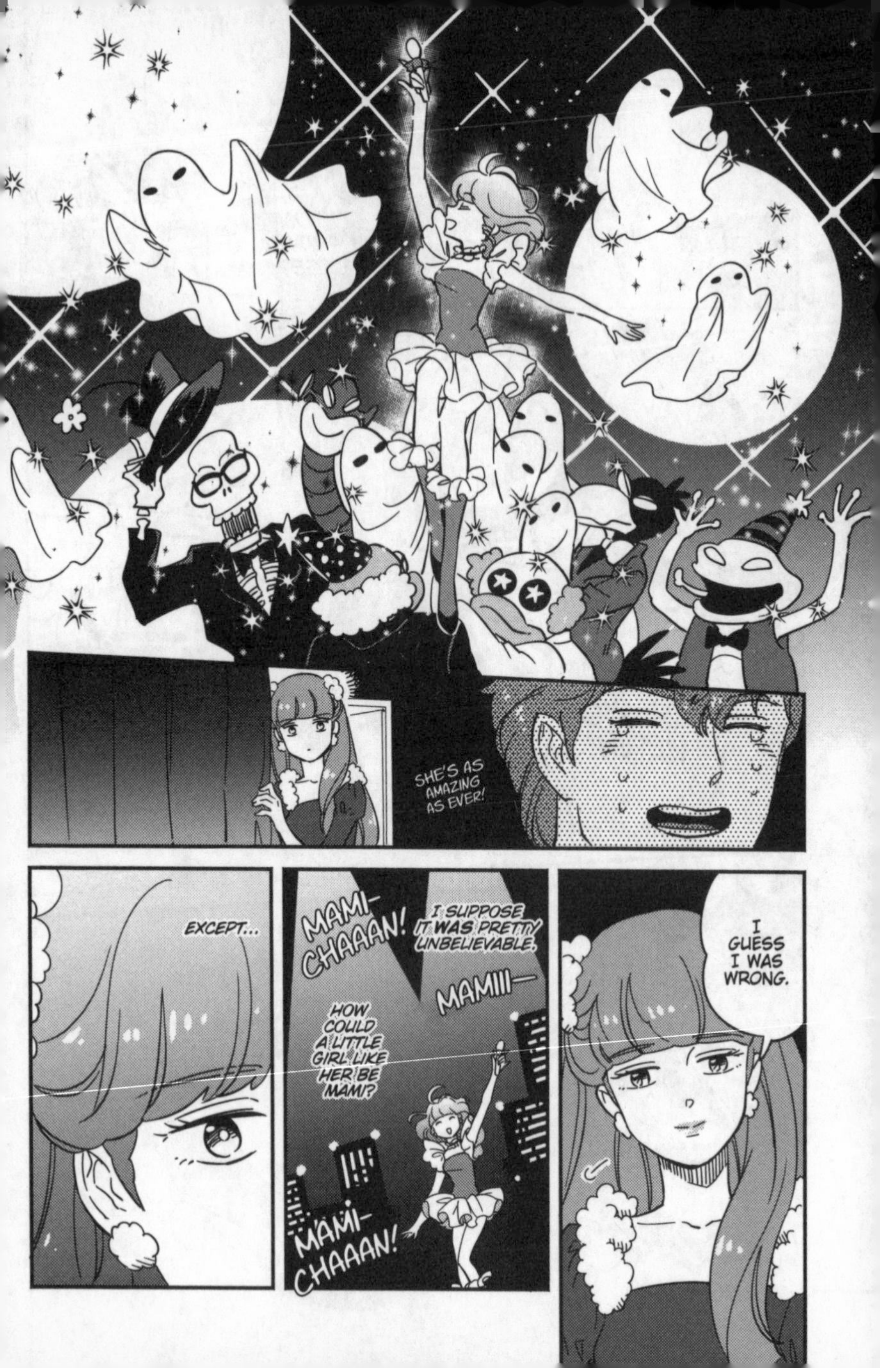
SHE'S AS AMAZING AS EVER!
I GUESS I WAS WRONG.
I SUPPOSE IT WAS PRETTY UNBELIEVABLE.
MAMI-CHAAAN!
MAMIII—
HOW COULD A LITTLE GIRL LIKE HER BE MAMI?
MAMI-CHAAAN!
EXCEPT...

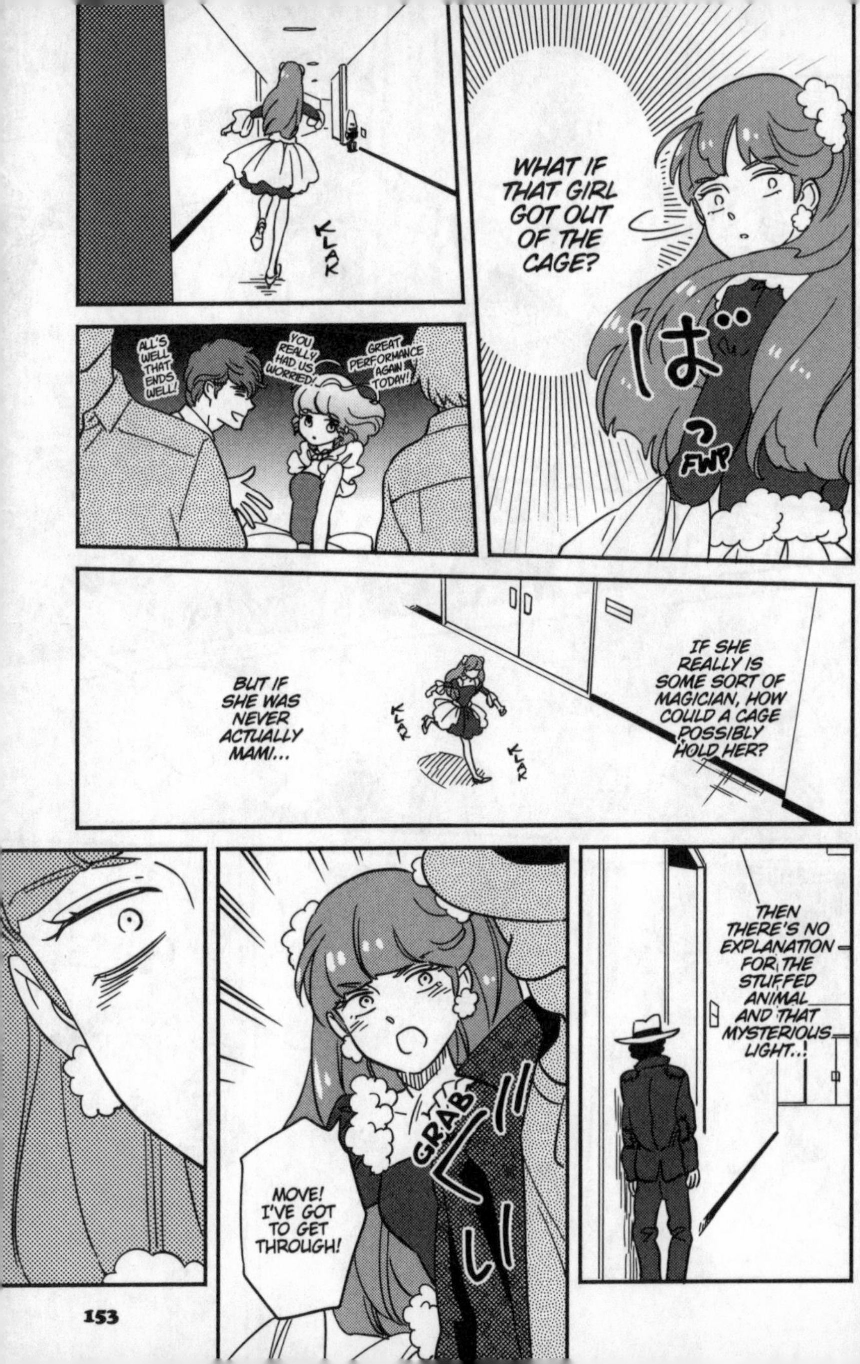
WHAT IF THAT GIRL GOT OUT OF THE CAGE?
ばっ
FWP
KLAK
GREAT PERFORMANCE AGAIN TODAY!
YOU REALLY HAD US WORRIED!
ALL'S WELL THAT ENDS WELL!
IF SHE REALLY IS SOME SORT OF MAGICIAN, HOW COULD A CAGE POSSIBLY HOLD HER?
KLAK
KLAK
BUT IF SHE WAS NEVER ACTUALLY MAMI...
THEN THERE'S NO EXPLANATION FOR THE STUFFED ANIMAL AND THAT MYSTERIOUS LIGHT...!
GRAB
MOVE! I'VE GOT TO GET THROUGH!

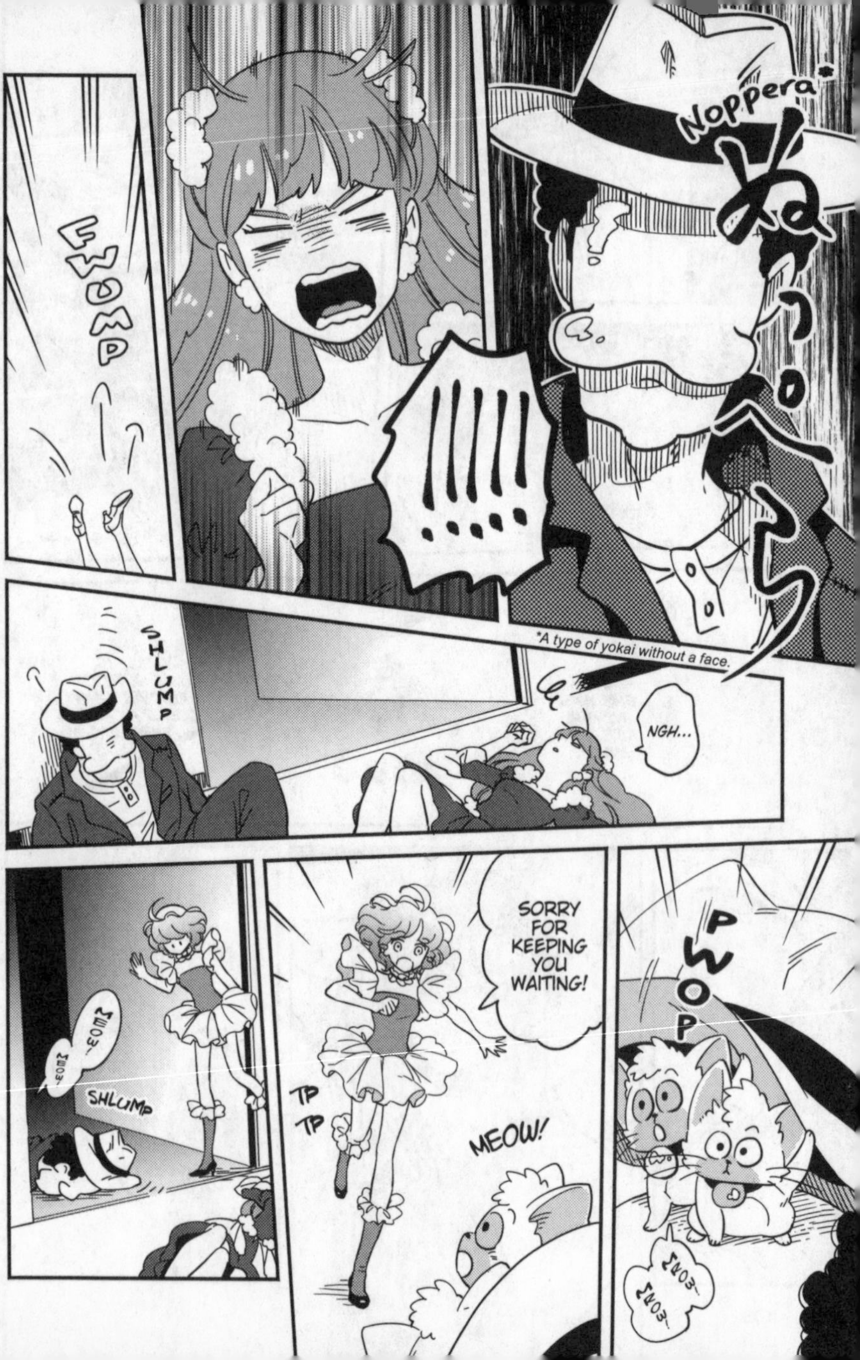
Noppera*
ぬっぺら
!!!!....
FWOMP
NGH...
SHLUMP
PWOP
MEOW~
MEOW~
SORRY FOR KEEPING YOU WAITING!
MEOW!
TP TP
MEOW~
MEOW~
SHLUMP

*A type of yokai without a face.

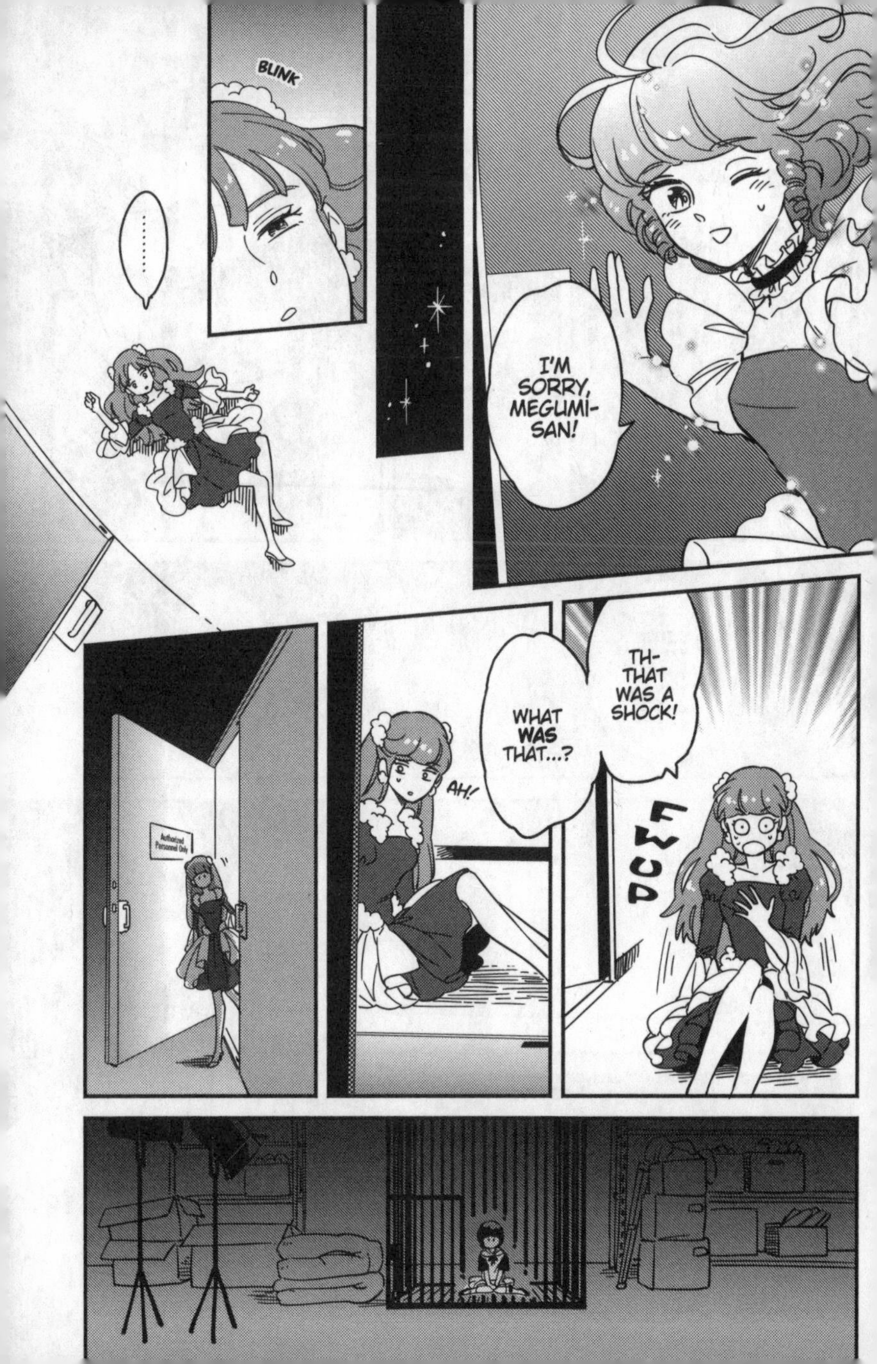
I'M SORRY, MEGUMI-SAN!
BLINK
......
TH-THAT WAS A SHOCK!
FWUP
WHAT WAS THAT...?
AH!
Authorized Personnel Only

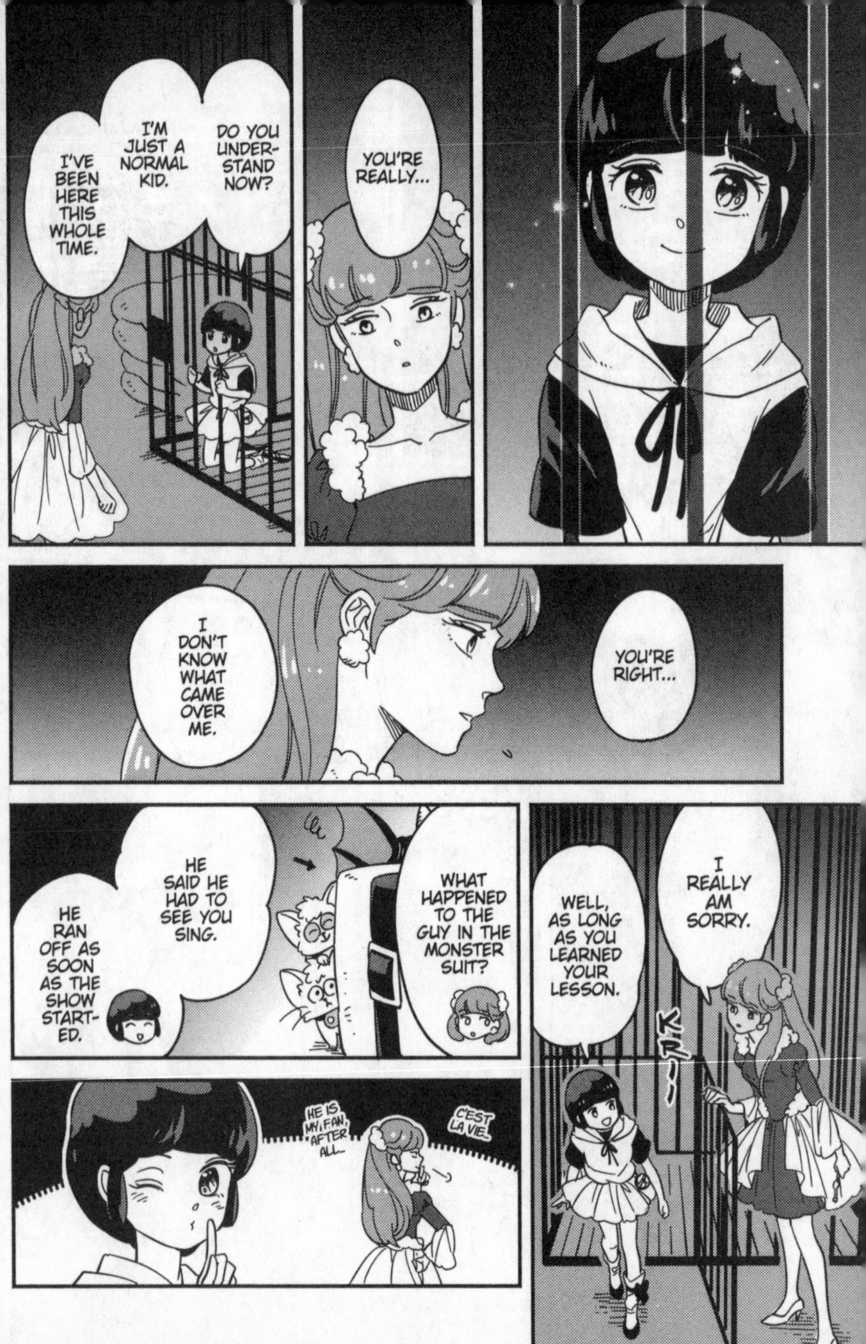
YOU'RE REALLY...
DO YOU UNDERSTAND NOW?
I'M JUST A NORMAL KID.
I'VE BEEN HERE THIS WHOLE TIME.
YOU'RE RIGHT...
I DON'T KNOW WHAT CAME OVER ME.
I REALLY AM SORRY.
WELL, AS LONG AS YOU LEARNED YOUR LESSON.
KRI
WHAT HAPPENED TO THE GUY IN THE MONSTER SUIT?
HE SAID HE HAD TO SEE YOU SING.
HE RAN OFF AS SOON AS THE SHOW STARTED.
C'EST LA VIE.
HE IS MY FAN, AFTER ALL.

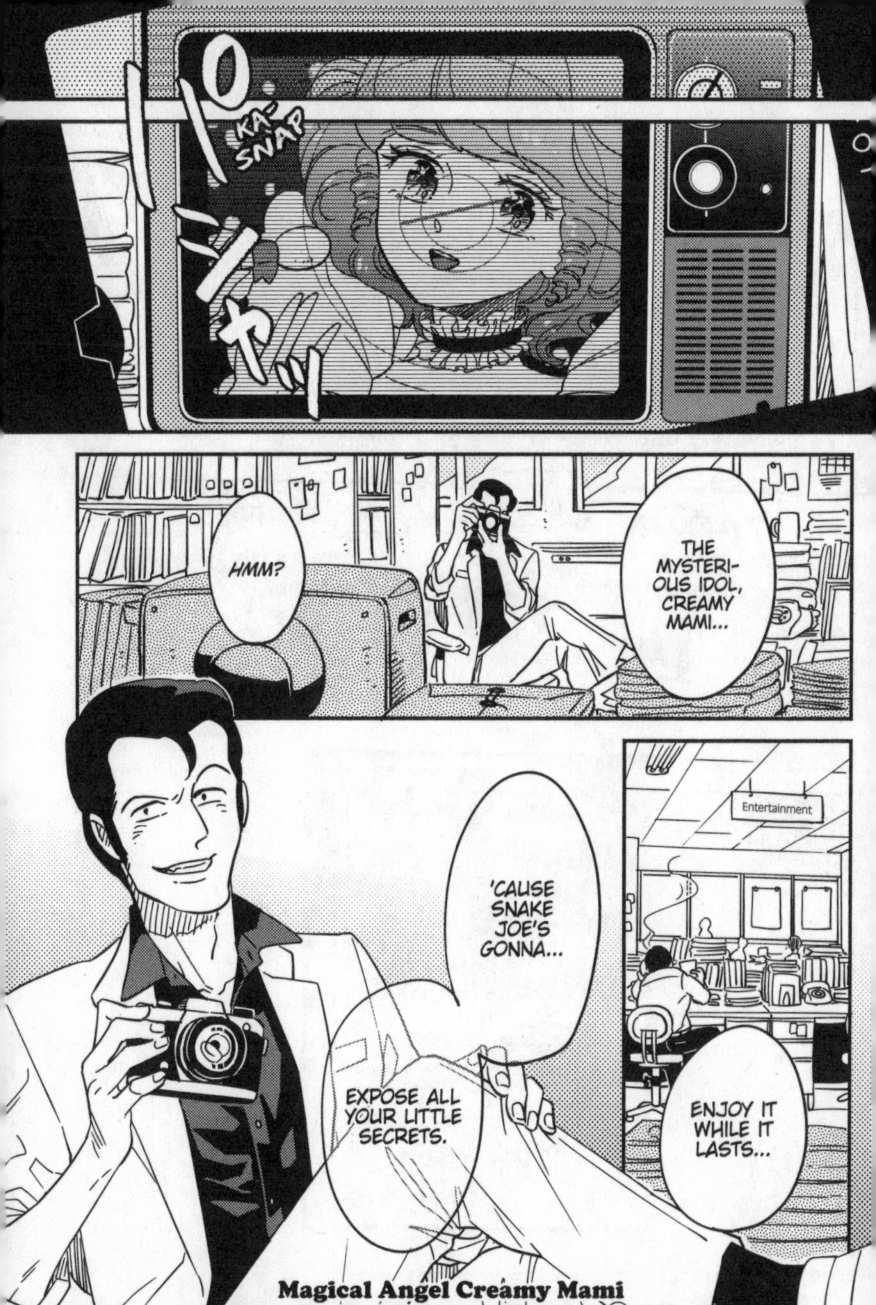
KA-SNAP
THE MYSTERIOUS IDOL, CREAMY MAMI...
HMM?
Entertainment
ENJOY IT WHILE IT LASTS...
'CAUSE SNAKE JOE'S GONNA...
EXPOSE ALL YOUR LITTLE SECRETS.

Magical Angel Creamy Mami and the Spoiled Princess Volume ① / End

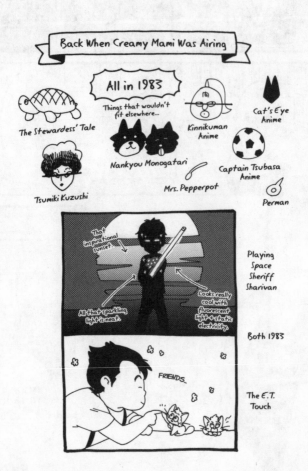

Back When Creamy Mami Was Airing

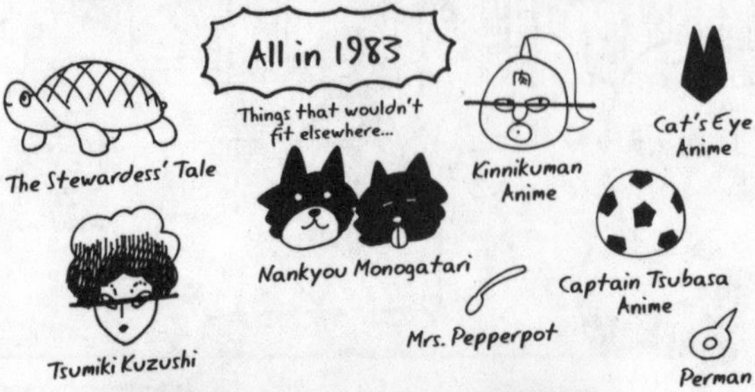
All in 1983
Things that wouldn't fit elsewhere...
Cat's Eye Anime
Kinnikuman Anime
The Stewardess' Tale
Nankyou Monogatari
Captain Tsubasa Anime
Tsumiki Kuzushi
Mrs. Pepperpot
Perman

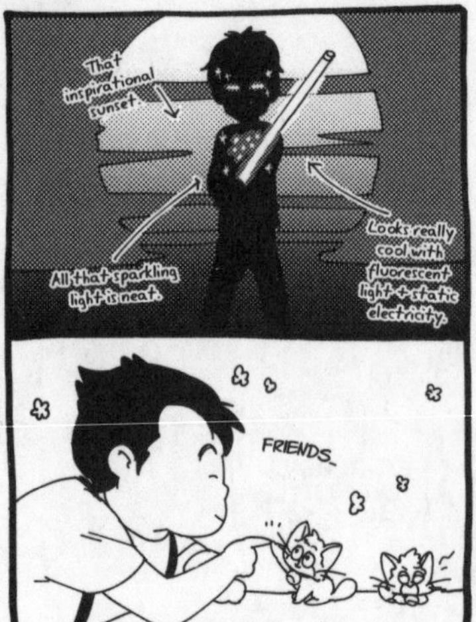
That inspirational sunset.
Looks really cool with fluorescent light + static electricity.
All that sparkling light is neat.
FRIENDS_

Playing Space Sheriff Sharivan

Both 1983

The E.T. Touch

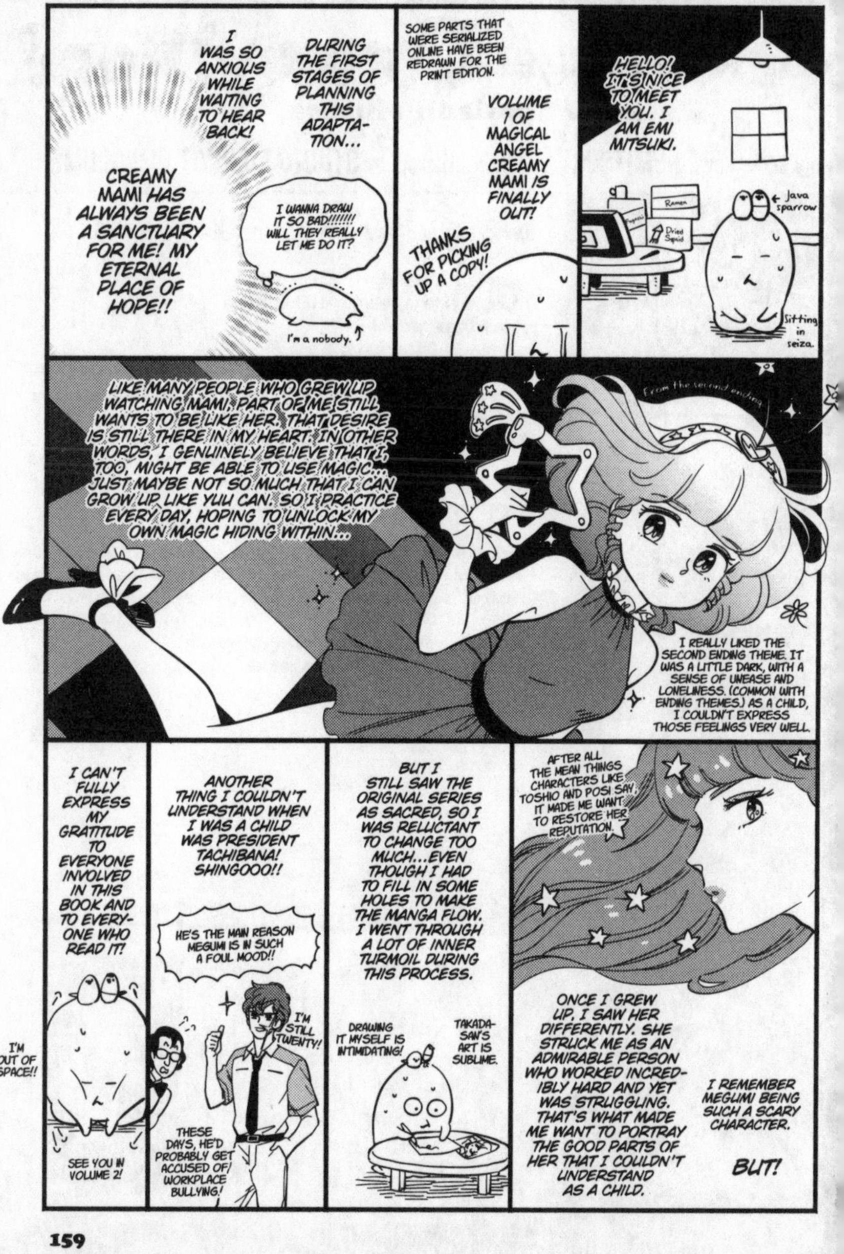
HELLO! IT'S NICE TO MEET YOU. I AM EMI MITSUKI.
Java sparrow
Ramen
Dried Squid
Sitting in seiza.
SOME PARTS THAT WERE SERIALIZED ONLINE HAVE BEEN REDRAWN FOR THE PRINT EDITION.
VOLUME 1 OF MAGICAL ANGEL CREAMY MAMI IS FINALLY OUT!
THANKS FOR PICKING UP A COPY!
DURING THE FIRST STAGES OF PLANNING THIS ADAPTATION...
I WAS SO ANXIOUS WHILE WAITING TO HEAR BACK!
I WANNA DRAW IT SO BAD!!!!!!! WILL THEY REALLY LET ME DO IT?
CREAMY MAMI HAS ALWAYS BEEN A SANCTUARY FOR ME! MY ETERNAL PLACE OF HOPE!!
I'm a nobody.
From the second ending
LIKE MANY PEOPLE WHO GREW UP WATCHING MAMI, PART OF ME STILL WANTS TO BE LIKE HER. THAT DESIRE IS STILL THERE IN MY HEART. IN OTHER WORDS, I GENUINELY BELIEVE THAT I, TOO, MIGHT BE ABLE TO USE MAGIC... JUST MAYBE NOT SO MUCH THAT I CAN GROW UP LIKE YUU CAN. SO I PRACTICE EVERY DAY, HOPING TO UNLOCK MY OWN MAGIC HIDING WITHIN...
I REALLY LIKED THE SECOND ENDING THEME. IT WAS A LITTLE DARK, WITH A SENSE OF UNEASE AND LONELINESS. (COMMON WITH ENDING THEMES.) AS A CHILD, I COULDN'T EXPRESS THOSE FEELINGS VERY WELL.
I REMEMBER MEGUMI BEING SUCH A SCARY CHARACTER.
BUT!
ONCE I GREW UP, I SAW HER DIFFERENTLY. SHE STRUCK ME AS AN ADMIRABLE PERSON WHO WORKED INCREDIBLY HARD AND YET WAS STRUGGLING. THAT'S WHAT MADE ME WANT TO PORTRAY THE GOOD PARTS OF HER THAT I COULDN'T UNDERSTAND AS A CHILD.
AFTER ALL THE MEAN THINGS CHARACTERS LIKE TOSHIO AND POSI SAY, IT MADE ME WANT TO RESTORE HER REPUTATION.
BUT I STILL SAW THE ORIGINAL SERIES AS SACRED, SO I WAS RELUCTANT TO CHANGE TOO MUCH...EVEN THOUGH I HAD TO FILL IN SOME HOLES TO MAKE THE MANGA FLOW. I WENT THROUGH A LOT OF INNER TURMOIL DURING THIS PROCESS.
TAKADA-SAN'S ART IS SUBLIME.
DRAWING IT MYSELF IS INTIMIDATING!
ANOTHER THING I COULDN'T UNDERSTAND WHEN I WAS A CHILD WAS PRESIDENT TACHIBANA! SHINGOOO!!
HE'S THE MAIN REASON MEGUMI IS IN SUCH A FOUL MOOD!!
I'M STILL TWENTY!
THESE DAYS, HE'D PROBABLY GET ACCUSED OF WORKPLACE BULLYING!
I CAN'T FULLY EXPRESS MY GRATITUDE TO EVERYONE INVOLVED IN THIS BOOK AND TO EVERYONE WHO READ IT!
I'M OUT OF SPACE!!
SEE YOU IN VOLUME 2!

SEVEN SEAS ENTERTAINMENT PRESENTS

lagical Angel Creamy Mami and the Spoiled Princess

tory and art by **EMI MITSUKI** original concept by **STUDIO PIERROT** **VOLUME 1**

TRANSLATION
Amber Tamosaitis

ADAPTATION
Ysabet Reinhardt MacFarlane

LETTERING
Jennifer Skarupa

COVER DESIGN
Nicky Lim

PROOFREADER
Stephanie Cohen

COPY EDITOR
Dawn Davis

EDITOR
Jenn Grunigen

PREPRESS TECHNICIAN
annon Rasmussen-Silverstein

PRODUCTION ASSISTANT
Christa Miesner

PRODUCTION MANAGER
Lissa Pattillo

MANAGING EDITOR
Julie Davis

ASSOCIATE PUBLISHER
Adam Arnold

PUBLISHER
Jason DeAngelis

Seven Seas press and purchase enquiries can be sent to Marketing Manager Lianne Sentar at press@gomanga.com. Information regarding the distribution and purchase of digital editions is available from Digital Manager CK Russell at digital@gomanga.com.

ISBN: 978-1-64827-079-6
Printed in Canada
First Printing: March 2021
10 9 8 7 6 5 4 3 2 1

READING DIRECTIONS

This book reads from ***right to left***, Japanese style. If this is your first time reading manga, you start reading from the top right panel on each page and take it from there. If you get lost, just follow the numbered diagram here. It may seem backwards at first, but you'll get the hang of it! Have fun!!

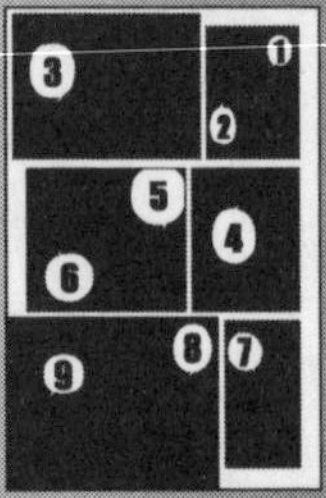
1
2
3
4
5
6
7
8
9

Follow us online: www.SevenSeasEntertainment.com